PRAISE FOR
ONWARD WE CHARGE

"In this well-written book, H. Paul Jeffers paints a colorful picture of William O. Darby, one of the remarkable commanders in recent U.S. military history, and the uncommon men he led into battle. On these pages, Darby comes to life, as do the many battles his Rangers fought in North Africa and Italy. Anyone who is interested in the U.S. Army Rangers should read this book."
—John C. McManus, author of *Alamo in the Ardennes*, *The Americans at D-Day*, and *The Deadly Brotherhood*

"[An] introduction to one of World War II's most storied units and the hero who led them."
—*Publishers Weekly*

"A thoroughly engrossing, can't-put-it-down history of a battalion of courageous men and their leader, who helped lay the groundwork for today's special forces. The book is a terrific read."
—Larry Alexander, author of *Biggest Brother: The Life of Major Dick Winters, the Man Who Led the Band of Brothers*

"Tough, decent, cocky, and fearless, Bill Darby was right out of an issue of *Boys' Life* or a fantasy of Teddy Roosevelt. But he was the real thing, the warrior who created America's most daring force in World War II, the Army Rangers. In *Onward We Charge*, H. Paul Jeffers brings Darby's story to life with verve and skill."
—Evan Thomas, *Newsweek* editor at large and author of *Sea of Thunder*

continued . . .

ONWARD WE CHARGE

THE HEROIC STORY OF DARBY'S RANGERS IN WORLD WAR II

H. PAUL JEFFERS

NAL
CALIBER

NAL Caliber
Published by New American Library, a division of
Penguin Group (USA) Inc., 375 Hudson Street, New York, New York 10014, USA
Penguin Group (Canada), 90 Eglinton Avenue East, Suite 700, Toronto,
Ontario M4P 2Y3, Canada (a division of Pearson Penguin Canada Inc.)
Penguin Books Ltd., 80 Strand, London WC2R 0RL, England
Penguin Ireland, 25 St. Stephen's Green, Dublin 2, Ireland (a division of Penguin Books Ltd.)
Penguin Group (Australia), 250 Camberwell Road, Camberwell, Victoria 3124,
Australia (a division of Pearson Australia Group Pty. Ltd.)
Penguin Books India Pvt. Ltd., 11 Community Centre, Panchsheel Park,
New Delhi - 110 017, India
Penguin Group (NZ), 67 Apollo Drive, Rosedale, North Shore 0632,
New Zealand (a division of Pearson New Zealand Ltd.)
Penguin Books (South Africa) (Pty.) Ltd., 24 Sturdee Avenue,
Rosebank, Johannesburg 2196, South Africa

Penguin Books Ltd., Registered Offices: 80 Strand, London WC2R 0RL, England

Published by NAL Caliber, an imprint of New American Library, a division of Penguin Group (USA)
Inc. Previously published in an NAL Caliber hardcover edition.

First NAL Caliber Trade Paperback Printing, June 2008
10 9 8 7 6 5 4 3 2 1

Grateful acknowledgment is made for use of quotations from Sergeant Thomas Sullivan's diary as
they appear in Mir Bahmanyar's *Darby's Rangers: 1942–1945*. The quotations appear on pages 31,
45, 47–48, 50–51, 55, 60, 68–71, 81, 84, 98, 114–15, 149–50, 152, and 158–59.

NAL CALIBER and the "C" logo are trademarks of Penguin Group (USA) Inc

NAL Caliber Trade Paperback ISBN: 978-0-451-22400-2

The Library of Congress has cataloged the hardcover edition of this title as follows:

Jeffers, H. Paul (Harry Paul), 1934–
    Onward we charge: the heroic story of Darby's rangers in World War II/H. Paul Jeffers.
        p. cm.
    ISBN: 978-0-451-22128-5
    1. Darby, William Orlando. 2. United States. Army. Ranger Battalion, 1st—History. 3. United
States. Army. Ranger Battalion, 3rd—History. 4. United States. Army. Ranger Battalion,
4th—History. 5. World War, 1939–1945—Regimental histories—United States. 6. World
War, 1939–1945—Campaigns—Africa, North. 7. World War, 1939–1945—Campaigns—Italy.
8. United States. Army—Biography. 9. Generals—United States—Biography. I. Title.
D769.311st.J44 2007
940.54'1273092—dc22   2006034782
[B]

Set in Adobe Garamond
Designed by Spring Hoteling

Printed in the United States of America

★ CONTENTS ★

CONTENTS

For Johnny and Judy

"Commanding the Rangers was like driving a team of very high-spirited horses. No effort was needed to get them to go forward. The problem was to hold them in check."

—Colonel William O. Darby, April 1945

★ PROLOGUE ★

"Where are their essays?"

"OF ALL THE ATROCIOUS PROBLEMS THAT ARE ASSIGNED TO THE MODERN high school student," wrote Bill Darby in 1929, "the writing of an essay heads the list."

In registering this gripe in the Fort Smith, Arkansas, Senior High School yearbook he recalled a feeling of "nausea and abhorrence" after having read on a blackboard a "diabolical" homework assignment to write at any length on a subject of his own choice.

He railed,

> Why should I have to write essays? Let those who
> will and wish write them but force me not. Alexander
> the Great at one time conquered all the known world.
> Where, pray tell, is a volume of his essays to be found?

If perchance he did write essays they must have been poor ones for they have never reached print. Let us take Napoleon Bonaparte, Frederick the Great, Maria Theresa, Catherine de Medici, Thomas Edison and Colonel Charles Lindbergh; I ask you, where are their essays? Why then, since I am given no answer and since I intend to become great, should I have to tax my soul with the writing of essays?

In the perfect perception provided by the long view of history, it is easy to read into this literary tantrum by a youthful future soldier not only the essence of his character but evidence that he harbored no doubt that one day his hometown would honor William Orlando Darby as a hero. It did so in 1944 with a parade and a ceremony on the steps of its historic courthouse, by naming the junior high school after him, and eventually making his boyhood home on a street re-named for him into a museum and headquarters of a foundation to enshrine his memory.

Nearly sixty years after he inscribed his feelings in the school publication about having been compelled to write an essay, Fort Smith's ninth-grade journalism students published a tribute entitled *William Orlando Darby: A Man to Remember*. Ironically, it consisted of a collection of essays. Among them were photographs and biographical data, as well as articles based on interviews with people who knew him from all periods of his life. For the students who created the fifty-five-page salute, their hometown's most famous figure was probably as distant as Alexander the Great and Napoleon must have seemed to seventeen-year-old Bill Darby, except that in 1958 there had been a successful movie about him called *Darby's Rangers,* starring James Garner, and in the year of the publication of their tribute the chief executive of Arkansas, Governor Bill Clinton, proclaimed his February birth date "William O. Darby Day."

What had occurred since publication of Darby's essay in 1929 to warrant honors in 1987 is one of the most astonishing tales of personal and historic achievements of the generation of Americans now universally described as the greatest. A U.S. Army historian wrote that as the organizer and leader of the Rangers, William O. Darby became "one of the truly legendary American combat commanders to emerge from World War II." Precursors of today's elite Special Forces in all branches of the military, Darby's men had led the way in four invasions and fought in twelve major battles in North Africa, Sicily, and Italy, while their colonel held his own with many of the war's most colorful and illustrious generals. For three years, he stood shoulder to shoulder, and at times toe to toe, with Dwight D. Eisenhower, Omar N. Bradley, George S. Patton, Theodore Roosevelt, Jr., Terry de la Mesa Allen, and Mark W. Clark.

Comparing the Rangers to the paratroops of the famed Eighty-second Airborne Division, Colonel William Yarborough noted that his jumpers always held to the "traditional esprit of the soldier" and "look sharp" even in foxholes, while "Darby's guys look like cutthroats" and "the sweepings of the bar rooms," with "stubble beards" and "any kind of uniform." Recruited for toughness, they came from all parts of the United States and as civilians had worked in steel mills and coal mines, on farms and factory assembly lines, in offices, a stock brokerage, and in a circus as a lion tamer. One was a bullfighter and another kept the books of a burlesque house. The official appeal for volunteers solicited "a high type of soldier with excellent character who is not averse to seeing dangerous action." It sought men who were "athletically inclined, have good wind and stamina," were good swimmers and mentally adapted "for making quick decisions in the face of unforeseen circumstances."

A thirty-one-year-old West Pointer, Major William O. Darby had begun soldiering in 1933 with the army's last horse artillery outfit. Tall, well built and with blue eyes, a million-dollar smile, dark hair and movie-matinee-idol looks, he could have been an army recruiting poster boy. In a farewell message to his Rangers in April 1945, he said of them, "Whether it was in training or in battle, your unwavering, indomitable spirit forged by painstaking and diligent zeal has always persevered. Your resourcefulness and initiative have earned for you the respect and esteem of all true fighting men the world over."

Four years before Fort Smith's journalism class undertook their memorial, the United States Military Academy published a "Golden Anniversary Yearbook," which cited the most famous graduates of each of West Point's classes. For the year 1933, there was one. The essay noted Darby's "legendary, restless, ranging spirit" as a combat commander, of whom another hero of the Second World War, Lieutenant General Lucian K. Truscott, said, "Never in this war have I known a more gallant, heroic officer."

When Darby began leading the Rangers in battle in 1942, I was an eight-year-old in the small steelmaking town of Phoenixville, Pennsylvania. For me the war was nightly reports of the latest action on the radio by Elmer Davis, Edward R. Murrow, Gabriel Heatter, and Lowell Thomas; newsreels at the Colonial Theater; daily accounts in the *Philadelphia Bulletin* and the Phoenixville *Daily Republican* and a newspaper for schoolkids, the *Weekly Reader*. The only person I knew who was actually in the war was my brother-in-law, Bob Devonshire, who drove a half-track in Patton's Third Army. During the Second World War, only a few fighting units were routinely identified in press reports by the names of their commanders. It was "Patton's Third Army," "Rommel's Afrika Korps," "Montgomery's Desert Rats," "Chennault's Flying Tigers," "Merrill's Marauders," and "Darby's Rangers."

Half a century later, I encountered William O. Darby and his Rangers while researching a biography of another World War II hero. The oldest son and namesake of the twenty-sixth president of the United States and a distant cousin of Franklin D. Roosevelt, Theodore

Roosevelt, Jr., known as Ted, had served heroically in the army in the First World War as a young man and returned to duty in the second at the age of fifty-three. A brigadier general in 1942, he was the second in command of the First Division's invasion of French North Africa and the Tunisian campaign. After action in Italy, he led the Fourth Division onto Utah Beach in Normandy on June 6, 1944. Learning about Ted in what was called the "Mediterranean theater," I necessarily found myself frequently in the company of Darby and the fascinating fighting unit that proudly carried his name as they stormed ashore ahead of Roosevelt's division in North Africa, engaged in battles that drove out the Germans and Italians, and then spearheaded the Allied drive onto Sicily and in two invasions in Italy.

Although Ted Roosevelt and Bill Darby stemmed from dramatically different cultural, social, economic, educational, and geographical roots, I found them amazingly similar in their character as boys, men, soldiers, and military leaders. They were admired, even adored, by their men, as both led from the front. Each was a military maverick who'd felt the stinging rebuke of General Patton for what he deemed their easy approach to soldierly decorum, but praise by "Old Blood and Guts" for their heroism.

While no one had written a biography of Ted Roosevelt, there were several volumes on the subject of Darby's Rangers. Yet, when my literary agent, Jake Elwell, told me that an editor had expressed interest in me writing a William Darby biography, I found a paucity of writing about him beyond accounts of the Rangers in World War II. The only biography was published in 1981 by Michael J. King. A visiting professor of military history at the Army Command and General Staff College, Fort Leavenworth, Kansas, who had served in Airborne, Ranger, and Army Special Forces units, he explained that his *William Orlando Darby: A Military Biography* was intended to be "a study of a soldier's life," emphasizing those elements of Darby's life that had an impact on his military career or his development as a soldier.

After a thirty-three-year career in journalism, I became a full-time author concentrating on nonfiction and biographies with a special interest in American military heroes. I'd written about Theodore Roosevelt as a colonel in the Spanish-American War, his namesake in two world conflicts, World War I "Ace of Aces" Captain Eddie Rickenbacker, and General William "Billy" Mitchell. Though I served in the U.S. Army for three years in the 1950s, I'd never seen combat. Consequently, this book is not intended to be a military analysis of Darby's Rangers in action, but an exploration for general readers of the life and times of an exceptional commander and the exploits of the unique fighting force he created and inspired for three years.

★ CHAPTER 1 ★

The Arkansas Kid

"They think you are being a little uppy."

BECAUSE IT WAS MEMORIAL DAY, EIGHT-YEAR-OLD BILLY DARBY DE-cided it would be fitting, and a lot of fun, if he and his cousin Will Hogan showed their respect to the occupants of Oak Park Cemetery by circumnavigating the hallowed ground atop the graveyard's stone fence.

He'd been told many times that within its confines reposed not only venerated people in the colorful history of Fort Smith, Arkansas, but the bones of seventy-nine men who'd been sent to meet their Maker at the end of a rope by the Honorable Federal Court Judge

Isaac Parker, who would be known in the chronicles of the American West as the "Hanging Judge." The last of these judicially decreed villains, Crawford Goldsby, better known as "Cherokee Bill," gazed at the waiting gallows and remarked, "This is as good a day to die as any."

Eight months to the day later, Judge Parker died of old age and Bright's disease. In his twenty-one years on the bench, he'd tried 13,490 cases, of which 344 were for capital crimes that resulted in convictions or pleas of guilty. Cherokee Bill was strung up at Judge Parker's decree on March 17, 1896, only fifteen years, one month, and six days before William Orlando Darby was born.

From the top of the narrow stone cemetery fence could also be seen the final resting places of thirty-three other outlaws; numerous U.S. marshals, deputies, and sheriffs; two Confederate generals (Richard C. Gatlin and James M. Macintosh); and numerous Civil War soldiers who'd worn the butternut gray uniform of the South. There, too, lay the remains of William Meade Fishback, the seventeenth governor of Arkansas and the only one from Fort Smith; and scores of citizens who had perished in the tornados that periodically ripped through the town off the plains of Oklahoma just across the Arkansas River.

The tour of the cemetery via the top of its bordering narrow wall by the daring cousins began very well, but about halfway into the sojourn Will lost his footing and tumbled down. Dismayed, disappointed, and disgruntled, Billy demanded that he go back to where they'd started and begin again. The command was obeyed, but as the boys resumed their balancing act, the cemetery caretaker appeared and ordered them to get down. Will did so promptly. Billy told the caretaker that he was not one to quit anything halfway through and if the caretaker wanted him off the wall, the caretaker would have to come up and remove him. When no attempt resulted, he continued on his mission, knowing that somewhere in the cemetery lay Sanford Lewis.

A year after William Darby's birth, Lewis was dragged from the city jail by irate Fort Smithians, beaten to a pulp, and lynched for having shot city police officer Andy Carr. The hanging took place on a trolley-car pole in front of the Hotel Main on Garrison Avenue, not far from the Church of the Immaculate Conception. Fort Smith's tallest landmark, the church stood on what had been the parade ground of the second army post called Fort Smith. The first had begun to rise at a spot named Belle Point on the Arkansas River on Christmas Day 1818, when Major William Bradford and sixty-four soldiers arrived with orders to keep the peace between the Cherokee and Osage tribes. They renamed the place Fort Smith. When General Winfield Scott, commander of the U.S. Army Western Division, arrived to take charge of the fort in March 1824, he ordered the post moved to the mouth of the Verdigris River and named the position Fort Gibson. The settlement the soldiers left behind kept the name Fort Smith. It got its first post office and postmaster in 1828. Ten years later, with Arkansas granted statehood, the Congress authorized construction of a second Fort Smith. Completed in 1846, it was designated "Mother Post of the Southwest." During the Civil War, it was alternately occupied by Union and Rebel forces. This fort was also eventually abandoned.

A departure point to the farther West for refugees and frontier pioneers during and after the war, the town found itself amid a growing roster of places romanticized in eastern papers, magazines, and cheap novels as the "wild and woolly West." Among the flamboyant personalities associated with Fort Smith in these yarns was Belle Starr. Although the notorious woman called the "Bandit Queen of the Indian Territory" and paramour of outlaw Cole Younger never lived in the town, she was ambushed and killed with a shotgun blast on a trail between Fort Smith and Oklahoma on February 2, 1889. Also contributing to this reputation as a den of outlaws and "six-gun justice" were tales of the Rufus Buck Gang. Six months before Cherokee Bill climbed the gallows, a mass hanging ended the reign of this quartet of youthful killers and rapists after they went on a fifteen-day rampage among the Creek Nation. They were executed by decree of Judge Parker on September 25, 1895.

As a frontier outpost, Fort Smith was a stop on the Butterfield Trail. Named for a former stagecoach driver, John Butterfield, and financed by the Wells Fargo, American Express, and Adams & Company stage lines, it stretched twenty-six hundred miles from Tipton, Missouri, to San Francisco, with 139 way stations. On October 13, 1858, the first eastbound coach arrived in Fort Smith, setting off a celebration unequaled until January 30, 1879, marking the laying of the last rail that completed construction of the Little Rock and Fort Smith Railway. Like all such towns on the western frontier of wagon trains, cattle drives, cowboys, and bands of desperadoes who stuck up stagecoaches and trains, Fort Smith had its rowdy side. Centered on Front Street along the river, it offered saloons, hotels, and brothels. The town was also home to individuals who sought to instill civilization and did so by putting down roots, starting farms and businesses, building houses and families, and erecting schools and constructing churches.

It was in this frontier era that William Darby's ancestors arrived in Fort Smith. After his parents, Percy and Nellie, settled in a small house at 311 North Fifth Street, their first child, Thelma May, was born in September 1905. William Orlando Darby arrived six years later (February 8, 1911). (When he was in high school, Thelma died before she had reached the age of twenty-one.) A few years later, Doris Nell was born.

Eight months after Bill's birth, Fort Smith was the site of the first Arkansas-Oklahoma State Fair. It ran for five days and drew a crowd each day that would be rivaled six months later by the throng that turned out to see and hear the most famous man in America, as former president Teddy Roosevelt took to the national hustings in a bid to return to the White House. Chagrined that his handpicked successor, William Howard Taft, had not lived up to his expectations, and appalled at the prospect of the Democratic New Jersey governor Woodrow Wilson becoming president, he had declared himself "fit as a bullmoose," announced "My hat is in the ring," and accepted the nomination of the Progressive Party.

The father of the future brigadier general with whom the son of Percy Darby would lead troops in battle in the Second World War had expressed the goal of fatherhood shared by Percy Darby—that the American boy "shall turn out to be a good American man." In defining this ideal, Roosevelt had written, "He must not be a coward or a weakling, a bully, a shirk, or a prig. He must work hard and play hard. He must be clean-minded and clean-lived, and able to hold his own under all circumstances and against all comers."

In all accounts by people who knew William Darby as a boy, he was exactly the sort of youth idealized not only by Teddy Roosevelt but by Americans everywhere in the innocent last years of an age that Mark Twain had labeled "Gilded." In the period that began with the 1876 Centennial Exposition in Philadelphia, marking the signing of the Declaration of Independence, and ended with the United States entering World War I, Americans embraced assertions by men such as Roosevelt that the United States of America was unique among the nations of the world, not only because the Almighty had ordained it, but by virtue of the American character defined by President Roosevelt. "Stout of heart," he declared in 1902, Americans "rejoice as a giant refreshed, as a strong man girt for the race; and we go down into the arena where the nations strive for mastery, our hearts filled with the faith that to us and our children and our children's children it shall be given to make this Republic the mightiest among the peoples of mankind."

Said Roosevelt on another occasion from the "bully pulpit" of the White House, "This nation is seated on a continent flanked by two great oceans. It is composed of the descendants of pioneers, or, in a sense, pioneers themselves, of men winnowed out from the nations of the Old World by the energy, boldness, and love of adventure found in their own eager hearts."

Growing up in the middle of this America with its "manifest destiny" to be great, Billy Darby was imbued with American can-do spirit by reading the magazines *American Boy* and *Boys' Life*, and adventure books by Horatio Alger and about the Rover Boys, Billy Whiskers, Tom Slade, and Tom Swift. His friend Franklin Wilder saw reflections of such fictional characters in Darby. "I think Bill was successful because he was a poor boy," Wilder recalled. "He didn't have everything dumped in his lap. He had to struggle like the rest of us and work for everything he got. Consequently, he was aggressive toward life and ambitious. He wanted to amount to something, be somebody, do something with his life."

As in many parts of the United States when Bill Darby was a boy, the foundations of life in Fort Smith were family, church, and school. The Darbys worshipped at First Methodist Church. Percy was a member of the men's Bible study group and Nellie was secretary of the women's group. Percy formed a partnership (Darby and Bly Printing Company) and subsequently had a sole proprietorship, Darby Printery, that he hoped would one day be known as Darby & Son. A talented musician (clarinet and saxophone), he added to his income by organizing the Darby Orchestra. The group of about thirty performed at the Electric Park amusement pavilion and provided musical accompaniment for the silent films at Fort Smith's movie theaters.

From time to time, Billy assisted his father in adding tunes to the actions on the silver screen. Franklin Wilder remembered, "The two nicest were the New Theater down on Tenth and Garrison, and the Joy Theater on Ninth Street between Garrison and Rogers Avenues. They would play regular music and then all of a sudden one of the cowboys would gallop up and they would increase the tempo of the music."

Darby's boyhood friend Charles "Chili" Brocchus recalled, "People in the neighborhood always looked forward to when we would go to Nellie's house to sing and play music. Bill also played saxophone and he and his daddy would play and we had many good times down there." Another remembered him as a talented musician who played in the school band and orchestra. "I can still see him," he said many years later, "walking after school with that saxophone case in his hand."

School chums at the Grove and Rogers elementary schools were consistent in observing no indications that he planned to become a soldier, but they agreed that he brimmed with self-confidence. Franklin Wilder noted, "Bill had a nice personality, was a good talker, and was bright. He was a hard worker, dedicated and ambitious."

Mavis Redding remembered Darby working as a delivery boy for Gardner's Groceries and thinking that anybody would have picked him out to be a success. Girls were keenly aware of his good looks. With dark brown hair and blue eyes, he was, said his young neighbor Martha Knapp, "a real special and handsome person" with "the most beautiful complexion you've ever seen." Recalling that her older sister, Catherine, was in love with him, she told an interviewer, "Bill had to walk by our house on his way to school when we lived on C Street. My sister would send me out so I could interrupt his walk. He walked fast and she wanted to walk with him. I remember one particular morning when he just came out and asked, 'Martha, did your sister send you out?' I said, 'Yes, Catherine wants to walk with you.'"

High school typing and shorthand teacher Virginia Gardner recalled, "Bill carried himself very erect with his head high. He looked good. It didn't make any difference what clothes he had on. Whether he was in work clothes or overalls, he was still handsome."

Perplexed after losing an election for high school class president, Bill asked Virginia, "Why? I thought I had a lot of friends. Why did people not vote for me?"

Virginia replied, "Bill, you walk with your shoulders back and your head high. So many people do not understand that is natural with you. They think you are being a little uppy."

"If I don't have pride," he answered, "I haven't got anything. Because I don't have anything else, I have to have pride."

This failure to win a school election surprised classmates who found Bill Darby to be a natural leader. Chili Brocchus noted that quality in Bill's membership in a church-related group called the Boy Rangers of America. For underprivileged boys, it was started in Fort Smith by businessman C. F. Wilman. "He led us all the time on our camping trips," Chili recalled of Bill. "We enjoyed his leadership." Telling a friend he was trying to enlist that the Boy Rangers were patterned on the Boy Scouts of America, Darby explained that they were "an outdoor group" that met at least once a month, "and a lot of time on weekends." When Ross Rhodes said he didn't have the money to buy a uniform and badges, Darby said the Boy Rangers' dues were five cents a month and the group did not require special uniforms. They would trek to Wild Cat Mountain, he said, "which is about the wildest place you can find anywhere to camp out." He continued, "We have plenty of good food to eat, cook on an open fire and have a good time."

Chili Brocchus met Bill in 1915 after the Darby house on North Fifth Street was destroyed by a fire and the family moved to Eighth Street, then later to North Greenwood Street. Because the Brocchus house was four blocks away, the boys grew up together. Three years older than Darby, Chili recalled, "Bill used to help on the neighbors' yards and gardens. He knew it had to be done right, because his family believed in hard work."

Depicting "typical boys," Chili noted that in high school the sport his pal liked most was track and that Bill mainly liked to run, high jump, and broad jump. "Quite often," he said, "Bill would run the tape measure when we were broad jumping. He would always measure it short an inch or two so we would try harder. Even though Bill loved music and sports, I think his primary goal in life came from receiving a BB gun for a present from his father. He loved it so and said he was going to be a marshal or soldier."

When Bill Darby left elementary school behind, he entered a high school that started with the eighth grade. Built in 1897, it was an imposing five-story edifice. Resembling a castle, with a pair of cone-roofed turrets, it was built and furnished at a cost of eighty thousand dollars. By the time he was a senior in 1929, the town's population stood at 31,400 and the old building had proved to be insufficient, requiring construction of a new high school capable of accommodating 3,000 students, with an auditorium that seated 1,000. Dedicated on February 15, 1929, it enrolled 848 pupils. He "sauntered happily through those great portals of learning" in the middle of his senior year, having earned membership in the National Honor Society and having served as its vice president, sat on the student council, and been business manager of the school paper, the *Grizzly*, and the school annual, the *Bruin*, for which he wrote his essay on writing essays. Nicknamed "Tuffy," he exhibited talents as an actor with roles in *The Lucky Break* and Fort Smith High School's version of *The Enchanted Cottage*, a 1923 Broadway hit written by Sir Arthur Wing Pinero that had starred Katharine Cornell. Accompanying his photograph in the *Bruin* was the quotation, "I smell the upper air."

The eighteen-year-old Darby had been settled on what he wished to do after graduation since the age of ten. The recipient of a birthday-gift subscription to the magazine *Mentor* by his aunt Pearle Bachle, his mother's childless sister, he had read a series of articles glamorizing cadet life at West Point. The appeal of what he found was not only the prospect of an exciting, adventurous career, but the fact that appointment to the U.S. Military Academy meant obtaining a superb education at no cost to his economically struggling father. Having set West Point as his goal, he understood that obtaining it required appointment by a member of Congress. In 1929, there were openings for two cadets from each congressional district, four from each state at large, and 122 from the nation at large. Representing the Fourth Congressional District of Arkansas was Democrat Otis Wingo. Because Aunt Pearle was employed as a court reporter and knew Wingo, she appealed to him to consider her nephew. Having already selected two candidates, Wingo agreed to name Darby as a second alternate. This meant that for him to gain appointment, the two nominees not only had to be disqualified, but the first alternate must also be found unsuitable. That all three would be eliminated seemed unlikely, but to Darby's amazement they failed to meet either the scholastic or physical standards.

Informed that he had survived the winnowing process, he reported to the Army and Navy General Hospital at Hot Springs, Arkansas, on March 5, 1929, for a physical examination. The doctor noted his height (five feet nine inches) and weight (144 pounds). He also recorded that after two minutes of exercise Darby's pulse rate exceeded the army's minimal requirements. Although the examiner reported him "disqualified for service" with the recommendation "he be rejected," Darby attributed the rapid pulse to nervousness and a panel of examiners elected to follow an army regulation that permitted relaxation of physical standards if there were "reason to believe that both the individual and the army will benefit thereby." Finding Darby to be "well muscled, healthy," and "desirable for appointment," they recommended approval by the surgeon general. It was granted on March 22, 1929. Two weeks after graduation from Fort Smith High School, he boarded an eastbound train for the longest journey of his life, far beyond Arkansas.

He arrived at West Point on the first of July and began two months of tough physical, mental, and psychological preparatory training. Known in the parlance of the U.S. Military Academy as "Beast Barracks," it began with a month of drill, learning military courtesy, and marksmanship. During the second month, the fresh cadets performed guard duty and took part in various ceremonies while receiving infantry training and instruction in service customs. At the end of the summer, as the full cadet corps returned to the academy from leave or training in the field, they were plebes (fourth-classmen) assigned to companies according to their height to assure a uniform appearance in formation. Of medium height, Darby was placed in Company D. His roommates ("wives") were John Baird Shinberger, nicknamed "Shinny," of Norfolk, Virginia, and George Wood Beeler of Seattle, Washington. They studied mathematics, tactics, military topography and graphics, English and French. At the end of his first year, his record listed forty-nine demerits for minor rule infringements of improper hanging of uniforms and being late for formation. The summer before his "third-classman" year was spent in a tent camp for field training. Studies resumed in the fall with the addition of physics and European history. It would be his best year, and he finished ninety-third in rank according to merit and was elevated to cadet corporal. Nonacademically, he played football in the fall and baseball in the spring, sang in the choir, was "hop manager," worked as a stagehand for the "Hundredth Night" annual show, and became a staff member of an annual handbook, *Bugle Notes*, commonly known as the "Plebe Bible," featuring West Point history, customs, and Cadet Corps traditions.

After summer leave spent back home, he plunged into the second-year curriculum of mechanics, hydraulics, aerodynamics, surveying, chemistry, electrical engineering, tactics, military topography and graphics, and Spanish. He finished it ranking 187 of 350, but found himself promoted on the basis of "leadership qualities" to provisional cadet captain. Whether it would be made permanent depended upon his performance in summer training at Fort Monroe, Virginia, and Fort Bragg, North Carolina. When the rank was confirmed on August 26, 1932, he was placed in command of a company the West Point annual, the *Howitzer*, characterized as "renegades, mavericks and misfits." That he was selected to take over such a company was a tribute to the sort of officer classmates such as Lyle B. Bernard observed. He noted that Darby's uniform looked as if it "had been poured on" and that he possessed the "innate leadership" that made his men want not only to follow him but to please him. In retrospect, Company I consisted of the sort of men Darby would choose to become Rangers ten years later.

Ranked 177 of 346 in the graduating class of 1933, he had a bachelor of science degree and a commission as a second lieutenant in the field artillery. After a seventy-four-day leave at home, he reported for duty at Fort Bliss, Texas, and was assigned to the First Cavalry Division, First Battalion, Eighty-second Field Artillery. His battery (A) was supplied with French 75mm guns dating to 1897. State-of-the-art in "the war to save democracy," they were as anachronistic to the artillery weaponry of other armies in 1933 as the unit's horse-drawn gun caissons were to the truck-towed artillery pieces of other nations and as cavalry charges were to attacks by columns of tanks.

Filled with revulsion at the mass slaughter of young men in the Great War that restored the United States' traditional policy of isolationism, feeling secure and invulnerable between two oceans, and mired in the worst economic depression in history, a vast majority of Americans and most leaders of their government exhibited no interest in maintaining a large army. They paid little attention to the rise of militarism in Germany under the Nazi regime of Adolf Hitler and the aggressive expansionism of the Empire of Japan. Consequently, when Darby reported for duty with the First Cavalry Division, he found it engaged in nonmilitary activities in the Arizona–New Mexico District of the Civilian Conservation Corps.

While serving in Texas, he wed Natalie Shaw of El Paso, but they divorced in 1939. A request for transfer to the Army Air Corps was denied, as was an application for assignment to the Philippines or Hawaii. After graduation from Field Artillery School at Fort Sill, Oklahoma, in 1937, he was assigned to the Eighty-fourth Artillery

Division at Fort Riley, Kansas, with much of the same duties as those in the First Division. A year later (a month after Germany triggered the Second World War by invading Poland), he was posted to the Eighth Field Artillery at Fort Lewis, Washington. As executive officer, Battery B, First Battalion, in June 1940 (as France capitulated to Germany), he was at Camp Beauregard, Louisiana, taking part in large army maneuvers that revealed the extent of American unpreparedness for modern warfare.

Cited in reports for outstanding performance and the ability "to get the maximum response from his men and at the same time keep them smiling," he was given command of a battery and quickly ordered to join the Ninety-ninth Field Artillery. Based at Fort Hoyle, Maryland, under command of Lieutenant Colonel George P. Hays, a Medal of Honor recipient in World War I, it was a "pack unit" with 75mm howitzers that could be partially disassembled and then carried by mules over terrain too rough for motor vehicles. Darby was promoted to captain on September 9, 1940, and ordered to command Battery A in joint army-navy exercises in amphibious operations in Puerto Rico. The training, carried out in mid-February 1941, introduced him to the virtues of the 4.2-inch mortar and its advantages in range, flexibility, and overall effectiveness in support of infantry. Originally designed for firing phosphorus and smoke rounds, the weapon was officially categorized as a "chemical mortar." Its use, the mountain operations learned, with a pack unit and tactics of beach assaults were to be hallmarks of the infantry unit that would become famous as Darby's Rangers.

"We are preparing for war, but hoping we're never in it," Virginia Gardner recalled her former pupil saying in late August 1941. As she drove him to Kansas City to board a plane at the end of a month's leave in Fort Smith following the exercises in Puerto Rico, he said with unusual solemnity, "But if we are, I will lead my men and will never be in back of them."

The year had begun with President Roosevelt asking Congress to approve a "lend-lease" program that involved Great Britain borrowing retired U.S. Navy destroyers and the United States being permitted to have bases in Britain's colonies in the Caribbean. Roosevelt also sought "authority and for funds sufficient to manufacture additional munitions and war supplies of many kinds, to be turned over to those nations which are now in actual war" with Germany and other "aggressor nations."

"Our most useful and immediate role," he had declared, "is to act as an arsenal for them as well as for ourselves. They do not need manpower, but they do need billions of dollars' worth of the weapons of defense. The time is near when they will not be able to pay for them all in ready cash. We cannot, and we will not, tell them that they must surrender, merely because of present inability to pay for the weapons which we know they must have."

At the end of January Adolf Hitler had promised a historic year for the "new European order." He boasted, "On land the number of our divisions has been mightily increased and their pay increased. War experiences have been evaluated by men and officers. Work has been done and work continues unceasingly. Equipment has been improved and our enemies shall see how it was improved. On the seas the U-boat war will begin in the spring, and they will see that there, too, we have not slept. And the air force will also put in an appearance, and all the armed forces together will force a decision one way or another. The German people stands behind its leaders, believing in their armed forces and ready to endure what destiny demands of it."

With the Lend-Lease Act approved on March 11, aid was extended to countries "whose defense is vital to that of the United States." Promising increasing assistance to Allies for a total victory, Roosevelt vowed, "The light of democracy must be kept burning. To the perpetuation of this light, each must do his own share. The single effort of one individual may seem very small. But there are 130 million individuals over here. There are many more millions in Britain and elsewhere bravely shielding the great flame of democracy from the black-out of barbarism. It is not enough for us merely to trim the wick or polish the glass. The time has come when we must provide the fuel in ever increasing amounts to keep the flame alight."

Predicting British defeat, Hitler asserted, "The world is not here for a few people, and an order based eternally on the distinction between the haves and the have-nots does not exist any more because the have-nots have determined to lay claims to their portion of God's earth."

On April 8, Vice President Henry A. Wallace retorted, "We of the United States can no more evade shouldering our responsibility than a boy of eighteen can avoid becoming a man by wearing short pants."

On May 15, President Roosevelt rebuked the vanquished French for collaboration with Germany. "The people of the United States can hardly believe," he said, "that the present Government of France could be brought to lend itself to a plan of voluntary alliance, implied or otherwise, which would apparently deliver up France and its colonial empire, including French African colonies and their Atlantic coasts, with the menace which that involves to the peace and safety of the Western Hemisphere."

A week later, British prime minister Winston Churchill warned the French government based in Vichy that if in pursuance of "their declared policy of collaboration with the enemy" the French took action or permitted action "detrimental to our conduct of the war or designed to assist the enemy's war effort, we shall naturally hold ourselves free to attack the enemy wherever he may be found." As he spoke, British forces were engaged in battle with a German force in the deserts of Libya. Commanded by General Erwin Rommel, the "Afrika Korps" of tanks and infantry had been rushed to North Africa following a crushing defeat in December 1940 of the Italian army in an attempt to seize Egypt and the Suez Canal.

On May 27, Roosevelt proclaimed an unlimited national emergency and noted that what started as a European war "has developed, as the Nazis always intended it should develop, into a world war for world-domination. Adolf Hitler never considered the domination of Europe as an end in itself. European conquest was but a step toward ultimate goals in all the other continents."

With the French government allowing Japan to take control of its colony of Indochina in July, the United States informed Japan's ambassador in Washington, D.C., that the United States could only assume that the occupation constituted notice that the Japanese government intended to pursue a policy of force and of conquest, and that, in the light of these acts on the part of Japan, the United States, with regard to its own safety in the light of its own preparations for self-defense, must assume that the Japanese government was taking the last step before proceeding upon a policy of totalitarian expansion in the South Seas and of conquest in the South Seas through the seizure of additional territories in that region.

In August, the government of Marshal Philippe Pétain in Vichy, France, announced full collaboration with Hitler. With Germany having attacked the Soviet Union and moved into the Baltic, the Balkans, and Greece, and having been freed from the prospect of French resistance in North Africa, Roosevelt and Churchill met on the American cruiser *Augusta* off Newfoundland to formalize their Anglo-American alliance and lay out their policy. Called the "Atlantic Charter," it asserted that they sought "no aggrandizement, territorial or other," and wished "no territorial changes that do not accord with the freely expressed wishes of the peoples concerned." After the "final destruction of the Nazi tyranny," the leaders hoped "to see established a peace which will afford to all nations the means of dwelling in safety within their own boundaries."

As Darby enjoyed his furlough in Fort Smith on August 17, 1941, Roosevelt consented to renew informal talks with Japan "for bringing

about an adjustment of relations" and to ascertain "whether there ex-
isted a basis for negotiations relative to a peaceful settlement covering
the entire Pacific situation."

Although the president said on September 2 that "every effort"
must be made to defeat "Hitler's violent attempt to rule the world,"
Darby believed war was much more likely to start in the Pacific. At
age thirty, he had been proudly wearing an army uniform for eight
years and had earned his captain's bars in routine assignments that
had imposed no challenges and offered no opportunities to fulfill the
prediction in his high school essay that he was cut out for greatness.
Consequently, when he was ordered in early November to prepare to
leave Maryland for a posting in Hawaii, effective at the end of the
year, he was delighted and excited. When the war he expected began
with the Japanese sneak attack at Pearl Harbor on December 7, he
recalled his pledge to Virginia Gardner that he would lead his men
into battle from the front and looked ahead eagerly to keeping the
promise in the Pacific.

★ CHAPTER 2 ★

ALL TYPES OF AMERICANS

"What do you say to that, Bill?"

OPENING SEALED ORDERS ON JANUARY 5, 1942, AT FORT HOYLE, MARY-land, and expecting to find instructions to proceed to Hawaii, Captain William O. Darby was astonished to discover that he was to report to New York City no later than January 7. He was to serve as the aide-de-camp to Major General Russell P. Hartle. Known as "Scrappy," Hartle was commander of the Thirty-fourth Infantry. His chief of staff, Colonel Edmond Leavey, was a forty-eight-year-old West Pointer.

The sequence of events that resulted in frustrating Darby's vision of attaining greatness in battle somewhere in the far reaches of the

Pacific Ocean had begun with the Atlantic Charter conference between Roosevelt and Churchill. They agreed on a plan called MAGNET Force that anticipated the United States ultimately entering the war against Germany. It called for the initial deployment of 158,700 American troops to the British Isles. A later War Department plan called RAINBOW-5 assigned approximately 30,000 to be based in Northern Ireland. On May 19, 1941, a Special Observer Group was established under command of Major General James E. Chaney in temporary headquarters at the U.S. embassy in Grosvenor Square in London. A meeting with the British Chiefs of Staff Committee to iron out coordination resulted in a plan for construction of bases in Northern Ireland and Scotland using $50 million of Lend-Lease funds. The first of the Americans in Northern Ireland would total 14,000 in two combat teams under the command of Major General Hartle.

Eight days after reporting to Hartle in New York City, Darby was on a troopship bound for Belfast and already registering with Leavey his disappointment with being assigned a staff post rather than command of a combat unit. When the Americans stepped ashore on January 26, 1942, they were greeted by the governor general of Northern Ireland, the Duke of Abercorn; the prime minister of Northern Ireland, John W. Andrews; the British troop commander in Ulster, General G. E. W. Franklyn; and the secretary of state for air, Sir Archibald Sinclair. Hartle set up the headquarters of U.S. Army Northern Ireland Force (USANIF) in Wilmont House. Seven miles southwest of Belfast in County Antrim, it had been built in 1859 by banker James Bristow at the junction of Dunmurry Lane and the Upper Malone Road.

Although General Hartle's frustrated aide-de-camp could trace his ancestry to Ireland, Darby found his duties in assisting in organizing USANIF left no time for exploration of either familial or Irish history. Because his temperament was deemed more congenial than Hartle's gruff and often brusque bearing, he was given responsibility for engaging socially with the Irish, who suddenly found not only their community inundated with thousands of American soldiers but their quiet countryside, narrow lanes, and scenic byways resounding to the rumbling and roar of military vehicles. With startling suddenness, it seemed Ulster was becoming Americanized as the USANIF expanded to include a U.S. Air Force maintenance depot at Langford Lodge and a Northern Ireland Base Command (Provisional) under Brigadier General Leroy P. Collins (former commander, Thirty-fourth Infantry Division Artillery).

On April 17, General Chaney, Brigadier General Robert A. McClure (military attaché at the U.S. embassy in London), along with roving diplomat W. Averill Harriman, presidential aide Harry Hopkins, and army chief of staff General George C. Marshall, began an inspection tour of American forces in Northern Ireland that would have a profound effect on William Darby's role in the war. The army chief of staff's purpose was to arrange for British officers who had combat experience in Commando tactics to train groups of American officers and enlisted ranks. These men could then train other American troops in such tactics. Back in Washington, D.C., in late April, Marshall met in his War Department office with Colonel Lucian K. Truscott.

Born in 1895, in Chatfield, Texas, Truscott had enlisted in the army in World War I. Selected for officer training, he was commissioned in the cavalry in 1917 but saw no combat. After the war, he served in a variety of cavalry posts and was an instructor at both the Cavalry School and Command and General Staff School. He had been picked by General Dwight D. Eisenhower, then chief of the War Department Operations Division, and General Mark Clark of Headquarters Army Division to lead a group of American officers to England to join the staff of Lord Louis Mountbatten's recently formed Combined Operations in England. Marshall told him there was no plan for the U.S. Army to create its own separate Commando units, but that hit-and-run methods were to become an integral part of existing forces in anticipation of an Allied invasion of Europe in 1943.

The Americans who trained with the British were to be temporarily detached from their units and return to them as instructors.

With this understanding Truscott headed to Britain carrying a letter from Eisenhower that defined four purposes of his mission. He was directed to (1) study organization, preparation, and conduct of combined operations, (2) initiate plans for participation of Americans as a means of gaining combat experience, (3) provide recommendations for training Americans in Commando operations, and (4) "promote a spirit of Anglo-American teamwork."

Before Truscott left Washington, Eisenhower had exhibited concerns about British sensitivities by urging Truscott to come up with a name other than "Commandos." The term had been coined by the British to describe guerrillas during the Boer War and was revived by Winston Churchill, who had been hailed as a hero in that conflict, to designate small British units meant to both harass Germans and boost British morale at the outset of the Second World War. Arriving in England, Truscott realized not only that Eisenhower was right about English sensitivity and the association of "Commandos" with the British, but that the Irish playwright Bernard Shaw had also been correct when he'd cynically observed that the English and the Americans were peoples separated by a common language.

Truscott quickly saw that grafting the British-style Commando operations to the American army would not be as easy a task as Mountbatten and Marshall had supposed, nor as prudent and practical as it had seemed. He recognized that Americans would eventually be using American-built landing craft and other equipment and arms. Perhaps motivated as strongly by national pride as by these military realities, he envisioned American "Commandos" who would be purely American in character, as well as in name, drawn from volunteers from the U.S. forces in Northern Ireland to form four or five troops with a total strength of four hundred to five hundred men. These suggestions were sent to Marshall on May 26, 1942. Two days later, a War Department cable gave the green light.

Promoted to brigadier general, Truscott drafted a letter to General Hartle to be signed by General Chaney directing Hartle to organize a "Commando-like unit" within the Thirty-fourth Division as soon as possible. Dated June 1, 1942, the letter explained that the War Department had directed organization of a unit for training and demonstration purposes under "British control and that after such training and experience as many men as practicable would return to their organization." The letter said that only "fully trained soldiers of the highest possible type" should be sought. The requirements were a natural athletic ability, physical stamina, and skills in self-defense, scouting, use of firearms and knives, mountaineering, boating, mechanics, electrical engineering, and operation and repair of radios. Physical specifications were twenty-twenty vision without eyeglasses, normal hearing, normal blood pressure for a man of twenty-five, no cardiac defects, no dentures, and no night blindness. Officers and noncommissioned officers were to "possess qualities of leadership of a high order," with emphasis on initiative, judgment, and "common sense."

The men were to be formed as a battalion at a site in Northern Ireland of Hartle's choice and attached to the British Special Service Brigade for training and tactical control, but using American methods and military doctrines as much as possible. The Thirty-fourth Division was to provide administration and supplies. Hartle would choose its commander. This decision was foremost in his thoughts as he, Leavey, and Darby traveled together to church services in Belfast.

"We can't get very far with this new job," Hartle said, "unless we have somebody good to put in charge. Any ideas?"

Keenly aware that Darby wanted to get into a tactical unit, Leavey replied, "Why don't you give the job to Bill?"

"What do you say to that, Bill?" Hartle asked.

By coincidence, Truscott's letter had been written on the same day that Darby had been promoted to major. Now, a week later, Darby was being offered an opportunity he had feared would never arise.

Envisaging "a rugged future in a job where a man could call his soul his own," he suddenly found himself being asked if he wished to be placed in charge of forging a battalion that was nothing more than the bare-bones concept of an irregular outfit on the lines outlined in Truscott's letter. Titled "Commando Organization," it began, "In order to provide battle trained personnel in ALL units, the 1st Battalion consisting of a Headquarters Company (8 officers, 69 enlisted) and 6 companies (3 officers and 62 enlisted men) each for a total of 26 officers and 441 enlisted men, will be formed from troops in the USANIF, preferably from volunteers."

This was to be completed within ten days.

Having no precedent in the history of the U.S. Army, the fledgling battalion also had no name. Eisenhower had urged a uniquely American designation, but had offered no suggestion. At some point, Truscott settled on a name that had blazed its way into history during the French and Indian War when Major Robert Rogers led a band of irregulars known as "Robert's Rangers." In 1937 they moved from the pages of the history books into American popular lore in novelist Kenneth Roberts's *Northwest Passage*. The best seller had inspired a 1940 movie of that title starring Spencer Tracy and Robert Young. In his memoirs, *Command Missions* (1954), Truscott recalled that while numerous names were recommended, "I selected Rangers."

Although Lord Mountbatten also laid claim to the designation, a former reporter for the *New York Times*, Captain Ted Conway, who had been present at a meeting where the name was chosen, stated in an article for the paper on August 20, 1942, that it was Truscott. The name appeared officially for the first time in a June 13 letter by Truscott to Hartle that stated, "The designation of this unit will be the 1st Ranger Battalion."

Darby's first decision was the selection of his executive officer. He chose a tall, thin, blond New Yorker. The same age as Darby, Captain Herman W. Dammer had graduated from Curtis High School on Staten Island in 1928 and was a National Guard cavalry lieutenant who had been called to active duty in July 1941. Adjutant of an anti-aircraft battery protecting Belfast, he had volunteered for the Rangers because he preferred to be in the infantry. As second in command of the Rangers, he was given responsibility for organizing an officer staff and serving as plans and training officer. Assisting him would be Captain Roy A. Murray. Six months older than Darby and his senior in time in service, he was an athletic Reserve officer from California and a hiker and runner with boating experience and excellent analytical and communication skills.

In selecting twenty-nine officers, Darby chose eleven infantrymen, four from the field artillery, three combat engineers, two cavalrymen, and one each from the Quartermaster, Signal, Ordnance, and Medical corps. Sixty percent of the enlisted men were to come from the Thirty-fourth Division and thirty percent from the First Armored Division. The selection criteria were personality traits and the man's motivation in volunteering. Looking beyond the physical demands, Darby attempted to determine whether a volunteer had "good judgment" and if his desire to become a Ranger was "genuine." The object was "weeding out the braggart" and anyone expecting "to be a swashbuckling hero who could live as he pleased if he exhibited courage and daring in battle."

These determinations were made during interviews with two thousand volunteers from Fifth Corps. Over a two-week period, Darby and his officers chose 575 men whom Darby described as "all types of Americans." In ages from seventeen to thirty-five, they were "boyish-looking soldiers just out of high school to an occasional grizzled 'old soldier' " from "practically every section of the Union."

Private First Class Thomas S. "Sully" Sullivan graduated cum laude from St. Michael's College in Vermont in 1941, with a dream of being a writer. Drafted into the army, he applied for training as a navigator in the Air Corps, but instead was assigned to Company G, 168th Regiment, Thirty-fourth Division, Fort Dix, New Jersey. On

February 19, 1942, the unit shipped out from New York City for North Ireland. When the news spread throughout his camp that "a new outfit was looking for some tough volunteers which would take the fight to the Germans," he was learning to be a radio operator. Though he passed the physical exam on June 8, he was unsure about "giving up radio." After an interview by a board of officers three days later he noted in his diary, "Evidently accepted for Rangers."

Technician Fifth Grade (T/5) Clyde Thompson of Ashland, Kentucky, told interviewers he wanted to be a Ranger because the recruiting letter said "they wanted men to work in small combat groups which would hit and run." Corporal James Haines of Kentucky had been a lion tamer in the Frank Buck Circus and ventured that being a Ranger "ain't no different." Samson P. Oneskunk was a private from South Dakota and a Sioux Indian. Private "Chico" Fernandez was a Cuban who'd qualified as an expert machine gunner. John Edmond Hill was from Poplar Bluff, Missouri. From the 125th Field Artillery Regiment, George Ostlund had lettered in football and hockey at Cathedral High School in Duluth, Minnesota. Dennis Bergstrom was a graduate of Duluth State Teachers College and William Arimond had majored in music at Duluth Junior College. Natives of Sioux City, Gino Mercuriali, Henry Peterson, and Zane Shippy were from the Headquarters Battery, 155th Artillery Regiment. An Iowa National Guard unit, it was mobilized in February 1941.

James Altieri from Philadelphia would demonstrate a talent for writing by vividly recounting his service with Darby's Rangers in a 1960 memoir, *The Spearheaders*. A Technician Fifth Grade in Battery A, Sixty-eighth Field Artillery, First Armored Division, he'd listened to a first sergeant read the letter calling for volunteers for a new unit "along the lines of the British Commandos" and said to himself, *"This is it."*

Recalling reading reports of the British hit-and-run raids along the Norwegian coast and in France, and noting that his heart pounded with excited anticipation of "taking part in swift night sorties on enemy coast fortifications," he pictured himself and his buddy Carlo Contrera returning from action "to rest up awhile and live in civilian billets as gentlemen." When asked later by the captain of Battery A to explain his desire to volunteer for the new Commando-type unit, Altieri replied, "That sort of fighting appeals to me because more and more emphasis is placed on personal initiative."

Acceptance depended on the outcome of an interview with an officer from the new unit. Noting Altieri's name, Captain Alvah Miller asked, "What would be your attitude about fighting hand to hand with Italians?"

Altieri answered, "Naturally, I would much prefer to fight the Germans or the Japs. I would feel bad about fighting the same people my father came from, but I feel that when the time comes, that factor won't interfere with my duty as an American soldier."

"Do you think you would have guts enough to stick a knife in a man's back and twist it?" Miller asked.

Replying that if it had to be done, he could do it, Altieri lied. "The mere thought of using a knife repelled me," he wrote. "But if knife-twisting was what these people specialized in, then I would be a knife-twister. What's the difference if you kill someone with a bullet or a knife? A dead man is a dead man regardless of how he is killed."

When he left the interview, Altieri began to doubt that he had measured up, but when a list of eleven names of those who had been accepted was posted the next day, he was the first. Carlo Contrera was second. They had become friends in basic training at Fort Knox, Kentucky. Of average height, stocky, with a thick neck and short brown hair, Carlo was from Brooklyn, though he confessed that he hated the New York City borough. Populated enough to rank as one of the largest cities in the United States, Brooklyn was the cause of bursts of affectionate applause from the studio audiences of radio shows whenever it and the name of its baseball team, the Dodgers, were mentioned. It was so famous for being teased that Darby felt it necessary to note that while the baseball team might be mocked as "dem Brooklyn bums," the soldiers who came from there "were no duds."

As Altieri and other potential Rangers boarded a truck that would join a convoy of recruits, their former commanding officer said, "If you don't like the new outfit or can't make the grade, you can always find your place waiting for you in Battery A. I don't want any of you to feel that your return will be considered a failure. There may be a thousand reasons why you may not like the life you are about to enter—and it's a man's privilege to change his mind."

Altieri understood that their CO was providing him and the others a means to reconsider without losing face, and hoped he would not have to take it. Their destination was a town on the north shore of Belfast Lough that in ancient Gaelic was *Carraig Fhearghais*. Meaning "Rock of Fergus," and identified on maps in English as Carrickfergus, it was the site of a twelfth-century Norman castle, an equally old Church of St. Nicholas, and the place from which the parents of President Andrew Jackson had emigrated in 1765.

When the convoy reached the town, the sun broke through leaden February clouds for the first time in two weeks, reminding the soldiers in the backs of the uncovered olive drab trucks with white U.S. Army stars on their sides why Ireland was called the Emerald Isle. Turning onto a narrow macadam road, the vehicles entered a large camp with rows of British army tents like those of American Indians. After the men dismounted and swung heavy barracks bags and gear to the ground, a group of dejected-looking men climbed into the trucks. Altieri asked a sergeant, "Where are they going?"

"Right back where they came from," the sergeant replied. "After three days most of them don't like the new outfit. Some are being sent back because they aren't qualified. You guys will understand what I mean after you've been here for a few days."

Carlo Contrera muttered, "What the hell can they do to a man in *three* days?"

★ CHAPTER 3 ★

THE CHOSEN FEW

"We don't intend to waste any time on foul-ups."

ON JUNE 15, 1942, MAJOR WILLIAM O. DARBY NOTED IN A PROGRESS report to General Hartle that personnel files of 104 of the 575 volunteers who arrived at Camp Sunnylands, Carrickfergus, Northern Ireland, with hopes of becoming Rangers had been stamped RTU (returned to unit). They either had been sent back already or were waiting for transport to their original outfits. This rate of elimination required dispatching six boards of officers to look for additional men throughout the First Armored and Third Infantry Divisions. Meanwhile, those who'd qualified were assigned to six companies that would each have three officers (a captain and two lieutenants) and sixty-nine enlisted men in two platoons. Companies were organized into three sections (two assault, one mortar). These and Headquarters Company constituted the First Ranger Battalion.

Assigned to Company F, and disappointed that his buddy Carlo Contrera had been put in Company D, James Altieri observed that the men of his company were from almost every branch of the army—infantry, artillery, antiaircraft, armored, ordnance, signal, and quartermaster. The company's loud-talking, self-assured acting first sergeant, Donald Torbett, had come from the Thirteenth Regiment, First Armored Division. Altieri guessed that Captain Roy Murray was about thirty years old, but noted that he moved with the agility of a nineteen-year-old. A native of Louisiana, Second Lieutenant Edwin V. Loustalot was small and wiry and had attended Louisiana State University. With the company having been given another physical, issued new uniforms, and heard an orientation lecture in the course of the first morning at Carrickfergus, the officers introduced them to a training exercise known as a "speed march" that Altieri would call one of the Rangers' secret weapons and Darby would describe as their trademark. In giving "maximum development to lungs and legs, and most importantly, to feet," he recorded, the long hikes "hardened" men so they eventually were able to march ten miles in eighty-seven minutes. No such steady pace was achieved on Company F's first speed march.

With Murray and Loustalot at the head of the double column, James Altieri wrote in *The Spearheaders*, they started off at a brisk pace down a narrow macadam road and out of the camp. With each man looking fresh, vigorous, and confident, he sensed a difference in spirit between his new outfit and the one he had just left. Alternately marching at a double-time rate for three hundred yards and a quick-time thirty-six-inch stride, they were sweating "heavily" and feeling "breathless" after doing five miles with full pack and equipment in one hour.

"Before we were dismissed for chow," Altieri noted, Lieutenant Loustalot "gave us a short talk—more or less a briefing on what to expect in the new outfit." In his Louisiana drawl, he said that they were there for the same purpose—to prove themselves qualified for the new American Commando outfit.

"We may be here for two or three weeks before leaving for Scotland, and during that time our training will be stepped up each day," he warned. "Any man who can't keep up will be sent back to his old outfit immediately, as will anyone who proves troublesome. Discipline in this outfit rests with the individual himself—it's up to you, as we don't intend to waste any time on foul-ups. And remember, you are free to request return to your old outfit at any time."

Questioning whether he could take it and wondering if each day would be the last for him, Altieri decided that giving up would mark him as a failure and "a would-be Commando: No guts, nothing but a lot of talk." Resolved to die rather than go back, he observed the men around him suffering as much as he was and felt proud to be one of them. He admired Sergeant Randall Harris. Thin, frail-looking, with difficulty in speaking without stuttering, Harris seemed to be more suited to be a clerk behind a typewriter. Altieri surmised that if a vote were to be taken among the men in Company F at the beginning of training as to who would be the first to be eliminated, Harris would have been unanimously elected.

"But Sergeant Harris," Altieri recorded, "besides being one of the smartest in the company, was proving that he had more guts and stamina than most. I was beginning to learn that what counted in this outfit was what a man had within him."

Under General Order Number 7, Headquarters USANIF and Fifth Corps (Reinforced), dated June 19, 1942, the First Ranger Battalion would be formally activated as follows:

Battalion Commander: Major William O. Darby

Executive Officer and Operations Training Officer: Captain
    Herman Dammer

Adjutant: First Lieutenant Howard W. Karbel

Supply Officer: First Lieutenant Axel W. Anderson

Medical Officer: First Lieutenant William A. Jarrett

Communications Officer: First Lieutenant George P. Sunshine

Company Commanders:

    A: First Lieutenant Gordon Klefman

    B: First Lieutenant Alfred H. Nelson

    C: Captain William Martin

    D: Captain Alvah Miller

    E: First Lieutenant Max Schneider

    F: Captain Roy Murray

Each company headquarters consisted of the CO, first sergeant (a master sergeant), company clerk (corporal), and messenger (private). A platoon had a lieutenant as platoon leader, a technical sergeant as platoon sergeant, a messenger (private), and a sniper (private). Platoons had two assault sections of eleven men each: Section Leader (staff sergeant), Assistant Section Leader (corporal), Browning Automatic Rifleman (corporal or T/5), five riflemen, and two scouts (privates). Their weaponry consisted of a .45-caliber pistol, an M1903 Springfield rifle with bayonet and grenade launcher, four A4 light machine guns, four Thompson submachine guns, two 60mm mortars, two 2.36-inch rocket launchers, eight Browning automatic rifles (BARs) for each company, and six 81mm mortars in Headquarters Company. Each company was also issued twelve brass knuckles. Steel helmets were World War I saucer-type model M1917A.

Communication equipment included semaphore flags, EE-8 telephones, and SCR-294 and SCR-536 radios. For transportation there were a lone one-and-a-half-ton truck, nine quarter-ton trucks (known as "peeps"), and six motorcycles. When a station wagon for use by the battalion commander did not arrive, Darby claimed a motorcycle that would become as associated with him in army photographs as a long-stemmed corncob pipe would be with Douglas MacArthur and a brace of ivory-grip pistols with George S. Patton.

The sight of Darby astride a World War I–vintage Harley-Davidson contributed significantly to an impression that quickly formed among officers and enlisted ranks of the battalion commander as a dashing figure upon whom fate had smiled at an early age. He seemed to have been endowed with a unique ability not only to command soldiers but to inspire them with the depth of his character. Accounts are universal in their esteem for him as a leader and a man.

To James Altieri, Darby seemed singled out by destiny to lead a group of men who required leadership of the highest caliber. Sergeant Peer Buck saw a boss who knew what he wanted, and when he said it you knew he meant it. Sergeant Warren Evans, who would earn a battlefield commission in North Africa, recalled that Darby followed the book on how to be a good leader. Although he was flamboyant at times, he was not demanding, but the men knew he meant what he said. Captain Dammer said that Darby conveyed "the tremendous impression of being in charge." He found him "tremendously proud" of being a West Pointer.

Pride, nature, and a desire to set a virtuous example by moderation in demeanor had combined with the ambition he'd exhibited as a boy to fashion an officer whose efficiency reports extolled both aggressive leadership and pleasing personality. While it had taken him seven years of active duty since graduation from West Point to rise to captain, he'd received promotion to major after only twenty-one months (June 1, 1942). But this exceptionally quick rise was eclipsed eighteen days later with his elevation to lieutenant colonel. When he received the silver-leaf emblem of the rank on June 19 (twelve days after his appointment as commander of the First Ranger Battalion), he achieved a unique place in U.S. Army annals by having gone from captain to lieutenant colonel in less than two years.

The date of his promotion to "light colonel" was also auspicious for the Rangers. In the words of Altieri, on that "big day for the outfit" the battalion was to be officially activated as a combat unit. A ceremony was scheduled featuring a British general of the Special Service Brigade. Rumor had it that he would speak about the British fighters known and venerated by soldiers on both sides of the Atlantic as the Commandos.

Born in London on April 18, 1907, Robert Laycock was the eldest son of Sir Joseph Frederick Laycock, a Royal Artillery officer who was knighted for his service in World War I. Educated at Eton and the Royal Military College at Sandhurst, Robert was commissioned in the Royal Horse Guards in 1927. When World War II broke out, he was appointed to the chemical warfare section of the British Expeditionary Force and later was chosen to lead one unit of the newly formed Commandos. He raised and trained a body of men drawn largely from his wide circle of friends. Much of the training was done in western Scotland. In a raid on the port of Bardia in the Italian colony of Libya, they learned the need to move quickly. During a campaign on the island of Crete in 1941, he thwarted a nighttime German attack on his headquarters by jumping in a tank that happened to be nearby and driving over the invaders. That year he also led a raid to capture General Erwin Rommel, which failed with significant casualties. Laycock evaded capture and after two months behind enemy lines made his way with a small group overland to British forces. In early 1942, he returned to England as commander of Special Service Brigade.

A month before Laycock arrived at Camp Sunnylands, three of Darby's officers and three sergeants had met with him and other British officers on a mission to observe and study Commando training methods at camps in Ardrossan, Inveraray, and Achnacarry, Scotland, followed by a visit to Southampton, England, to watch infantry units in combined training. A report to General Lucian Truscott written by First Lieutenant Alfred H. Nelson expressed the belief of the observers that "it is possible by use of some of the British methods, plus some that I am sure will be devised by our own commanders, to train Americans to do a better job in any situation than that done by their British forerunners."

In bright sunlight on a soccer field on June 19, with a Signal Corps band playing martial tunes and Rangers in fresh uniforms "trying to look serious and soldierly," the five companies of Darby's battalion paraded past a reviewing stand where Darby stood next to General Laycock. Announcing that Laycock would be in charge of the next phase of Ranger training in Scotland, Darby reminded the troops that they now bore a name honored in American military history. "Men have come and men have gone," he said, "until now the chosen few remain."

Slight of build, with iron gray hair, his right hand holding a riding crop, Laycock began with a greeting that sent a surge of pride through the ranks: "American Rangers." Calling them "an experiment, novel in modern American military history," he said, "You are pioneering in a daring field of warfare at a critical time when our fighting forces, reeling from early defeats, must rebound and assume the offensive. In the British army, Commandos have provided the spark for that offensive spirit. You men are destined to provide that offensive spark for the American forces in Europe."

While Darby and Laycock addressed the Rangers in Northern Ireland, seven of Darby's officers and twelve sergeants were en route to temporary duty on the Isle of Wight. They were to observe the Second Canadian Division as it prepared to take part in a British raid on the French port town of Dieppe in early July, code-named Rutter. When President Roosevelt learned from Prime Minister Churchill that it was scheduled for the Fourth of July, he insisted that it include Americans. He hoped that news of even a handful of U.S. troops taking the war to the Germans on the continent of Europe, however briefly, would have the same morale-boosting effect as the recent Doolittle Raid. The bombing raid by Mitchell B-25s launched from the aircraft carrier USS *Hornet* and led by Lieutenant Colonel James "Jimmy" Doolittle attacked Tokyo, Japan, on April 18, 1942, the anniversary of Paul Revere's famous ride in 1775.

Eisenhower's concern about Americans not offending British sensibilities was not shared down the chain of command by First Lieutenant Nelson and enlisted men, such as T/5 Altieri. Their chests swelled with pride when Laycock predicted the Rangers would make American military history and when, more important, Darby named them "the chosen few."

★ CHAPTER 4 ★

El Darbo

"The great adventure was about to begin."

On June 28, 1942, a misty morning that the Irish called a "soft day" broke more noisily than usual in Carrickfergus. Instead of the thumping boots and rattling equipment from columns of American soldiers beginning speed marches that residents had come to expect, the town awoke to a rumbling convoy of olive drab one-and-a-half-ton trucks as the First Ranger Battalion began a three-day trek by road, boat, and train to whatever General Laycock had in store for them in the rugged highlands, rolling glens, streams, rapids, and lochs of Inverness in northern Scotland.

Diligent chronicler Altieri recorded that twenty-six hours after boarding boats at a small port on the Irish Sea, the Rangers crawled, staggered, and limped from rickety railway coaches as they arrived on July 1 in light rain, having endured being cramped into small compartments like sardines. As he and the men of the company slung barracks bags over their shoulders, he decided that no Commando training could outdo the rigors and discomforts of what he called "that train ride."

First Sergeant Donald Torbett bellowed to the dazed men, "Let's go! Let's go. You're holding up the war!"

Darby's memory of that moment was more romantic. "In high spirits, with their future before them," he recalled, "the men of the First Ranger Battalion stepped down from the train at Fort William, Northern Scotland. A Cameron Highlander band was piping its shrill music from bagpipes, sounding the call of battle. The great adventure was about to begin."

Greeting the Americans at the train station as the bagpipes played was the British officer who had almost single-handedly forged Winston Churchill's concept of a Commando force into reality by organizing the training of "Talent Operation Groups" (TOG). Authorized in February 1942 at the direction of Eisenhower and deemed "of the utmost importance in all upcoming Allied offensives," the TOGs were to be "the first and best line of defense against Axis Talent [forces]." Appointed to set up and run the "School for Unconventional Warfare" at Achnacarry, Scotland, Lieutenant Colonel Charles E. Vaughan, Order of the British Empire (OBE), was a veteran of World War I and had participated with distinction in the Commando raids in Norway and elsewhere in 1940. Barrel-chested, six feet two, with a ruddy countenance that could change from sunny to stormy with the suddenness of an Arkansas sky in tornado season, he defined TOGs as small, autonomous, and self-sufficient "strike first" squads attached to regular army units with the purpose of disrupting the enemy and taking the initiative from him. This would be achieved by scouting the enemy line, locating Axis Talents and "causing damage and demoralizing the regular enemy forces as they go."

Chosen as the location of Vaughan's Commando school, Achnacarry Castle was the historic and legendary domain of the warrior clan of the Camerons. The name derived from the Gaelic "wry" (crooked) and "sron" (nose or hill). Lying between Loch Arkaig and Loch Lochy, it had stood for centuries as the seat of clan chieftain Lochiel. In the eighteenth century the castle had provided refuge for Bonnie Prince Charlie. Also known as the Young Pretender and Young Chevalier, Charles Edward Stuart was claimant to the British throne and led a Scottish Highland army in rebellion. The son of James Francis Edward Stuart and grandson of James II of England, he was born in Rome in 1720. After his father obtained the support of the French government for a projected invasion of England, Charles Edward went to France to assume the command of the French expeditionary forces. When unfavorable weather and mobilization of a powerful British fleet to oppose the invasion led to cancellation of the plan by the French, he persisted in his determination to drive George II from the British throne. As he arrived in Scotland in 1745, a number of Highland clans came to his assistance in taking Edinburgh, defeating a British force at Prestonpans, and advancing as far south as Derby, England, before being forced to retreat. In April 1746 his forces were routed at Culloden Moor. Hunted as a fugitive for more than five months, in which the Highlanders never betrayed him, he escaped to France in September 1746. During the fighting, Achnacarry Castle was ravaged by the Duke of Cumberland's army.

The present owner, Sir Donald Cameron of Lochiel, had loaned the castle and grounds in Inverness to His Majesty King George VI's government for the war's duration. With formation of the Commandos, it became their primary training facility. One of its attractions was craggy Ben Nevis. Eighteen miles from the castle, the mountain rose 4,406 feet and proved to be an ideal destination for speed march-es. Its surrounding woods and seemingly countless streams, bogs, and numerous lakes provided natural training obstacles.

Following the bagpipers and marching beside Vaughan, Darby led the Rangers onto a steep road. "With the lift given by the band," he recalled, "we stretched our stride, lifted our heads, and set out behind them for the hills in the distance. The first mile or two was fun. The band played on and the Rangers' enthusiasm sparkled. The hill got steeper, the band played louder, and feet began to drag. Mile after mile, we plodded ahead, packs getting heavier, and perspiration trick-ling down our backs."

James Altieri admired the scenery as the road twisted uphill through richly tufted fields, dotted with quaint, picturesque farmhouses and flanked by steep hills. The Scottish countryside, now basking in sun-light after a mild rain, was a beautiful sight. When the column turned a sharp bend beside a towering hill and he saw a huge ivy-covered castle with ancient battlements that towered over rows of British army tents, he felt as though the uphill hike with pack and rifle had not been seven miles but seventy. Private First Class Sully Sullivan's simple note in his diary for July 2, 1942, read, "Met by the Highlanders band in kilts and all. March to Achnacarry, Commando depot. We live in tents."

Altieri described the tents as wigwamlike, made of canvas and spaced six feet apart in a row for each company. He thought that no more than four men could possibly squeeze in, but a tall Commando lieutenant explained that eight men could be comfortably housed per tent if they slept with their feet toward the supporting post at the center, like the spokes of a wagon wheel. The Commando officer also advised digging a ditch around the tent to prevent flooding by heavy rains common to the Highlands. The intrepid diarist Sullivan wrote, "We sleep on ground in shelter bags. During day, blankets folded, clean towel at top, with [barracks] bag in back, equipment on top—a neat but trying arrangement in cramped quarters."

Training instructors for each Ranger company (officers and enlisted men) were veterans of the British SS (Special Service) Brigade and Commandos. They consisted of one officer and two or more sergeants. Believing that no American soldier would refuse to go as far forward in combat as his officer, Darby not only required his officers to participate in the hard training by joining the enlisted ranks, but "to be the first to tackle every new obstacle, no matter what its difficulty." He and Herman Dammer alternated their training between companies.

The schedule designed by Colonel Vaughan extended from early morning to late at night, seven days a week, with every minute accounted for. Constantly in the field, participating in, observing, and criticizing the training, Vaughan insisted on rigid discipline. Darby noted that the schedule would have delighted the heart of a Napoleon, and saw the regimen as a trilogy of physical conditioning, weapons training, and battle preparedness. These steps involved speed marching and running increasingly difficult obstacle courses; practice with all types of firearms, and using bayonets and the British "Sykes" knife; and learning the skills of stalking a sentry, scouting, gathering information in enemy territory, knocking out pillboxes and street fighting.

Finding northern Scotland ideal for physical training, Darby extolled the rugged, scenic terrain of mountains, valleys, bogs, and heavily forested country with stout heather undergrowth. Augmenting these natural advantages were man-made devices, including high walls, ladders, ditches, and hedges positioned around the Commando Depot. Looking back on the period spent at Achnacarry, he proudly reported, "We marched swiftly, swam rivers or crossed them on bridges made of toggle ropes—a length of cord with a wood handle at one end and a loop at the other. Each man carried one. There were cliffs to climb, slides to tumble down, and when all that was not quite enough, we played hard games."

Log exercises, borrowed from ancient Scottish games, became a ritual of the training as a group of men carrying a six-inch-thick log on their shoulders tossed it about in an attempt to keep it off the ground. There was also boxing and close-in fighting. While there was no particular emphasis on jujitsu, some men were given a few good usable holds that each would be expected to remember and utilize when needed.

Famous and cursed by the Rangers were speed marches at the Commando Depot that began with three-mile hikes and worked up to courses of five, seven, ten, twelve, and sixteen miles that averaged better than four miles an hour over varied terrain, with full equipment.

In Highlander kilt and wearing a jauntily cocked green wool Scottish cap, Company F's British training officer, Lieutenant Cowerson, predicted, "Before this month is over many of you will hate me. You will curse me under your breath every time I take you through an obstacle course. On every road march some of you will hope that I meet with an accident. Some of you will spit on the ground every time you see me."

On the first full day at Achnacarry (July 3), Tom Sullivan noted that Company A's Commando instructor, Sergeant Major McCaughan, an Irishman with sixteen years in the army, ordered a march at a speed of five miles an hour with packs and rifles. The next day, he marked U.S. Independence Day by "working the pants off" his American students.

In the first real test of how well the American "GI" and the British "Tommy" could get along together, Darby observed that the British Commandos did all in their power to find out what sort of men the Americans were. That at least one Commando was dubious about the quality of American soldiers did not go unnoticed by Altieri. "I don't know too much about you Yanks," Lieutenant Cowerson said on the first day at Achnacarry. "You are supposed to be the best the American troops have—so they say."

As commander of the Rangers, Darby quickly learned that his men and Vaughan's were divided not only by a common language, style of uniforms, military customs, and experience in warfare, but separated by the most basic element of soldiering, expressed in the timeless maxim "An army travels on its stomach." Darby, with an acute awareness of British sensibilities that would have pleased Eisenhower, described the food provided to the Rangers by the British as "rough fare." Consisting mainly of tea, fish, and beans for breakfast, and tea, beans, and "bully" beef for lunch and dinner, the menu was varied occasionally by porridge without sugar or milk and by what Darby called "some ungodly concoction peculiar to the British" known as "duff." To Tom Sullivan the food was "wholesome but scarce, no seasoning." He wrote, "Mess officer has temerity to ask if we like it."

When the food evoked howls of anguish from troops used to starting the day with eggs and ham or bacon, cold cereal and fruit, or even the chipped beef on toast commonly called "shit on a shingle," Darby cast aside concerns about offending the British and requested that an American mess team be sent from the Thirty-fourth Division. The result was the arrival of a staff of cooks under Master Sergeant Peer Buck. The son of an American, he was born in Denmark but grew up in the United States and graduated from the University of Minnesota's School of Agriculture. He had been a middleweight boxer. While the British continued to provide the meals, Buck and his cooks supplemented them with American rations. Although cooks did not participate in training, they frequently went on hikes and assisted by performing odd jobs during various field exercises and maneuvers.

The centerpiece of Colonel Vaughan's combat-training plan for the month the Rangers would spend at Achnacarry was a three-day exercise ending in a sham battle. It was based on Vaughan's observation that any trained soldier can march the first day, even over obstacles, up- and downhill, and through swamps, and that the good soldier will finish out a second day, but only the top-notch soldier would complete the march on the third day and still be able to fight effectively. After the Rangers' first three-day exercise and mock battle, Darby discovered the validity of Vaughan's notion when 20 percent of his men were separated from the unit and returned to their original outfits. This reduction in strength would amount to more than those killed, wounded, or sick throughout the Rangers' actions during the campaign in Tunisia. The only death during exercises at Achnacarry was that of Private Lamont Hoctel. He drowned as he swam across a stream. The single casualty under fire was First Sergeant Donald Torbett. Shot in the buttocks during an amphibious landing exercise, he returned to Company F after two weeks of rest and discovered he'd been given the nickname "Butt."

In a close call during an amphibious exercise, a Commando tossed a hand grenade into a boatload of Rangers. "Luckily, a quick-thinking lad picked it up after it bounced off another's head," James Altieri recorded, "and threw it far out into the lake, where it exploded harmlessly." The man whose head had been hit was admonished by a lieutenant for "being unobservant."

Altieri, confessing that the part of Commando training he feared most was cliff climbing, wrote that he'd seen men who were not the least bit fazed by bullets twanging close to their heads, by grenades exploding several feet from where they lay, by swimming in the racing, ice-cold river with full equipment, and by all the other dangerous Commando courses, become taut, worried, and unsteady when it was their turn at the cliffs. Consequently, on the night before Company F was to have its first lesson in cliff climbing, Altieri was overcome with fear. The thought of climbing and descending the jagged rock cliff made him tremble.

Deciding that there was only one way to prove to himself that he wouldn't falter the next day, he headed that evening for the cliff and forced himself to climb it. When his feet touched the ground after the nightmare of sliding down a rope from the top, he felt as if he had conquered the world. Completing the climb and descent the next day, and hearing a Commando laud him for taking the cliff "like an old hand," he felt guilty because he'd had two tries at it while they had only one.

In a more daunting challenge designed to test a man's courage called "the death slide," the trainee had to climb a forty-foot tree and descend it on a single rope that was strung at a forty-degree angle and attached to a tree on the opposite bank of a roaring river while under fire. This test of courage was surpassed by a leap from a tower of the castle. It required a trainee to jump from the top of the stone battlement and lower himself with a rope looped under his left leg and through bare hands while using his feet against the wall as a brake. Tom Sullivan did it on July 12 and wrote in his diary, "Most of us [have] burns or blisters [on] hands and thighs."

On a "bullet and bayonet" course men worked in pairs. With one covering the other, they were required to scale difficult obstacles and leap with fixed bayonets into mud so deep that an instructor frequently had to pull a man out. The course included firing at targets that popped up and ended with a climb up a steep slope under fire and bayoneting other pop-ups. The firing of live bullets from rifles and machine guns by Commandos at trainees was so realistic that one Ranger exclaimed, "Sometimes I think those bastards are actually trying to kill us."

Darby said with a laugh, "It took only one such sniper shot and the Ranger who insisted on crawling with his tail in the air hugged the earth, from forehead to instep, forever afterward."

On a training ground that Colonel Vaughan called the "me and my pal course," Rangers in teams of two were challenged to watch after one another as they dealt with stone fences, barbed-wire obstacles, streams, steep hills, and pop-up targets that required one man to shoot over the other's head. "Dangerous as this was," Darby explained, "it stressed the confidence that a soldier must have in his friends and the type of cooperation necessary in the Rangers." In another of these exercises, a pair had to secure a building. One covered the other as he approached it to knock out a window and toss in a grenade. With that done, the one who had been providing cover entered the building to make sure it was clear.

The typical day began with reveille at 6:45, followed by company formation and inspection. Breakfast was at 8:30. Training hours varied according to the day's program and the whim of the instructors. Sully Sullivan's diary for July 9 listed a speed march over mountains, assault courses "galore," mountain climbing and toggle-rope bridges across streams. On July 15: "All-day hike over three mountain ranges—cold, rainy on peak where we bivouac for dinner. Up and down hills, mountains, streams—return 8:15 at night."

The nature of a day's training for Ranger enlisted men and their officers was entirely up to the British instructors. The favorite training exercise of the Commando in charge of James Altieri's Company F was amphibious landings under fire from Commando marksmen on the shore. As the men hit the beach and scrambled up a hill to attack a target, they were met by explosions of dynamite while Bren gun bullets peppered the ground. Described by Altieri as a man without emotion who could be cruelly direct in his admonishments, the instructor for Company F had complete control from eight in the morning until five thirty in the evening. Except for military courtesy, he expected from the Ranger officers of the company the same performance demanded of the enlisted ranks. "In a way," Altieri observed, "their lot was a little worse than ours because [by Darby's orders] they were always the first to be initiated into the hellish training devices that Lieutenant Cowerson concocted for Company F."

Altieri found Captain Roy Murray and Lieutenant Edwin Loustalot to be aggressive but not overbearing as they instilled spirit and morale by their leadership, encouragement, and understanding of each individual. They achieved this not by arbitrary power but by developing a spirit of mutual helpfulness and cooperation in which all ranks seemed to strive to assist their leaders with their responsibilities.

The portrait of the commander of the Rangers in Altieri's memoir of his army service provides an enlisted man's observations and insights into William Orlando Darby as he shouldered complex responsibilities for supervising a military organization with no precedent in American history. Recording that Darby set the pace for his officers and inspired the enlisted ranks by being constantly in the field with his troops, Altieri wrote, "One day he would go out with A Company as they went through the assault landings, the next day he would be with B Company on an overnight problem, the next day with C on a forced march, and so on. Full of energy, poise, and an amazing endurance, he cut a rugged, well-polished figure that exuded confidence. Nothing escaped his attention, not the slightest detail. At the end of the day's training he called his company commanders together and made remarks as to what he had observed."

Altieri also observed that Darby "was keen on making quick decisions" and that there "was nothing vacillating about him." He was direct, forceful, and sometimes explosive, and he was at times "so cutting" that "both officers and men when called down by him would remember the incident for the rest of their lives." To look at him, Altieri wrote, "it was hard to visualize him as a one-time, pencil-pushing aide-de-camp."

At some point in the training at Achnacarry, the Rangers bestowed on their commander the nickname "El Darbo."

In contrast to Darby, Altieri found the second in command, Major Herman Dammer, to be a leavening influence, with a faculty for saying a tremendous amount in very few words. The result was a well-synchronized team in which one added to the other's stature.

During training at Achnacarry, the overshadowing and often overwhelming figure for the GIs and their officers alike was the burly, ruddy-faced Colonel Vaughan. It was his "tremendous personality," in Darby's words, that pervaded the Commando Depot's atmosphere. Constantly in the field, he reminded Americans who had played football in school of coaches pointing out the errors in plays, or scolding them for not showing the proper team spirit. Vaughan explained to Darby that he was quick to think up means of harassing "the poor weary Rangers" in order to "give all members the full benefit of the course." The problems he devised were written with imagination and had a sense of both the dramatic and a thorough knowledge of the enemy that the Rangers would be facing in combat. Each exercise or maneuver was outlined like a movie scenario in an information sheet. In one that Darby found amusing, "MacDarby's ragamuffins" had been "cutting up" at a local hotel and carrying out "their usual looting and pillaging." The plan was for them to be attacked on their way back to their camp by "good" Rangers. Details of the attack were left to unit commanders.

Another story began with the information that Ranger officers were heading to a nearby fort, where they had "outclassed" Commando officers with "the local blondes and brunettes." Commando chief MacVaughan, aided by his henchman, Private Samson Oneskunk, vowed to teach the Rangers a lesson. The contenders in the resulting confrontation would be Martin Sharpshooters (Commandos) and the Meade Rangers. The purpose of injecting sexual rivalry as the motivation was to "heighten" interest. The exercise centered on the village of Spean Bridge and its small hotel, operated by two middle-aged Scottish women. They enjoyed the experience of grenades exploding nearby and young men with rifles attacking their premises so much that when the battle ended in a Ranger victory, they served both sides tea.

One Ranger tactic in carrying out a Vaughan scenario to victory left its author feeling disgruntled. The Ranger objective was to capture a Commando command post in Fort William. They achieved this by dressing a Ranger in a borrowed nurse's uniform and sending him into Fort William with a Tommy gun under the cape, "getting the drop" on occupants until the entire Ranger force arrived. Vaughan pronounced the ruse effective but "not exactly cricket."

In a report to Headquarters Special Service Brigade on the Rangers' progress, with a copy provided to Darby, Vaughan noted "good feeling" between Commando Depot instructors and that Rangers accepted arduous training "cheerfully and willingly," but recommended that more attention be given to training of the noncommissioned officers. He recommended platoon and section mobility by pooling mortars in headquarters companies, placing the air-cooled .30-caliber machine guns under battalion control, and equipping the sections with Bren guns or the Browning automatic rifles (BARs). Darby accepted all these recommendations and stated in his own progress report his confidence that Ranger performance with weapons would improve as they gained more practical experience under Vaughan's realistic training programs.

During an inspection on July 7 by the head of the British army's Scottish Command, the Rangers demonstrated what they'd learned as each company carried out a particular exercise. For Company A it was use of the toggle-rope "Death Ride." B staged a landing using folding boats. C ran an obstacle course, D attacked a pillbox, E demonstrated rope climbing, and F Company exhibited skills in shooting from the hip and bayonet fighting. The day ended with tea served on the firing range.

Altieri, summing up his company's progress, wrote, "Our bodies were now trim and muscular; our confidence and spirit high. And far from hating Lieutenant Cowerson, the men looked upon him with great admiration and respect. He and his sergeant assistants had molded us into a closely knit, sturdy and aggressive unit."

Six days after the tactics demonstration for the Scottish general, a contingent of eighteen officers and fifty enlisted men arrived at Achnacarry to begin two weeks of learning Commando methods in order to teach them to troops in the United States, as had been intended by the men at the conference in London that created the Rangers.

The July 18 entry in Tom Sullivan's diary read, "Spirit and devil-may-care attitude of Americans amazes British and Scotch." Sully also observed that the Commandos "go wild" over an addition to Darby's Rangers' equipment in the form of a new American rifle. Replacing their World War I–vintage Springfield, the M1 Garand was a .30-caliber, semiautomatic gas-operated combat rifle that had entered the U.S. arsenal in 1936 but was now being mass-produced as the standard infantryman's weapon. Designed by John Cantius Garand, it was 43.6 inches long and weighed eleven and one-quarter pounds when fully loaded. It fired eight rounds from a clip that ejected after the last shot. Its effective range was 440 meters.

The day after the arrival of the M1, the Rangers repeated the demonstration they'd given the Scottish general for General Hartle, but with the companies switching roles. As training resumed, Sully Sullivan diligently recorded in his diary:

7/19/42:   Lt. Whitfield of the No. 1 Commandos is best liked of all officers—very tall, lithe—can out-walk any man I ever saw.

7/21/42:   Don't know about [British] army, but British Commandos are real fighting men—London Police training.

7/22/42:   Hathaway, Wallsmith et moi fifth columnists disguised as sheepherders. We meet Mr. Camerun and ten sheep inside Spean Bridge. Problem a success.

7/23/42:   Old Mr. Camerun's sheepdog was a marvel to behold—the way he handled those sheep. We got captured only because of GI shoes.

7/24/42:   Fell out on speed march to Spean Bridge—
               ran a country mile—but couldn't catch up.
               Whitfield views with disgust. Tsk. Tsk.

7/25/42:   Run opposed landing under heavy fire, live
               ammunition of course. Associated Press re-
               porter impressed as Bren gunner slashes 303s
               about him.

7/29–30/42:   Speed march about 12 miles around Loch
               Lochiel—bivouac for dinner, scouted by
               enemy—cross canal by rope—all night
               march and dawn attack across river on castle.
               After 3 hour layover in cold and wet we force
               march thru underbrush to Achnacarry and
               attack castle at 6 a.m. The river was swift and
               cold as Vermont winter.

The next day, the First Ranger Battalion completed training at Achnacarry with yet another review, but this time under the scrutiny of only Vaughan and Darby. The morning of August 1, 1942, was brisk and sunny as the battalion formed on the parade ground. With the ancient castle that they had climbed, jumped from, and assaulted again and again looming over them, they heard Vaughan confess, "You Yanks bloody well surprised us. We expected to grind you to bits. Instead, some of my best Commando instructors have been hard put to keep up with you. A cracking good bunch, you Rangers."

Marching to the music of kilted bagpipers, the companies passed in review. Although they had qualified to wear the Commandos' green beret, Darby did not permit it. Ceremonies completed, they loaded onto trucks that would convey them down the long hill to Fort William for transportation to the next phase of their education. Summarizing the birth of the Rangers, Darby said, "Though volunteers, they had been welded into a close-knit unit able to operate in any kind of warfare. Their bodies were physically hard, wits sharp, hands firm on the trigger, bayonets and knives ready. They were not supermen. They were not thugs or cutthroats. They wore their uniforms correctly, they saluted smartly, and they had confidence in their leaders."

★ CHAPTER 5 ★

WE KNOW BETTER NOW

"Oh, what a wonderful war we're fighting."

AS THE MEN OF COMPANY F, FIRST RANGER BATTALION, MUSTERED to leave Achnacarry on August 1, they did so without Captain Roy Murray. He and two sergeants (Thomas Sorby and Edwin C. Thompson), three PFCs (Howard Andre, Stanley Bush, and Pete Preston), and Private Donald Earnwood of Headquarters Company, along with officers, sergeants, T/5s, PFCs, and privates from the other six companies, for a total of fifty men, were detached to be sent to the south of England. The stated reason for their separation was that they had been selected for specialized training in demolitions. What the Rangers did not know was that Darby had volunteered, but was turned down. Whether he knew the Combined Operations chief Lord Mountbatten was planning to carry out the raid on Dieppe that had been canceled in July is not known. Darby stated only that he "hoped to join the party," but that Brigadier Laycock, in charge of Ranger instruction, had insisted he remain with the Rangers because "training must come first."

Phase two would take place around the rugged western Scottish islands of Mull, Rhum, Eigg, Canna, and Soay in a region known primarily to American connoisseurs of whisky for distilling single-malt Scotch. With such alluring names as Glenfiddich, Aberfeldy, Convalmore, Laphroaig, and Tobermory, they invoked images of Scots taking the high road or low road to the "bonnie, bonnie banks of Loch Lomond," in the words of the Scottish poet laureate Robert Burns and jazz singer Maxine Sullivan's musical rendering of the poem, and the nostalgia of Burns's "Auld Lang Syne" that Guy Lombardo and His Royal Canadians orchestra had made a New Year's Eve anthem through radio broadcasts from New York's Waldorf-Astoria Hotel every December 31.

For the Rangers in August 1942, the Scottish islands and peninsulas of Argyll, with a mixture of sandy and rocky beaches, some opening inland and others leading directly to cliffs, were perfect for practicing amphibious assaults. No finer place could have been selected, Darby felt, than the Royal Navy's amphibious training facility at Kentra Beach, centered on the permanently docked ship HMS *Dorlin*. The region offered every type of terrain and beach for landing operations and for practicing knocking out coastal batteries. In a month of training, companies would be paired and stationed on Roshven (A and B) and Glenborrodale (C and D), and the peninsula towns Glencripesdale (E and F) and Salen and Shielbraige (battalion HQ).

Recording that Company F was transported to Glencripesdale island by a "flat-bellied, faded, gray, Royal Navy launch," James Altieri found "very little Ranger spirit in evidence" as the men gazed at mountains with steep cliffs "rising perpendicular from the water's edge." A gauzelike mist left their summits barely discernible in what seemed to Altieri to be "the most forlorn, forsaken, dismal piece of real estate in the United Kingdom." Because the role the Commandos had filled at Achnacarry was assumed by the British navy, Commando Lieutenant Cowerson was replaced by a "dapper-looking Royal Navy officer armed with a cocky smile and the inevitable swagger stick." Introducing himself as Lieutenant Nye, he assured the men of F and E companies that while they had not arrived at "the most lavish training site," they would find "the solitude of the mountains most conducive to keen concentration" on their training. Nye informed the Rangers that the only inhabitants of the island besides themselves were a herd of the king's deer, and warned that George VI was "very touchy about his private deer preserve" and that the penalty for "the assassination of one deer is forty pounds."

Housed in two-man pup tents that relentless winds frequently blew down, in daily rain and cold nights, and tormented by mosquitoes that Altieri called "the most vicious that ever harassed flesh and blood," the Rangers commenced a month of training that he termed "even more exacting than at Achnacarry." Tom Sullivan found Roshven a "most desolate spot" with "a pip of an obstacle course." Describing "the most miserable stretch of training" they had endured, Altieri recorded that about twice a week His Majesty's Royal Navy called to pay their respects in the form of a flotilla of Higgins assault craft to convey Rangers down the firth for an exercise in amphibious landings along the coast. Some would be opposed landing on a beach by Commandos waiting with Bren guns and mortars. With bullets crackling inches above the heads of the Rangers and live mortar rounds landing as close as six yards from the landing craft, the Rangers reached the beach, tumbled out of the boats, and streaked for their beach objectives.

"After blowing up coast guns, we would withdraw, still under fire," Altieri recalled. "We often made landings at night against rocky cliffs from boats lashing about precariously in huge swells, and often a Ranger would miscalculate his leap from the boat and fall into the waves, narrowly missing being dashed to bits against the rocks."

Darby, participating with the troops, found the training site an excellent assault area in which machine guns nestled in the cliffs overlooking a rocky beach. One of the companies or larger groups would move out to sea in wooden R-boats (sharp-prowed forerunners of the wide-prowed assault craft in use later). Because there was no ramp for exit, the Rangers crowded to the front in columns on two plank runways along the inner side of the hull and jumped into the surf when they neared the beach. Real bullets from the defenses zinged around the craft and cut up spurts of water. Ashore were booby traps with light charges.

The objective in a landing exercise on the island of Mull was capturing its only town. Founded in 1788 as a fishing port, Tobermory was famous for Glengorm Castle, built in 1880, and for making single-malt Scotch until the distillery (started in 1798) closed in 1930. With a population of less than a thousand, it stood at the northern entrance to the Sound of Mull, where, it was said, the Spanish Armada treasure ship *Galeon de Florencia* sank with a cargo of gold in 1588. The nature of Tobermory's residents was extolled in a folk song:

> Their Highland hearts are truer gold believe me,
> Than all the gold in Tobermory Bay.

Informed two days before the war game by Lieutenant Max Schneider, commander of E and F companies, that capturing the town would be the main objective of a three-day exercise, the residents welcomed the opportunity to test the readiness of their small police force and the town's "home guard" volunteers. With Schneider's men in the role of defenders, Major Dammer was to attack from the water with four Ranger companies (A, B, C, and D) and seize the town in no more than twenty-four hours. The immediate goal was to destroy a simulated radio station on the site of an old stone fort. The Ranger assigned to this objective, Lieutenant Frederic Saam, Jr., would carry a large quantity of TNT. With the target eliminated, the attackers would move to capture the town.

While explaining the exercise to the people of Tobermory, Dammer enlisted a few of them to play "collaborationists" whose role was to assist the attackers in infiltrating the town ahead of the main attack. Several fishermen were recruited to man small boats and patrol the rocky shoreline. Dammer also explained that all the Americans involved in the sham battle would fire their weapons, but the bullets would be altered to render them harmless. This would be achieved by removing bullets from their cartridges and replacing them with soap pellets. The men would be directed not to fire them closer than two hundred yards, "because at fifty yards they would sting dangerously."

The exercise commenced at night in a heavy rainstorm with the attacking Rangers in small British navy landing craft. One of them, commanded by Captain William Martin, ran into two of Schneider's patrol boats. In a running battle in pounding surf, Martin and several of his men were captured. Meanwhile, Dammer's force landed. As a demolition party made its way toward the "radio station," the main body headed for the town and met tough resistance. In the excitement, one of the Rangers forgot the firing restriction and shot one of the defenders in the face. (The injury proved slight.)

"Fighting through houses, inns, and fields," Darby recorded, "the assault force finally drove the American and home guard defenders into Tobermory and surrounded them."

With the battle over, the problem facing Darby, Dammer, and Schneider was rounding up the men from both sides in driving rain. Four Rangers who had "holed up in dry spots" couldn't be found and were left behind. (They returned to Glencripesdale on their own the next day.) As the Rangers gathered on a dock to board boats to return to their bases, women of the town served them cakes and sandwiches. With this "warm demonstration" of Scottish-American friendship in full swing, Darby was informed that a "distraught" woman had telephoned to explain "between tears" that her house had just caved in. Situated a thousand yards from the old fort that Saam and his men had blown up, the cottage was so shaken by the concussion that plaster fell from walls and windows shattered. Darby designated four officers to "investigate and pay damages."

With E and F companies stationed together at Glencripesdale, James Altieri found himself reunited with Carlo Contrera and able to compare notes. Each time, Altieri wrote, Carlo came up with a new gripe. His arches were falling. He was starving from the British rations. His girl in Brooklyn wasn't writing often enough. His relations with his first sergeant were deteriorating. "All this was harrowing enough," Altieri complained, "but his most humiliating misfortune was to be fined forty pounds for being caught red-handed killing one of the king's deer."

After Carlo fired ten rounds and missed, he and another Ranger crept up on the deer and stalked it into a mountain defile, trapping it in a narrow cleft. Out of ammunition, they clubbed the deer with their rifle butts and killed it. As they prepared to put the skinned carcass on a fire, a king's warden appeared and arrested them. Carlo feared losing his PFC stripe, but Darby let the punishment of the fine suffice. A second miscreant stood before Darby not because he had shot a Royal deer, but for mistakenly killing a prize bull calf. After some negotiation, Darby recalled, the accused Ranger compensated the owner.

Finding it hard to believe that a Ranger's eyesight was that bad, Darby observed that for some time the Ranger "took a good-natured hazing."

After three weeks of training among the remote islands, Darby allowed his men a brief break by granting the battalion a two-day leave in the town of Oban. Meaning "little bay" in Gaelic, the town on the Firth of Lorn considered itself the gateway to the Hebrides and was the site of ruins of the twelfth-century Dunollie Castle and the "Dog Stone." A huge rock, it was said to be the place where the Gaelic hero Fingal chained his giant hound Bran. Given their first pay call in two months, the Rangers pocketed British pounds (a pound was the equivalent of four dollars) and looked forward to a place that Company F's Sergeant Donald Torbett promised would be "a real live town, full of bars and lonesome gals" who'd never seen any Yanks and were "waitin' to welcome us."

Around noon on August 20, fortified with his pay and an additional sixty pounds won in a crap game, Altieri joined rollicking Rangers surging from the Royal Navy's *Alicia* onto the town's cobbled quay before hawser lines were made fast. Carried away by their first encounter with "Scottish maidens," Altieri wrote, several Rangers "ran up to the terrified girls and, in full view of the townspeople, embraced them with bear hugs."

The boisterous scene was halted by Sergeant Torbett blowing a whistle and shouting, "F Company, fall in, you're not dismissed yet. Any more of that and we're gonna load on that boat and go right back."

To Altieri's dismay, Torbett appointed him and a corporal from second platoon military policemen for the entire forty-eight hours. "To me," he wrote, "MP duty was the most ignoble assignment a soldier could draw. It didn't matter so much that I was deprived of the opportunity to raise hell in Oban like the others. What really infuriated me was that I, who hated MPs, was now going to be a watchdog and policeman over my own buddies. This was a stigma I could never erase."

While Darby's Rangers caroused in Oban, Scotland, the fifty officers and enlisted men who had been detached for training in "demolitions" in the south of England were writing a page of Ranger history by becoming the first Americans in battle on the soil of France since 1918. Despite Winston Churchill's desire for a British victory on the continent and the demand by President Roosevelt that Americans get into battle against Germans as quickly as possible, the raid on the French port of Dieppe that Mountbatten's Combined Operations had planned for the Fourth of July (Operation Rutter) had been pushed back to August 19. It was renamed Jubilee. Crossing the seventy-mile stretch of the English Channel would be two hundred fifty ships, including nine destroyers, one gunboat, nine landing ships, and seventy-three personnel landing craft (LCT), carrying a combined force of Commandos and Royal Marines, Canadians, and Rangers totaling 6,086 men. The Americans were divided between two Commando groups attacking four beaches on the flanks of the assault, with Canadians attacking Dieppe at the center. Yellow I and II were on the left (north), Orange I and II on the right (south), and two Canadian regiments in the center (blue, red, white, and green).

Whatever surprise the raiders hoped to achieve was scuttled seven miles from the coast when they were spotted by a convoy of German gunboats escorting a tanker. During the ensuing battle and in the first attempts to land troops, the Rangers suffered their first wounded (Stanley Bush, Charles Reilly, John J. Knapp, and Edwin Moger). As Second Lieutenant Edwin Loustalot dashed across a field of poppies to attack a German automatic weapons position, he became the first American officer killed on French soil. Twenty-three-year-old Lieutenant Joseph H. Randall (Company C) of Washington, D.C., never made it ashore. He was killed at water's edge on White Beach. The first American ground troops to be taken prisoner were Albert T. Jacobsen, Walter Bresnahan, and Edwin R. Furru, all from Company B. The American credited with the first killing of a German in World War II, Corporal Franklin Koons, was decorated for the distinction by both the Americans and British. The Rangers lost two officers and four enlisted men, with seven wounded, one of whom would die in a hospital, and four men taken prisoner.

Describing the purpose of the Dieppe Raid and analyzing its result in *U.S. Army Special Operations in World War II*, published in 1992 by the Center of Military History, Department of the Army, David W. Hogan, Jr., noted that the ostensible purpose was to test the defenses of the port and force the German air force to give battle. The Luftwaffe did respond, resulting in a dramatic air battle with the Royal Air Force in which the British lost ninety-eight planes while inflicting greater casualties on the Germans and protecting the landing forces. To clear the way for the main assault on the town by the Second Canadian Division, two Commando battalions with Rangers attached were to seize a pair of coastal batteries flanking the port. While one of these was knocked out, boats carrying the second battalion were dispersed by German torpedo craft and only a handful of troops landed. Meanwhile, the assault on the town proved disastrous. Of the five thousand attackers, thirty-four hundred were killed, wounded, or captured.

"As a raid, Operation Jubilee had been a dismal failure," wrote the military historian Richard Yule. "The attempt to seize Dieppe had failed on the beaches and surrounding shallows and died. The enemy defenses had been tested, but overall the Germans had not been seriously alarmed."

The day after the Rangers who had been on forty-eight hours' leave in Oban returned to their training bases, the Rangers of Dieppe rejoined the First Battalion in Scotland. "They all looked weary, much older and deadly serious," Altieri wrote, "[and] seemed very bitter that the overall plan had met with failure. They had seen the full impact and horror of a large-scale landing gone wrong. Their baptism of fire under the worst possible conditions brought home to us the deadly career we had chosen voluntarily for ourselves."

Sergeant Ed Thompson said of the calamitous raid, "It was murder, pure murder."

With a shell-fragment wound in an arm, Sergeant Marcell Swank said of the experience of combat, "In training we used to be made to do a lot of things that seemed silly to us. Well we know better now. Every bit of Ranger training we had came in useful."

Lieutenant Colonel Darby assessed the outcome of Dieppe and found reason for optimism. Despite a third of the Allied attackers having been lost, he felt that in the landing and the ground battle his Rangers performed well. He believed they'd demonstrated "the meaning of discipline in overcoming fear and in making an assault through flying lead." Dieppe had also indicated that more training was needed, that planning for such assaults must be more careful and more detailed, and that intelligence and reconnaissance must be more complete if an invasion of Europe via the coast of France were to succeed. For him, the only questions were the significance of the role to be given to the First Ranger Battalion and the date. He was confident his men were training for an invasion that would occur soon, but when and where were matters to be decided by men far above his pay grade.

That the testing of the First Ranger Battalion would occur not in France but in North Africa had been decided on July 30, 1942, by Franklin D. Roosevelt. During many months of debate between him and Churchill, and strategic and tactical discussions among American and British generals on the place and timing of an Allied confrontation with Hitler's armies, the Americans argued for an invasion of France in early 1943. Operation Sledgehammer was meant to both relieve pressure from the Soviet Union for a "second front" and meet Roosevelt's demand that U.S. forces engage the Germans as early as possible. Urging an invasion of French North Africa, Winston Churchill envisioned an occupation of Morocco, Algeria, and Tunisia that would trap Rommel's Afrika Korps between the Anglo-American force in the west and the British Eighth Army in Egypt. By taking the Mediterranean rim of Africa, he said, "the soft underbelly of Europe" would be vulnerable to invasion. Insisting that "it is of the highest importance that U.S. ground troops be brought into action against the enemy in 1942," Roosevelt approved the North Africa invasion plan in July.

In early August, American and British officers under the newly created commander in chief of the European theater of operations (Eisenhower) met at Norfolk House in St. James's Square, London, to begin planning Operation Torch. On September 5, 1942, they agreed that landings would be made in Morocco by American troops from the United States and by Americans and British out of Great Britain around the coastal cities of Algiers and Oran in Algeria.

Two days before this decision, Darby's Rangers were on the move from the west coast of Scotland to the eastern port of Dundee. Darby described this period of training with Commando unit Number One as "preparation for a landing operation somewhere."

Because Dundee had no military or naval bases to provide barracks, posters had been put up in the city seeking room and board for as many pairs of Rangers as possible in the homes of voluntary residents. When they arrived by train on September 3, arrangements were in place for four companies, requiring the other two to be billeted in the city hall. This lasted one night. Darby and the troops awoke on the floors in their sleeping bags to find "an excited group of women" offering rooms. By mid-morning, Darby noted happily, "all my Rangers had homes."

Given four pounds in subsistence money and slips of papers with names and addresses, but no directions from the railroad station, the Rangers were expected to use their ingenuity to find their way to the homes. Tom Sullivan walked from city hall to become the guest "in civilian billets" of "Misses McClaren" at 39 North Court Street. He and his buddy Roy Brown found the "younger sister, about fifty, haughty, domineering." The other, "about sixty, was rather deaf, but likeable." The men shared "a big wooden bed with spring mattress" and had their "own bureau, fireplace and commode." The sisters cooked breakfast and dinner, made the bed, cleaned the room every day and washed their clothing.

James Altieri and Corporal Oscar Runyon, a small, wiry BAR gunner of the Second Section, from Sioux City, Iowa, were guests of Mrs. N. Gibson. To reach 104 Granston Way, they hailed a taxi. En route, the driver told them that Dundee had the largest cinema houses in Scotland with daily showings of "the best American" films, several nightclubs, two dance halls, fine tea shops and restaurants, and numerous pubs. Deciding that joining the Rangers was "the best thing I ever did," and relieved that "the rigorous Spartan life in the Hebrides" of sleeping in pup tents in the rain and "living on skeleton rations" was behind him, Altieri said exultantly, "Oh, what a wonderful war we are fighting."

Darby, presented with a situation in which his men were housed with civilians, saw the arrangement as "excellent training" for future occasions when the Rangers would have to act as independent small groups on their own initiative. Telling them that he expected every man to know where their commanding officer stood concerning "personal deportment," he believed that if any of them "were inclined to be rowdy," they would "not have the heart to get drunk and disorderly as might be the case in barracks where, at a late hour, they would only disturb other soldiers." The men were advised that the penalty for misdeeds was life in pup tents in a field and only packaged C rations for meals.

The Rangers were well rested after sleeping in civilian beds and having had English breakfasts in quaint cottages and houses with trim gardens. Carrying paper bags of homemade food for the entire day, they headed in pairs or small groups to morning formation in Baxter Park. Tom Sullivan noted in his diary on September 4 that residents leaned out of windows and cheered as the men marched past. The next day, he and Roy Brown rode a tram with other Rangers "hanging from the rear platform and everywhere."

Because billeting men in homes eliminated a need for mess facilities, Darby decided that the American cooks who were added to the battalion in Ireland should become "actual Rangers" by joining in the combat training.

Altieri found the schedules the most interesting he had ever encountered. One day they concentrated on street fighting in an abandoned housing project. The next day they might attack the huge coastal batteries flanking Dundee. Other days involved combat field problems, with the Commandos and Home Guard units playing the role of enemy forces. Frequently, they would go out of town as a unit to a distant objective and each man would have to make his way back to Dundee using his own ingenuity.

Darby envisioned the purpose of three weeks of training with the Commandos at Dundee as development of the responsibility of the individual. This included officers. Falling in ranks with the enlisted men, they were required to leave the leadership of each unit to the sergeant and were barred from giving commands or advice. Before an exercise he designed to challenge "Yankee initiative," Darby quoted an order given by Major Robert Rogers to the original Rangers: "When all else fails, the thing to do is forget your instructions and go ahead." One of Darby's tests of his battalion's self-reliance was an order to move twenty-five miles within five hours to the ferry dock in the town of Arbroath using any means to reach it, but without hiring transportation. As Darby waited on the dock, most Rangers arrived on foot, a few appeared on horseback, some in horse-drawn wagons, and others by hitching rides in cars, trucks, or trains. Several managed to persuade a local aviator to fly them to the town.

At the end of each day's training, the Americans invaded Dundee looking for a night of entertainment and female companionship. Sullivan's diary for September 6, 1942, recorded, "Plenty of good restaurants, theaters and even a beauty of an ice rink. People bubbling over with friendship and enthusiasm for us. We get canteen cards for food and sweets." Two days later, he wrote, "Have had two dates with cute good-looking brunette—Sarah Rice, about 19—she does welding. All of them [Scots] hate the English." At the movies on September 11 he watched a newsreel showing A Company "under fire in assault landing" and enjoyed seeing the feature film *How Green Was My Valley* by director John Ford about a Welsh family, starring Walter Pidgeon, Maureen O'Hara, and young Roddy McDowall. Sully's diary entries noted that a popular eating place was Green's Playhouse Café and that on September 12 he'd had Coca-Cola at Café Val D'Or, a "swell restaurant."

The purpose of the Dundee training was to prepare the Rangers for participation in raids by Number One Commandos on fortifications and gun positions on the mountainous Norwegian coast. Training for the mission required scaling the Van Arbirth cliffs, described by James Altieri as "towering perpendicularly hundreds of feet above the sea," but this time the climbing would be done without the aid of ropes that had been used at Achnacarry.

On the final day of training at Dundee (September 11), as the officers led the way in "the long ascent," Altieri was "frightened and gasping for breath" when he followed his buddy Simon Gomez to a narrow cleft two-thirds of the way up. At that point someone above shouted, "Rock! Rock!" Looking up, Altieri saw a boulder hurtling toward him. Pressing against the cliff wall and praying, he heard a dull thump. Gomez fell with arms outstretched, struck an abutment, bounced into space, and plummeted a hundred feet or more to hit the ground with a "resounding thump." Unconscious with a severely injured head, he was taken by an ambulance that always stood by during training to a hospital.

While shaken Rangers stood silently at the foot of the cliff, Captain Roy Murray began climbing "faster than a mountain goat." Without ordering Company F to follow him, he was joined by Lieutenant Nye and Sergeant Torbett. Moments later, the entire company completed the climb. "I knew then," James Altieri wrote, "that never again would I be afraid of the highest heights. And I believe every man of F Company felt the same way."

On a speed march back to Dundee, the men of Company F learned that a worse tragedy had occurred as another company practiced landing tactics. On a beach that was supposed to have been cleared of land mines, Private James R. Ruschkewicz had been killed and T/5 Aaron A. Salkin had been hit in an eye by shrapnel. Altieri remembered that Salkin, a shoe salesman from Baltimore, and he had been together in basic training at Fort Knox, Kentucky, and that Salkin's "fondest hope was to become a three-stripe sergeant."

Confronted for the first time with the responsibility of arranging a funeral service for one of his men, Darby turned to the only chaplain at Dundee. A Roman Catholic assigned to the British Special Service Brigade, Captain Albert E. Basil wore his white priest's collar along with the uniform and green beret of the Commandos. At the close of the ceremony in a tent, he asked Darby for permission to meet with all the Catholics among the Rangers.

"That's all right for the Catholics," said Darby, "but what about the rest of us poor damned Christians?"

"You mean you want me to speak to the Protestants as well?" Basil replied.

"Yes, Father. You see, you're our only chaplain. As far as we Americans are concerned you represent the God we worship no matter what our particular creed may be. So if you don't mind, we would appreciate your taking care of all of us."

Private Carl Lehmann provided this colorful and eloquent memory of meeting Basil:

During the drench of a Glasgow fall, a slender British Army Chaplain appeared at the flap of Headquarters tent, 1st Ranger Battalion. His erect figure in battledress, topped with the green beret was militarily correct except for a cleric's collar and the effect of the ruinous rain. Muck of the Company street compelled him to roll his trousers mid-thigh and carry boots and gaiters. Clydesdale mud sheathed his legs to the knee.

With a toothy grin and mischievous eyes dancing behind enormous horn-rims, he announced he'd come to "look after" the Rangers. His lilting, melodious tones filled the tent and stifled tongue and typewriter; it slowed traffic slogging by in the Company street. Cheery small talk and wisecrack in faultless diction and sculpted phrase stamped him master of the tongue, honed as at Eton and Oxford. He charmed lately bored clerks and surly NCOs, quickly learning their names and origins and regaling them with jolly quip and query.

James Altieri remembered Basil visiting each company and getting to know each man individually. "He never imposed himself on people," said Altieri. "He merely introduced himself and chatted amiably about their families, their hometowns, their civilian occupations. If a man was interested enough to seek guidance and counsel on religious matters, he would bring him to his quarters and enlighten the individual in accordance with the size and scope of his problem."

The priest held mass for the Catholics each morning as required, but the remainder of the day he spent seeing all creeds. With sharp, intelligent features, he was at times amusing, satirical, and witty, but always approachable.

Darby was so impressed with Basil that he obtained permission from Special Service Brigade commander Laycock for "the Rangers' popular adopted Chaplain" to remain with the Rangers until after they landed in North Africa.

The morning after the funeral service for Private Ruschkewicz, Darby's Rangers assembled on Dundee's parade ground dressed in olive drab Class B uniforms and their trademark cut-down leggings for a last review before marching to the railway station. Altieri's account in *The Spearheaders* depicted Darby "looking poised and seemingly unperturbed by the previous day's disasters." With the aid of a field loudspeaker, he said, "Rangers, today we leave Dundee for our staging area near Glasgow. I am very proud of the way you conducted yourselves as guests of Dundee. The Lord Mayor has asked us to come back whenever the fortunes of war permit, which is a good indication of the esteem you have earned from the good people here. We leave Dundee deeply saddened by the terrible incidents that occurred yesterday. However, I want all of you Rangers to remember that these men who were wounded and killed in training are as much heroes as anyone killed in battle. No one could have sacrificed more for their unit and their country."

Altieri wrote that if anyone else had been saying those words, "we would have felt that we were being loaded with the usual patriotic pitch," but Darby "somehow put sincerity and strength and true meaning into his words." With the speech concluded, Darby took his place at the head of the battalion and led it out of the parade grounds and through thronged streets to the train station "teeming with civilians." Gathered to say good-bye, Altieri observed, "were many of the townsfolk whose houses we had shared and many of the young ladies whose affections we had shared." When Darby "magnanimously allowed" a fifteen-minute break before train time for good-byes, a "wild surge of females converged on the troops like a tidal wave." Elderly ladies carried pots of hot tea, warm biscuits, and cookies. Young women "thronged about, offering the choicest gifts young soldiers could ever receive—warm, vibrant embraces, some mingled with passion and affection, others with remorse and sorrow, all with thoughts of the many joyous experiences shared together."

When the Rangers left the troop train at Corker Hill, near Glasgow, they gazed forlornly through fog at rows of the ugliest, messiest, soot-stained pyramidal tents that seemed to sprawl for miles in muddy fields. Once again housed in eight-man British tents with canvas cots, the Rangers scraped mud off their boots and pants and settled down for what they hoped would be a short stay at Corker Hill. They learned that they had been attached to the Eighteenth Infantry Regiment of the First Infantry Division. Under command of General Terry de la Mesa Allen and his deputy, Brigadier General Theodore Roosevelt, Jr., the "Big Red One" (named for its arm patch with a red numeral one) was often called the "Fighting First." It was the first U.S. force to arrive in England in 1942 and had been the first in France in World War I, gaining fame and glory at Cantigny, Soissons, St. Mihiel, and the Argonne Forest.

"We knew immediately what that meant," Altieri recalled. "Our impending operation was no small-scale raid. With an entire division behind us, we were scheduled for something real big—perhaps a full-scale invasion." Meanwhile, the training continued. Mornings consisted of calisthenics, followed by a ten-mile speed march. Afternoons were filled with weapons drills, bayonet practice, unarmed combat, and map and compass reading. The Rangers' main function, Altieri noted, "was simply to wait; wait till the ships were assembled in the Firth of Forth to take us off to the great adventure" in a place and at a time that only high commands in Washington, D.C., and London knew. Evenings were spent in Glasgow to "make the usual rounds of pubs and dance halls, meet the usual Scottish lassies, share the usual joys and come back to camp in time for reveille."

After a few days of this routine of training and Glasgow nights, awaiting the start of the great adventure, and shepherding by a British Catholic chaplain, the ranks of Darby's Rangers were expanded by a figure Altieri described as "a strange-looking apparition." A moon-faced, stocky sergeant, loaded down with seven or eight cameras and a pack full of film, he appeared as the Rangers returned from a speed march, fell into stride, and ran alongside them puffing heavily and snapping pictures.

Born in Philadelphia, in 1919, Phil Stern began a career in photography at age sixteen in New York City as a studio apprentice by day and as a crime photographer for the *Police Gazette* at night. Sent to Los Angeles by *Friday* magazine, he freelanced for *Life*, *Look*, and *Collier's* magazines, launching a career of photographing Hollywood celebrities. As a combat photographer, given the nickname "Snapdragon" by Darby's Rangers, he would take thousands of pictures during their training at Corker Hill and in action from North Africa to Italy. After the war, his camera would provide an archive of movie stars for half a century, including an iconic portrait of James Dean playing peekaboo with a sweater half over his face.

Asked by Darby why he'd volunteered to become the Signal Corps photographer with the Rangers, Stern replied that he was tired of living in the plush quarters of U.S. army headquarters in London, "shooting pictures of generals at social events" with "a feeling of being nonessential to the war effort." Having read the Rangers were "a colorful outfit with a colorful commander," he said, he decided their "deeds should be recorded" by "the best cameraman in the army."

Altieri noted with satisfaction that Stern "adopted" F Company and bragged that Stern did so because F Company was "the very best in the battalion." As Stern regaled the men of the company with tales of Hollywood, Altieri felt that he was either the film capital's most-sought-after photographer or "the world's best liar."

After two weeks in Corker Hill, the Rangers moved by train to the port of Gourock to board three former ferryboats—*Ulster Monarch*, *Royal Ulsterman*, and *Royal Scotsman*—that the Royal Navy had converted to troop landing ships. Darby saw a confident group, drawn together by their success in passing the rugged Commando course. The Rangers were "held to a rigid standard of discipline and conduct."

Their code demanded that when "we got into a scrap, we must not come back to bivouac unless we had won."

The tableau of F Company boarding boats that Phil Stern photographed on October 13, 1942, was later put into words by James Altieri:

> Squadrons of seagulls crisscrossed the misty October sky as we trudged across the creaking gangplank into the moldy hold of the *Royal Ulsterman*. Dock workers and sailors stopped working to stare and listen as we sounded off in lusty song:
>
> Commandos said they'd make it tough.
> But they couldn't make it tough enough,
> Darby's Rangers . . . Rugged Rangers
> We trained like hell to fight a war,
> We're ready for a foreign shore,
> Darby's Rangers . . . Ready Rangers.

"So with jaunty air, we shouldered our packs," Darby recalled. "Where the trail led, we could not be certain. We knew only that we would acquit ourselves as the best-trained unit in the American army."

★ CHAPTER 6 ★

LIGHTING THE TORCH

"They'll be dead pigeons."

IF EVER A SHIP HAD BEEN MISNAMED, GRUMBLED JAMES ALTIERI, IT was the *Royal Ulsterman*. As he dropped his gear in the "low-beamed, hammock-lined, pipe-crossed, evil-smelling" hold that was to be Company F's living quarters, he saw nothing regal.

From the moment they were told they would be boarding the ships, speculation began as to their destination. PFC Peter Preston ventured, "We're heading for Dieppe again. The Limeys don't like the beatin' they took there, so we're all going back for revenge." Ray Rodriguez, who rarely expressed an opinion, thought they were headed for Spain to attack the Germans through France. Sergeant Jack Mulvaney envisioned sailing around Africa to the Red Sea to give a hand to General Bernard Montgomery in the defense of Egypt and the Suez Canal. PFC Junior Fronk insisted they were bound for the Panama Canal and across the Pacific to Guadalcanal to help out the Marines.

As others proposed Marseilles in France; Palermo, Sicily; ports in Italy; Dakar; Norway, and even New York City for a parade up Broadway to boost home-front morale, Sergeant "Butt" Torbett discerned in the heated debate a chance for someone to profit. He proposed that each man write his prediction on a slip of paper and put five pounds in a pool to be held by Torbett until the announcement of the destination by Captain Murray on "Torpedo Day," the date on which operation planners felt it would not present a risk to the security of the convoy from German submarines to reveal its course to the troops.

Altieri picked Bordeaux, France.

To everyone's disappointment and dismay, the three boats made their way into the Firth of Forth in the Clyde region for what Captain Murray announced would be more rehearsals in making landings against simulated gun positions, perfecting night tactics, and refining assault techniques. Centered on Loch Linnhe, the maneuvers would consist of eight nighttime landings and had been given the code name Mosstrooper. The regimen would consist of boat drills, loading and unloading, fire drills, sinking drills, and aircraft attack drills. For three weeks, the flotilla would sail into some remote island harbor and drop anchor. In pitch-black darkness, loaded with full battle gear, the men scrambled into the assault boats and shivered in the piercing cold as they were lowered into the choppy waves. Manned by veteran sailors who had already participated in many Commando raids, the assault boats rendezvoused with the assault craft of other ships. With perfect timing, the attack waves formed for a swift, steady dash to the shore.

During these drills it became clear to Altieri and his buddies that the mission of the First Ranger Battalion was to make a surprise night landing, silence a pair of gun batteries, occupy a waterfront area, and protect a large landing of infantry and armored units. They were told that a failure by the Rangers would require a naval bombardment that the planners obviously preferred to avoid. The only information not provided was the location and date of the invasion.

When Darby learned these facts is unclear. He recorded only that he knew the details of the plan a month before the Rangers began the additional training in the Firth of Forth. Their objective was the small port of Arzew in the French North Africa colony of Algiers. Located to the west of Oran, the invasion's ultimate objective, Arzew was protected by a harbor boom that could be closed and two coastal artillery batteries named Fort de la Pointe and Batterie du Nord. The latter had a four-gun installation with a range of five miles. Between Arzew and Oran were two beaches. One lay four miles northwest of Arzew near a hump of land called Cap Carbon. The other, with the ominous name Cemetery Beach, was blocked by numerous offshore rocks that could break up assault boats. The challenge for planners of the attack by Rangers was not only in selecting a beach, but knocking out both coastal batteries at once. Darby explained, "If the entire battalion attacked the smaller fort at the water's edge [Fort de la Pointe] we would very probably alert Batterie du Nord on the hill. If the Rangers attacked the larger fort first, its defenders would be alert and at 'action stations' at Fort de la Pointe and other coastal defenses, and the boom in the harbor would be closed."

Pondering the strategy of the mission, Darby appreciated that the men of his battalion had been selected to spearhead the first entirely American invasion in a war with the ultimate goal of liberating Europe. Named Operation Reservist, the plan to seize the port of Oran was part of a broader scheme called Torch for invasions of Algeria and Morocco that would trap the Afrika Korps between Americans and British in Algeria on the west and the British Eighth Army in the east. The Algerian assaults would consist of the British at the city of Algiers (a British division, three Commando units, and a U.S. regimental combat team) and the U.S. Army Second Corps under Major General Lloyd Fredendall at Oran, with Rangers attached to the First Infantry Division under Major General Terry Allen, sailing from Great Britain on Royal Navy ships. The Moroccan operation, under Major General George S. Patton, Jr., would consist of American troops sailing on U.S. Navy ships from the United States.

Tactically, Darby and his Rangers had been assigned the task of clearing the way for a landing by General Terry Allen's reinforced Sixteenth Infantry Regiment (Combat Team Sixteen), the Eighteenth Infantry Regiment (Combat Team Eighteen), and Combat Command B of the First Armored Division. Called Task Force Red, these forces were to land at Arzew. At the same time, the Twenty-sixth Regiment and part of Combat Command B would land west of Oran to form a pincer movement with the Arzew forces to take the city. Oran would provide a port for the following forces to debark and a base from which to expand and move eastward to link up with the British at Algiers.

Darby was also aware that in their first action as a battalion the Rangers would not be fighting Germans. The garrisons at Arzew would be forces of the French Vichy government. He had been provided intelligence data on Arzew's terrain, obstacles to landings and defenses, but no one could answer the crucial question: What would the French do? Would they fight bitterly, or would they give up after their "honor" had been satisfied by token resistance?

While Darby contemplated these factors, Rangers impatient for genuine combat raided sham fortresses in Scotland until, as Altieri noted irritably, "We could go through the entire operation with blindfolds." Tom Sullivan wrote in his diary, "Getting real proficient."

On October 15 at Glasgow, Sully inscribed, "Gigantic convoy forming. Three airplane carriers, *Queen Elizabeth*, destroyers and troopships as far as the eye can see."

Recalling an "awe-inspiring" panorama of a harbor choked with ships, large flat battlewagons, sleek cruisers, narrow gray destroyers, tiny corvettes, ponderous carriers, and bulky troopships, Altieri wrote, "We knew our time had come."

In the third week of October 1942, a war strategy that had been conceived by Roosevelt and Churchill in the Atlantic Charter conference aboard a U.S. Navy cruiser in 1941, developed by American and British army and naval officers in countless meetings since July 1942, and placed in the hands of General Eisenhower to finalize and execute was now two vast armadas an ocean apart. In Churchill's elegant prose, they would "fit together like a jeweled bracelet." Heading out for Morocco from Hampton Roads, Virginia, Western Task Force Thirty-four would land troops under Patton at Fedala, about ten miles northeast of Casablanca. Loading onto ships in England and Northern Ireland were seventy-two thousand men in a ratio of two Americans to one British. Designated "Eastern Task Force," they consisted of the Thirty-fourth Infantry Division (under command of Major General Charles W. Ryder), which would land at Algiers, and the U.S. Army Second Corps (commanded by Major General Fredendall), with the objective of taking Oran in an operation to be spearheaded by the First Ranger Battalion at Arzew. In Glasgow Harbor on October 26, Lieutenant Colonel William Darby compared the trio of ferryboats assigned to his men to trusty old streetcars being sent out on a new untried rail line and chickens in a barnyard protected by the mother hens of the fleet.

To T/5 James Altieri on the *Royal Ulsterman* the spectacular tableau extending for miles ahead consisted of stately lines of troopships, guarded by a strong cordon of destroyers, cruisers, and battleships. At the rear of the convoy, the former ferryboat was trailed by a speedy corvette as observation planes circled lazily on the alert. Standing near the starboard bow in a cluster of Rangers astounded by the power of the mighty armada they were a part of, he heard a familiar voice.

Turning around and finding Chaplain Albert Basil, he exclaimed, "Father, what are you doing here?"

With green Commando beret at a jaunty angle, Basil grinned and replied, "Well, lads, you may consider me a bona fide stowaway. I decided that you Rangers needed me and I need you. I was a little jealous that you would be going on this important adventure while I was back in Scotland, so here I am."

As the excitement of sailing out of Glasgow Harbor subsided, life for troops on the large ships became what the historian Rick Atkinson in *An Army at Dawn* termed a "weirdly languorous" voyage, as if they were going to war on a Cunard cruise, with stewards serving them morning tea, printed menus in the dining rooms, and Indian cabin boys in black-and-white livery filling tubs with hot seawater for evening baths. An American officer on the *Duran Castle* noted that he and other officers wore Class A uniforms at dinner and had coffee in the lounge afterward. On the *Monarch of Bermuda*, Brigadier General Ted Roosevelt not only entertained fellow officers by reciting passages from Rudyard Kipling, but recalled meeting the famous British poet when he'd visited President Theodore Roosevelt at the White House.

While the convoy was getting under way on October 26, Ted had written to his wife, Eleanor, "Cleared to strange ports—that's what we are."

Although the *Royal Ulsterman* skipper cheerily wished his American passengers a fine voyage, existence on the refitted ferryboat was less than comfortable. On October 27, the captain told the Rangers they were part of Combat Convoy C and their course was due west, but he omitted their destination. Five days later (Monday, November 2), Captain Murray assembled Company F on the lower stern deck and drew a canvas tarpaulin from a large table to reveal a minutely detailed model of the topography of their landing zone. "Fellows," he said, "D-day is November eighth. The port we are going to take is probably a place none of you have ever heard of. It's in French Algeria, thirty miles west of Oran, the French naval base. It is called Arzew."

"All in all," wrote James Altieri, "there was no particular enthusiasm among the Rangers about fighting the French. Personally I was let down. I didn't relish the idea of slaughtering people who were not really our enemies, regardless of the military gains achieved."

Because no one had predicted the location of the Rangers' first combat, the men of F Company agreed that rather than using the betting pool to throw an after-battle victory party, the money should be donated to Father Basil as a "fund for the uplifting of the lost souls in the First Ranger Battalion."

After stopping for oil and water at Gibraltar on November 5, the convoy slipped past the Pillars of Hercules and into the Mediterranean Sea. The armada would soon divide and twenty-seven thousand men would head for Algiers while the remainder descended on the region of Oran, with the Rangers as the invasion spearhead at Arzew. Nervously scanning the ships, Darby was certain that the five hundred men under his command, trained by Commandos and with the experience of landing exercises in all kinds of weather on the islands of western Scotland, would fight smartly and courageously.

As the leader of the Rough Riders in the Spanish-American War, Lieutenant Colonel Theodore Roosevelt had said, "All men who feel any joy in battle know what it is like when the wolf rises in the heart." On November 5, 1942, his son, Brigadier General Ted Roosevelt, second in command of the First Infantry Division, wrote to his wife, "The die is cast and the result is on the knees of the gods."

"At Gibraltar," wrote diarist Tom Sullivan, "gigantic convoy—five lanes of transports and two of warships on flanks as far as eye can see. A magnificent sight."

Saturday, November 7, 1942, began with a Royal Navy breakfast that many, if not most, of Darby's Rangers thought but did not say could be their last. Letters home that might be their final words to loved ones were dropped into collection bins. A British voice sounding over the loudspeakers announced the smoking lamp was lit and that assault sections were to report to their designated briefing areas. Each man recited his role. Aerial photos and maps were reviewed. Differences between these briefings and those they'd had in Scotland were the warm Mediterranean climate and the knowledge that in less than twenty-four hours the force that opposed them would be shooting to kill.

At two in the afternoon on the *Royal Ulsterman*, Father Basil held a service for the entire ship's complement, followed by confessions and mass for Catholics. Having tended to the state of their souls, the Rangers did calisthenics for half an hour, ran in single file around the deck, and continued exercising individually by climbing mast lines and in pairs by wrestling and boxing. Weapons and equipment were checked and double-checked.

"We were assured and confident," Altieri recalled. "Despite some personal reservations about fighting the French, we knew we were well equipped to accomplish our mission. We knew we were led by the best officers in the army. We knew we were surrounded by men who had proved themselves again and again through grueling tests of courage, endurance and ability."

At ten o'clock, British cooks served the Americans a dinner of hamburger steak.

At eleven, F Company listened to a few final words from Captain Murray, Lieutenant Nye, Sergeant Torbett, and Father Basil.

Half an hour later, the troops began assembling on decks to await the order to climb into landing craft that would be lowered into the sea beginning at eleven thirty (2330).

On the bridge of HMS *Ulster Monarch*, Darby peered through fog to locate the other boats. Feeling pricks of apprehension, he considered what lay before them. Arzew was thirty miles off the starboard bow. Barely visible were misty outlines of the *Royal Scotsman* and

Royal Ulsterman. The sea was calm. Moving to the port side of *Ulster Monarch's* bridge, he stared down into the water and saw to his horror two silvery objects racing toward the Rangers' ships. He shouted, "My God! Torpedoes!"

Certain the invasion fleet had been detected by a submarine, he watched in terror as the streaks closed to within twenty-five yards. He instinctively raised his hands to cover his head and he braced for explosions. Barely ten yards distant, two porpoises leapt up gracefully, plunged back into the sea, changed direction, and swam playfully alongside the ship.

Minutes later, British sailors began lowering the motorized landing craft. Noting that the Rangers couldn't see ten feet ahead, Altieri wrote in *The Spearheaders,* "We were loaded to the gills. Besides his own ammunition and weapons, each man carried a stick of dynamite for gun demolitions, two mortar shells, a Commando toggle rope, a deadly sharp Commando knife and a Mae West life preserver twined around his waist."

A British voice commanded, "Lower away all boats! Lower away all boats!"

With Rangers packed together like spoons in a drawer, as historian Rick Atkinson vividly described the loading process, and the winches of davits on the two troopships making eerie, grinding noises so loud that Altieri was certain they could be heard by the French on the shore six miles away, fourteen LCAs (landing craft, assault) inched downward. Each held a platoon (thirty-two to thirty-five men) and five British crew. Carrying no troops, one LCS (landing craft, support) was armed with machine guns and other weapons to fight off any French torpedo boats that might appear and to return enemy shore fire.

In a loading and lowering process that had been practiced over and over in drills in the Scottish islands, Darby's men had become letter perfect. Half a world away in the Pacific, Americans who landed on the island of Guadalcanal in August had traveled a relatively short distance from New Guinea and stormed ashore in American landing craft launched from U.S. Navy ships. The Rangers had sailed for thousands of miles for two weeks in converted, cramped ferryboats that carried British landing craft. By utilizing large ships carrying a number of small landing craft in such a ship-to-shore operation, Darby said, "fighting men can travel distances of more than a thousand miles and be disembarked several miles out to sea from the beach."

Proud of his men's achievement and confident they would meet the challenge of their first invasion as the misty shapes of the LCAs moved forward to rendezvous off the bow of the leading ship, he watched with horror as a cable of an LCA being lowered from the *Ulster Monarch* broke loose, dropping the bow and pitching its platoon of Rangers into the water. Hearing a loud whip crack, James Altieri looked back from his LCA and saw "a dozen or so Rangers" in the sea, weighted down with heavy gear.

Among soaked and cursing men pulled from the sea, Altieri noted, was destiny-minded photographer Phil Stern, wailing about his precious film being ruined at this historic moment. Lieutenant Saam found his handlebar mustache drooping and shouted epithets at the British navy. Other men were roaring curses. While none of the men lost their rifles, an officer who was to lead a demolitions team had to abandon fuses, explosive caps, primers, and packs of TNT to keep the weight from dragging him down. Also lost was a two-way high-frequency radio for use after the landing to communicate with the fleet, along with several flares that were to be used to signal the main invasion force that the Batterie du Nord had been taken.

With the disabled LCA hanging by its stern and the soaked Rangers loaded into others, the boats formed an assault flotilla around guide craft and headed for their landing points. Led by Major Dammer, A and B companies were to enter the port of Arzew, slip past the harbor boom, land on a jetty (mole number one), follow it to the shore, and attack Fort de la Pointe. Darby and the remainder of the battalion would come ashore on a beach and take Batterie du Nord.

In a haze that limited visibility to under two hundred feet, the British sailors steering the landing craft had to depend on compasses and the fog-dimmed glow of a lamp in a lighthouse. Tense, silent Rangers gripped their weapons tightly. As Altieri imagined thousands of enemy troops waiting on the beach to pick off the Rangers like sitting ducks, he looked around at combat veterans who'd been baptized in the Dieppe Raid—Mulvaney, Andre, and Preston—and wondered if their stomachs were twitching like his. Shifting his eyes, he settled on Captain Roy Murray in the front of the LCA. Another Dieppe Ranger, he appeared as he always seemed in training exercises—relaxed and confident.

In the leading boat, Darby peered through thinning fog and recognized the mass of Cap Carbon that he'd studied in dozens of photographs and maps. Stretching southeasterly toward Arzew lay a small scramble beach—one hundred yards wide and thirty to forty feet deep—that in a few minutes would be swarming with Rangers. Thundering from nine LCAs, their objective was to get off the beach, scale overlooking cliffs, move rapidly to a coastal road, head southward, and capture Batterie du Nord. With it taken, Darby would fire colored flares to signal the troopships five miles at sea that the way had been cleared for General Fredendall to commence his portion of the invasion.

On course and on time, the first LCA lowered its ramp. With Darby in the lead, Rangers debarked. "As if rehearsing a play," he recalled, "the men ran swiftly across the beach and tore into the cliffs. They knew they had a difficult climb ahead, and they wanted to get all the momentum possible. The enemy was nowhere in sight."

Landing close behind Darby's LCA, Altieri found the scene unfolding before him on Red Beach exhilarating. Of his first action, he wrote, "Quickly and quietly we hurtled across the narrow beach and bunched up against the side of a small cliff. Frantically we tugged and pulled at our cumbersome Mae Wests and threw them onto the sand."

Sagging under the burden of mortar shells, the men of F Company's first platoon cleared the cliffs, bounded across a road to take up positions along a ditch facing the hills, and waited for the second platoon to catch up. When Lieutenant Nye said the landing had been a complete surprise, Altieri felt "real good." No longer afraid, he was "once again a brave Ranger."

When the second platoon arrived, the men moved forward in single file across a field into rocky hills with rifles uncocked and at the hip-ready position. Marching two and half miles up tortuous draws, they halted at the base of a ravine that was to be the jumping-off point for the attack on the gun battery. After a sentry wandered from his lookout post on Cap Carbon and was taken prisoner by Darby's group before he could give warning, Darby observed that the men seemed like football players who made the first tackle and were now unconcerned about the crowd at the big game. As they started southeast across rolling African foothills toward Batterie du Nord, they heard bursts of machine-gun fire from the direction of Arzew Harbor, indicating Major Dammer's Rangers had run into resistance.

In five LCAs, Companies A and B had left the *Royal Scotsman* at 0100 and moved into the harbor in a column along an outer jetty. Guided by lights at the harbor's entrance and finding the protective boom open, they proceeded to the site that planners had chosen for the landing. Although analysis of intelligence photographs had provided an estimate of the height of the dock's seawall, the angle at which the pictures had been taken did not show that it was steeply sloped. Consequently, the Rangers clambering from the boats found themselves slipping on a wet, angled wall coated in green slime. Some slid back into the water. A few became snagged in ropes tied to small buoys used as fenders for boats. Wet, with green-stained uniforms, cursing and disgusted, Captain Jacob Manning's platoon scrambled to the top of the dock and came face-to-face with two French soldiers and an Arab. Carrying bundles of laundry toward Fort de la Pointe, the bewildered trio earned the distinction of being the Rangers' first prisoners of war.

Moving stealthily from the dock into a nearby cemetery, B Company's first and second platoons set up mortars and blocked avenues of approach to the fort. At the same time, Company A located the fort's barbed-wire embankment, cut it, and rushed the fort to seize its gun positions. As they surged forward, a lone French sentry evidently heard noises. He sauntered toward the sounds to investigate and a Ranger struck him on the head from behind. As he fell unconscious, A Company swarmed into the fort and after a few shots captured the gun emplacements and sixty French soldiers, including the commandant and a woman in bed.

In the fifteen-minute operation, the Rangers suffered two casualties. A sniper had shot Lieutenant Earl Carran through the shoulder and Private George W. Grisamer died later from a stomach wound.

At 0215, Dammer fired flares to signal General Allen's command ship that the guns of Fort de la Pointe would present no obstacle to the invasion. By walkie-talkie, Dammer exultantly reported to Darby, "I've captured *my* objective."

Of Dammer's emphasis on the personal possessive adjective, Darby recalled, "I got the implication all right, that my subordinate had succeeded quickly. Now it was to be seen if I could do as well."

With a support ship offshore to provide flanking protective fire if needed, the Darby force had reached a wadi leading from the coastal road into the hills. Companies C, E, and F advanced abreast. Five hundred yards to the rear, D Company carried four 81mm mortars. Their objective, Batterie du Nord, was surrounded by concentric circles of barbed wire fourteen feet deep and eight feet high. Behind them lay the fort's big guns, protected by four machine-gun emplacements.

After consulting with Captain Murray, Lieutenant Nye passed the order to the men of Company F to form a skirmish line and fix bayonets. As PFCs Ray Rodriguez and Pete Preston crept toward the double-apron barbed wire with cutters, the silence was shattered and the night lit with crisscrossing streaks of orange and green tracer bullets from the machine guns. During Altieri's first experience under enemy fire, with dirt from the impact of the bullets kicking up everywhere, Darby arrived on the scene. Nye gave the command to fire and the men cut loose from prone positions, aiming at orange and green flames from enemy weapons. A Ranger fired a long burst at the right flank of the machine gun. The burst was answered by the French. Bullets whistled past, stitching into a low embankment behind the Ranger line, but Altieri discovered he wasn't scared. Because of the Commando training, close-landing bullets had become a familiar experience. The battle was so completely absorbing that there was no time to be concerned about personal fears. The only pressing concern was what happened next.

The answer came from Darby. On a walkie-talkie to D Company, he ordered its mortars to lay down a barrage and told Murray to pull his men back a few yards, "then hit 'em when the barrage stops." A moment later, the mortars fired and Altieri heard the loud flutter of a round directly overhead, followed by an earthshaking crash and the loud swishing and fluttering of mortar shells speeding earthward. The whole hillside shuddered with the impacts of the fierce, two-minute bombardment. The French guns fell silent.

Nye yelled, "Assault!"

Showered by rocks and debris from a shell that fell short and landed behind them, the men of F Company surged off the ground screaming wordlessly, rifles at their hips, toward the gaps that Rodriguez and Preston had hacked in the barbed wire. Through swirls of acrid smoke, they dashed thirty yards to the first gun battery. Leaping a low concrete parapet into a dugout and finding seven half-dressed "whimpering Frenchmen, dazed by the mortar barrage," Altieri shouted, *"Nous Americains."*

Depicting the silencing of the French machine guns by the mortars "as if someone had pulled a switch," Darby recalled that the Rangers needed no orders. Several rushed the big guns, thrusting Bangalore torpedoes (four-foot sections of steel pipe crammed with explosives) into the muzzles. At the same moment, a larger party of Rangers slammed through the main entrance of Batterie du Nord, shooting the sentry barring their path. The battle was practically over. The French soldiers had barricaded themselves in a powder magazine underground thinking the mortar shells were aerial bombs. When they did not answer an order in French that they give themselves up, grenades were pushed down the ventilators along with a Bangalore torpedo.

Sixty French came up with hands in the air. The guns were demolished and outposts were established.

Unaware of the fall of Fort de la Pointe to Dammer's force and the surrounding of his fort, the French commander of Batterie du Nord found himself ordered by Darby to come out carrying a white flag. He replied, *"Oui, oui, mon colonel."* When Darby and five Rangers started toward the fort, a machine gun opened fire.

"We were now thoroughly aroused," said Darby, "and fighting mad."

As Rangers charged toward the fort, the French garrison threw their guns into a well and surrendered. Moments later, wearing a naval coat over pajamas and with feet in slippers, the commander appeared waving a white flag. The remaining French position to be taken was a convalescent home for the French Foreign Legion. Demanding its surrender, Darby was told by a French colonel that the commander could not do so without at least a token of resistance by his men to show they had displayed "valor."

Darby replied, "Tell him his troops can fire their rifles just once, then I want them to march out of the fort to surrender at 0800 or they'll be dead pigeons."

With the two forts taken and Arzew captured, Darby was to signal the accomplishment by radio and by firing four green flares, followed by four white star shells. Because the radio and the white star flares had been lost when the boat carrying them had tipped during the lowering of the landing craft, Darby had only the green flares to fire. Fortunately, a British observer party that had come in with the Rangers had a radio with which to inform a British destroyer of the victory. It relayed the message to Generals Fredendall and Allen.

In the two attacks, the Rangers had lost four men killed and eleven wounded.

★ CHAPTER 7 ★

SNAPSHOTS

"Now we can get down to real business."

IN THE STREAKY PURPLE AND RED OF AN ALGERIAN DAWN, WITH OC-casional bursts of gunfire in the distance, James Altieri stood with his F Company buddies beside the silenced big guns of Batterie du Nord and gazed down at the Mediterranean Sea. Like water bugs, dozens of assault craft carrying men of the Sixteenth Infantry Regiment moved toward Beach Green far below. Reliving the panorama two decades later in *The Spearheaders*, he wrote, "Although we were sleepless and hungry, the nervous excitement of the fantastic scene unfolding beneath us gave us renewed energy. Our situation seemed incredible. Here we were sitting a half mile above the harbor watching the drama of the first American invasion unfold beneath us. In one swift stroke we had secured as a base of operations a port with all its facilities intact and with a minimum of casualties. We had opened the way to Oran."

Presently, photographer Phil Stern bounded up the hill. Grinning, he carried the booty of war in the form of a German Leica camera dangling from a neck strap and a bulky canvas bag crammed with rolls of captured film slung over a shoulder. Having shot several rolls of Rangers in action, from their landings to the seizure of their objectives, he demanded that Butt Torbett pose hugging the barrel of one of the four-inch guns.

"Listen, fellows," Stern said dramatically, "these pictures will soon be seen by millions of people back home. These pictures will tell the story of what we Rangers accomplished in opening the gates for the attack on Oran."

No man with a camera since Matthew Brady in the Civil War would enshrine in black and white images of so many colorful American warriors, from generals to privates, than a photographer of Hollywood celebrities who had chosen to ally himself with Darby's Rangers. Through Stern's photos they would become as familiar to Americans as the faces of movie stars or character actors from central casting that every moviegoer recognized but couldn't name. In formal portraits and candid shots, he memorialized men with stars, oak leaves, and bars on collars; guys with stripes on sleeves and rifles slung over shoulders; a GI shaving with cold water in a helmet and another washing in an Algerian bathtub; an infantryman eating C rations; another with full pack and shouldered M1; Rangers dug in on a hill above Arzew; Father Basil in a white robe as Rangers buried their dead; and their commander, Lieutenant Colonel William O. Darby, striding along a landing beach, conferring with Captain Roy Murray and Major General Terry de la Mesa Allen and chatting with Brigadier General Ted Roosevelt.

Of the central figures of Torch, there was no more mismatched trio of officers in terms of age, background, and personal deportment. The leader of the Rangers was the youngest, more properly soldierly, and the only graduate of West Point. While Allen had completed three years at the U.S. Military Academy, he had failed in ordnance and gunnery in his final year, dropped out, and finished college at Catholic University. Taking an army commission in 1912, he was wounded at St. Mihiel in World War I. At the Army Command and General Staff College in Fort Leavenworth, he was called by the commandant "the most indifferent student ever enrolled" and was near the bottom of a class in which Dwight Eisenhower ranked first. While facing court-martial on a charge of insubordination and contemplating quitting the army in 1940 as a lieutenant colonel, he was amazed to learn that he had been promoted two grades to brigadier general on the same day as his old friend, polo partner, and military individualist George S. Patton, who wrote him, "My dear Terry: Congratulations!! The army has certainly gone to hell when both of us are made. I guess we must be in for some serious fighting and we are the ones who can lead. All we need now is a juicy war. At least they have had the sense to promote the two damn best officers in the U.S. Army."

Given two stars and command of the First Infantry Division in 1941, Allen took it to war aboard the *Queen Mary*. Nicknamed "Terrible Terry," he told his men, "Nothing in hell must stop or delay the First Division."

When Ted Roosevelt was named Allen's deputy, General George C. Marshall wrote to Allen, "T.R. and you are very much the same type as to enthusiasm. I am a little fearful." That Roosevelt was described by one officer as "the most disreputable-looking general" he'd ever met had no effect on Marshall. Calling him his "favorite swashbuckler," Marshall said Roosevelt was "an A-No. 1 fighting man with rare courage, and what is even rarer, unlimited fortitude."

While Darby's divided Ranger Force attacked Arzew's two fortifications, Roosevelt was off Oran to the east and leading his old World War I outfit, the Twenty-sixth Infantry Regiment, and part of Combat Command B. With him was his son Quentin. An artillery battery commander, he was the namesake of Roosevelt's youngest brother, who as an aviator had been shot down and killed in France in 1918. On June 6, 1944, Ted and Quentin would be the only father and son to land in Normandy, but on separate beaches. Ted would be in command on Utah and Quentin would lead men as a captain on Omaha.

Coming ashore in Algiers east of Oran just before dawn on a November Sunday in 1942, Ted was fifty-five years old. With a Colt Army .45 automatic pistol in hand, a dog-eared copy of *The Pilgrim's Progress* in a pocket, and a history of medieval England in his knapsack, he saw the first wave of invaders as "little, scarcely seen black shapes" and shouted to them, "March to the sound of the guns."

Aboard the *Reina del Pacifico* facing Arzew, Terry Allen had kept in shape during the long voyage from Britain by jogging three miles after breakfast, exercising with Indian clubs, and throwing and receiving a medicine ball. Described by one observer as "looking nearly as ugly as Ted Roosevelt" and by a newspaper reporter as "a champion rioter and rebel," he commanded the U.S. Army's oldest division and embodied its unofficial motto, "Work hard and drink much." His battle order was "ride around 'em, over 'em, and through 'em." Officers of the Fighting First were told, "A soldier doesn't fight to save suffering humanity or any other nonsense. He fights to prove that his unit is the best in the Army and that he has as much guts as anybody else in the unit."

Through field glasses from the silenced Batterie du Nord, James Altieri looked down on the beach as launches unloaded "the sinews of war" and toward the captured harbor at transport ships "easing majestically toward the docks." He decided that everything seemed "well in hand." A few moments later, he saw a berthed transport bracketed by two shell bursts. Training his glasses farther east, he observed a flash of the French gun as it "belched out another salvo" and was horrified that the shells hit the transport amidships, tearing a gaping hole. Hearing the roar of aircraft, he looked up and saw two low-flying Spitfires wheel "gracefully" and swoop down on the gun "like vengeful eagles." Firing cannon and machine guns, they silenced it.

Recording that for the remainder of the day it was "all quiet on the Fox Company front," Altieri gleefully watched Rangers trading C rations for oranges and eggs with "six wandering Arabs riding jackasses." This windfall was combined with chickens confiscated from the fort commandant's own coops and a barrel of Algerian wine found near a French dugout. "Like good Rangers," Altieri noted, "we ate, drank and tried to convince ourselves that we were really pulling important duty guarding the gun battery."

As night fell, Company F settled down on the windswept battery with canteens "full of vin rouge," chicken, eggs, and oranges, "egos full of pride" for their D-day accomplishments and hearts grateful that they had "pulled through without a single casualty."

In the bustling port that night, Tom Sullivan had time to jot in his diary: "At 1:30 a.m., A Co. lands on dock inside harbor at Arzew taking fort in one hour. One Arab killed at entrance. C. D. E. & F. take F. Du Nord with mortar fire preceding. Am guarding oil refinery."

With Arzew taken, the two regimental combat teams of the First Division ashore, and the attack moving inland, Darby received requests for Ranger assistance in two actions. The first was for a company to join a battalion of the Sixteenth Infantry at Port-aux-Poules. Darby gave the assignment to Lieutenant Max Schneider's Company E. The mission was to clear a road to the town of La Macta. The road, including a bridge over an unfordable gorge, was defended by a long-range Hotchkiss machine gun and a French force threatening a counterattack. The Rangers, traveling by train, came under harassing fire and had to deploy about a mile from the town. Arriving at the blocked road at 0200 on November 9, they borrowed two self-propelled 75mm guns, broke the resistance, entered La Macta with the infantry, and provided "close-in protection" until 1400 the next day. They returned to Arzew by train.

A few hours after E Company had departed Arzew to aid the Sixteenth Infantry, Darby received an appeal for assistance from General Allen. In a drive eastward from Arzew to join Roosevelt's force in enveloping Oran that Allen had told the men of the First Division "nothing in hell must delay or stop," the general had established his command post at the nearby village of Tourville. Lieutenant Gordon Klefman's Company C arrived late in the afternoon on November 8. While they stood guard throughout the night, the Eighteenth Regimental Combat Team under Colonel Frank Greer was engaged in an assault on a village astride the Arzew-Oran highway. In a wide, bowl-shaped expanse of farmland, St. Cloud was defended by a battalion of the French Foreign Legion and the Sixteenth Tunisian Regiment. With machine guns, artillery, and mortars, and with the advantage of unobstructed fields of fire, they stopped Greer's First Battalion. When the Second Battalion joined the fray, the result was the same.

Allen, determined not to be held up in the push on toward Oran, decided that St. Cloud was a tough nut to crack and that his division would bypass the town, leaving it to one of Greer's battalions to contain the French, with the assistance of Klefman's Rangers. Marching from Tourville, they arrived to link with Greer's First Battalion at two o'clock in the afternoon on November 9. With orders from Greer to block the town's exits and prevent the enemy force from escaping, C Company deployed after dark in an encircling movement to the south of the town. As dawn broke on November 10, they found a French column on the road and moved to attack. When heavy fire from artillery, mortars, and machine guns blunted the assault about a quarter of a mile from the column, Klefman ordered one of his platoons to return fire. Leading the second in an attempt to flank the dug-in French, he was mortally wounded. As he lay in an open field, he shouted, "Keep going! Keep going to the right and don't worry about me."

When the French commander in Oran surrendered the city and ordered the forces in St. Cloud to cease fighting at three o'clock in the afternoon, Darby learned that C Company had been badly shot up. Inheriting command of the company, Lieutenant Charles Shunstrom reported eight wounded and Klefman, PFC Elmer Eskola, and Private Alder L. "Bud" Nystrom killed. As Darby made arrangements for burial of the first of his Rangers to die in an entirely American battle, he recognized irony in the date of the ceremony. On November 11, 1942, U.S. soldiers who had been killed on French territory by French troops would be laid to rest on the twenty-fourth anniversary of the armistice that had ended a war in which the intervention of the U.S. Army had saved France from defeat by the Germans. Nor did the significance of the day go unnoticed by James Altieri. "Without fanfare," he wrote, the Rangers turned over Batterie du Nord to the French, "who were now our allies," and the fort was "now flying the French tricolor alongside the American flag."

Assembled in a small field overlooking Arzew Harbor, Companies A, B, D, and F of the First Ranger Battalion stood stiffly at attention with rifles at "present-arms" while Father Basil, in the black-and-white cassock of his faith, conducted the funeral ceremony. Altieri and four others fired three saluting volleys. Three plain wooden coffins were slowly lowered into the graves. A moment later, with Darby and Dammer in the lead, the battalion filed onto a road that wound past landing beach Red, into rocky ravines and onto a steep mountainside.

On a march that Altieri called "a nightmare," Darby's Rangers found themselves moving at breakneck pace for ten miles over treacherous mountainsides, now climbing, now sliding downward, now running in short spurts on occasional stretches of level terrain. Recalling six of the most memorable, miserable, heartbreaking miles he'd ever experienced, Altieri wrote, "Several times I was on the verge of falling out, joining the swelling ranks of the stragglers. But more than pride, fierce anger prevented me. Darby and Dammer were up there. This was killing them as much as it was the men. If they could take it, so could I."

Darby explained later that he drove his men because he'd recognized that after one battle they "considered themselves heroes and experienced soldiers" and "looked for a pat on the back, a chance for rest and recreation." Instead, they found their commander marching them for long distances on short rations that made training in Scotland seem "easy in comparison." In night problems and landings "practiced again and again," the Arzew operation was replayed "like a phonograph record," but in varied weather and tide conditions. Believing that veteran soldiers, even between campaigns, required "continual training to prepare them for new and unusual enemy attacks," Darby converted Arzew and the surrounding region into an amphibious army assault-training center.

In a period of the most strenuous, ambitious, versatile training program in U.S. Army history, Altieri observed, "Colonel Darby, ably assisted by his efficient executive officer, Major Dammer, devised an ingenious schedule designed to condition us physically and mentally for any type of combat we might be called on to perform."

After several weeks, Darby announced, "Now that I'm satisfied you men are hardened enough to be called Rangers, now that I know that every man here is physically equipped to endure any march over the most challenging terrain—now we can get down to real business."

While the men of F Company exchanged opinions in their quarters in the former Foreign Legion convalescence facility on what El Darbo meant by "real business," photographer Phil Stern barged in, waving copies of the Army newspaper *Stars and Stripes* and a three-week-old *New York Times*. "The whole country knows about Arzew. Look! My pictures!"

The *Stars and Stripes* headline read:

DARING RANGERS SILENCE COASTAL GUNS

CRACK NIGHT FIGHTERS TAKE ARZEW ON D DAY

THEN SMASH WAY TO ORAN

Stern's pictures, Altieri wrote, had not only made the public aware of the Rangers, but "they had given us a new surge of pride and spirit at a crucial time," when many were beginning to doubt the wisdom of joining the Rangers and felt disappointment that they were not being used for Commando raids as they had envisioned. Recording that the Rangers "were vain enough to bask momentarily in the national spotlight" provided by the articles and Stern's photos, Altieri wrote, "Even if Darby didn't let us know how good we were, the rest of the world knew it."

In addition to his personal demand that the Rangers keep in fighting shape, Darby had been instructed to prepare them for a night raid on an Italian radar and radio installation on the island of Galita in the Straits of Sicily off the Tunisian city of Bizerte. They were to board the British assault ship *Queen Emma* on Sunday, December 27, and spend three days practicing landings from it to the Arzew beaches in preparation for assaulting the rocky coast of Galita. On December 30, they were to march over mountains to knock out the facilities and occupy the island by New Year's Day.

Informed of the mission, Altieri eagerly anticipated a no-holds-barred period of street fighting at its dirtiest that "we had all been yelling for, because this was the kind of fighting we had joined the Rangers for and were trained for."

On Christmas Day, the Rangers stood bareheaded in hot sun on Red Beach for alternate Catholic and Protestant services conducted by Father Basil. Accompanied by a small portable organ Basil had somehow located, Darby's re-toughened warriors sang carols and hymns in honor of the birthday of the Prince of Peace. On Sunday, December 27, they gathered on the wharves of Arzew Harbor to watch the troopship drop anchor. Wearing sunglasses, Darby gave the order to board a small armada of assault boats to take them to a vessel that, compared to the Irish ferryboats that took them to North Africa, was a sleek aristocrat of the Mediterranean. The *Queen Emma* provided the Rangers remarkably good chow, freshwater showers, and a system of loudspeakers offering recordings of American swing music. After three days of boat drills, landing rehearsals, and general orientation, the ship pulled up anchor and sailed out of Arzew Harbor without naval and air escort.

Anticipating her standing off their destination that night and Rangers clambering into assault craft, Altieri stood on the port side of the bow and decided he'd never seen the battalion in higher spirits. Chatting with his buddy Carlo Contrera, he noticed the ship making a wide turn. A few minutes later, the voice of the ship's captain boomed out of the loudspeakers, "Rangers, we are returning to port. Colonel Darby will now speak."

He told the stunned and disappointed Rangers, "We have just received instructions from Supreme Headquarters that owing to changes in the overall strategic situation in the Mediterranean, our island raid has been called off. Our orders are to return to Arzew. I'm sorry, damned sorry. I know you would have put on a good show."

Describing the Rangers' mood as "ugly" when the ship reversed course, Altieri wrote, "Once again the future was uncertain. Once again we would go back to training. Once again we wondered for what."

Summing up the role of the Rangers in Torch, Darby said, "The battle for Oran was won." The attack on the Arzew batteries was carried out as planned. They had hit the ground, fired their weapons, crawled or run forward without deliberate or conscious thought, sustained light casualties, inflicted heavy enemy losses, and taken several hundred prisoners.

In two actions after the successful landings, two of the companies had been called upon to fight as conventional infantrymen and did so with distinction. While this alteration in the concept of the role of Rangers elicited no complaint from their founder and commander, the use of Rangers in this manner and the aborted raid on the island troubled James Altieri. He wrote, "Gone were the bouncy zest, the cocky wisecracks, the enthusiastic efforts of our daily routines. The terrible letdown of the raid that wasn't, the impatience for action, the uncertainty of our status as a fighting force—all combined to pervade the outfit with a futile sense of melancholia, the most insidious enemy an army can have."

He and the others asked, "What was the purpose in organizing and training Rangers for Commando-type operations if they were going to be frittered away in mass battles?"

★ CHAPTER 8 ★

APPOINTMENT IN TUNISIA

"A man doesn't talk about what he does with a bayonet."

PERHAPS BECAUSE CAPTAIN WILLIAM O. DARBY OF THE THIRTY-FOURTH Division in Northern Ireland in the spring of 1942 had exhibited such a natural ability and personal charm as aide-de-camp to General Hartle in smoothing relations between American soldiers and Irish civilians, Lieutenant Colonel Darby of the Rangers found himself appointed military mayor of Arzew. He confronted a dual challenge of keeping his men battle-ready and restoring everyday life to the small city of Arabian and French heritage and culture that had been engulfed by thousands of young Americans. To help deal with the problems of running a city, providing water, and keeping electricity flowing, he installed Arzew's former mayor in an adjoining office in the town hall.

When Rangers who regarded themselves as blooded warriors were required to patrol the streets like policemen, they chafed at what they considered both a waste of their soldierly skills and a demeaning assignment. Bitterness grew to such an extent that occasional respites from training and weekend passes for excursions into Arzew and Oran failed to boost morale.

"We were plain bored with Arzew," Altieri complained, "and the pleasures of Oran no longer appealed to us, particularly since Oran was literally infested with GIs from all over Africa. Not that we minded the competition, but the sheen of the city had worn off." The wine "tasted lousier, the girls looked harder, the prices were higher," and souvenirs reflected "inferior workmanship." Barroom and street brawls with soldiers from other units increased. Company commanders began reporting men "absent without leave" (AWOL). When they returned or were brought back in custody, they found themselves face-to-face with Darby and then confined to a barbed-wire stockade with a pup tent for housing and C rations for meals. An increasing number of Rangers became so disillusioned and frustrated by lack of action that they sought transfers to combat units. Because the battalion was a volunteer unit, Darby could appeal to them to remain with the Rangers, but he could not compel them. "If this keeps up," cracked one embittered Ranger, "there won't be anyone left but Darby."

While individual Rangers were choosing to leave the ranks in the belief that it had no future as an elite outfit of "spearheaders," the battalion's accomplishments at Arzew and St. Cloud sufficiently impressed Eisenhower and his European theater of operations staff that a letter had been sent to the War Department on December 2 stating, "Experience has proven that specially trained units of this character are invaluable in landing operations, for the reduction of coast defenses, and similar missions." The result was authorization for formation of the Second Ranger Battalion to be drawn from volunteers in training units in the United States and men of the Twenty-Ninth Infantry Regiment in North Ireland. The cadre would be the "provisional" Ranger battalion that had been established by a directive to General Mark W. Clark (Second Corps commander) in September.

While formation of a second battalion patterned on the first was a tribute to Darby, he faced an alarming attrition of disgruntled men that threatened to render his battalion ineffective as a fighting force. This required an appeal for volunteers from other units in Algiers and from Morocco through notices posted on division, battalion, and company bulletin boards, word of mouth and personal visits by Darby, Dammer, and other officers. By January 26, Captain Jack B. Street, five other officers, and a hundred enlisted men had passed Darby's screening process. When they arrived in trucks, on Red Beach at Arzew to begin Ranger training, they found "a rousing reception" consisting of cheers from men of the six companies, bursts from M1 rifles, machine guns shot into the air, BARs fired under and around the trucks, and an occasional hand grenade lobbed into the sea. Darby assigned some of the replacements to undermanned companies and the remainder to a new company (G) under Street. As training of the new men commenced, he climbed into a C-47 transport plane for a trip to Eisenhower's headquarters in Algiers.

Fresh from a conference between President Roosevelt and Prime Minister Churchill at Casablanca from January 13 to 23, Eisenhower had recently named a new deputy chief of staff. To replace Mark Clark he had chosen the general who had been given the task of organizing the U.S. version of the Commandos and had been the principal American observer when Rangers participated in the Dieppe Raid. Now a major general, Lucian Truscott had been in command of Operation Goalpost in the landings in Morocco under Patton.

The objective had been not only to seize the port of Lyautey but to secure a strategic airport located three miles to the north. The planning called for the landing of four battalions at five different points along the shore at precisely 4:00 a.m. Once the troops were ashore, a special unit of seventy-five men would secure the airfield. Unfortunately, the French were not surprised. At the time when the troops were scheduled to land, the plan went awry. A premature broadcast of a recording by President Roosevelt calling on the French forces to capitulate alerted them to the impending invasion. Meeting fierce resistance, Truscott led his force ashore. After securing the beaches, they faced the daunting task of attacking the Casbah, a heavily fortified French concrete fortress just inland from the beach. With his troops bogged down by skillful snipers, he waited for reinforcements. After Wildcat fighter-bombers destroyed the gates, the attackers stormed into the fortress, forcing the surrender of two hundred and fifty French soldiers. The special units were then able to capture the airfield.

Of Truscott's elevation to Eisenhower's deputy chief of staff, General Patton said, "His promotion has been well deserved and he has invariably done a good, though never brilliant, job. I am very proud of him."

Sixteen years older than Darby, with flecks of gray in his hair, the godfather of the Rangers found in their handsome, dashing thirty-two-year-old leader the most important trait required of a successful officer. "Character," Truscott said, "is what you are. Reputation is what others think you are. The reason that some fail to climb the ladder of success, or of leadership if you want to call it that, is that there is no difference between reputation and character. The two do not always coincide. A man may be considered to have sterling character. Opportunity might come to that man; but if he has the reputation for something he is not, he may fail that opportunity. I think character is the foundation of successful leadership."

As the two officers who had been key figures in taking Casablanca and Arzew met for the first time since Darby took command of the Rangers in Northern Ireland, the objective for Eisenhower was to clear the Germans and their Italian allies from Tunisia and capture the port of Tunis. Without enough forces to drive out the Germans and Italians, the Allies had established defensive positions in the Tunisian mountains between the Mediterranean Sea on the north and the Sahara Desert on the south. While Darby's Rangers were training in the months after their victories at Arzew and St. Cloud and the aborted raid on Galita, the Allies had moved east into Tunisia as Germans moved west until they faced each other on a curving front from Medjez-el-Bab in the north to El Guettar in the south called the Mareth Line. With Italians in the fore, Rommel's Panzer Army Africa was ready to rush forward from Libya while Colonel General Hans-Jurgen von Arnim's Fifth Panzer Army stood poised at a base near Tunis in the north. The headquarters of the Second Corps under Fredendall was at Tebessa in Algeria at the head of a region called Speedy Valley, located to the west of a mountain range (Grand Dorsal) that was cut by numerous passes.

With the bulk of the U.S. armed forces in Algeria committed to protection of extended lines of communication, Eisenhower decided to detach the Second Corps, of which the First Armored Division was the nucleus, from Center Task Force at Oran in order to concentrate it for a new combat mission in Tunisia. On January 1, 1943, he appointed Fredendall to command the Second Corps, including a French force at Constantine, Algeria, and a British paratroop brigade, with orders to concentrate these forces in the Tebessa and Kasserine area to prepare for "offensive action against the enemy's lines of communication."

With Second Corps having completed its concentration in the area in mid-January, Eisenhower ordered Fredendall to be ready to launch an attack by January 23. Success depended on perfect coordination of its movements with those of the British in order to contain von Arnim's forces. It was estimated that he was receiving 750 men a day with necessary supplies, and that his forces numbered about

65,000. To build up Allied strength and interdict the enemy's buildup became the guiding principle of Eisenhower's strategy. Late in December, before Second Corps arrived in the south, his headquarters learned that Rommel had an accurate appreciation of the situation. He was still far away, Eisenhower noted, but he was in full retreat from the victorious British Eighth Army since it defeated him at El Alamein. In a captured document dated December 16, 1942, titled "Appreciation of Situation," Rommel stated that the enemy "probably lacks cohesion and suffers from the inherent weakness of an Allied Command." On the basis of these observations, he had outlined an ambitious strategy to capitalize on the weaknesses. He proposed holding the British Eighth Army with a minimum force and using the remainder to "attack and cut the enemy lines of communication in Tunisia." He calculated that two divisions could either hold the Eighth Army or delay its pursuit in a slow withdrawal under air cover and by minefields. He proposed to advance the bulk of his force on Allied lines of communications in the south, which he saw as "not well guarded." Von Arnim's mission was to keep a corridor open for Rommel's force to advance northward from Libya along the coast of the Gulf of Gabes and link up with von Arnim's Panzer Army to form a front from which to push westward to attack the Allies and keep them from taking the ports of Tunis and Bizerte.

In the scenario described by Eisenhower at the meeting to which Darby was summoned from Arzew, Ranger skills in amphibious assault were useless in a desert. "This time there was to be no spearheading of strong U.S. formations," Darby noted. Uniquely trained for carrying out hit-and-run operations at night, the Rangers were to locate enemy outposts, eliminate them, take prisoners, gauge the enemy's strength, and create the impression that the Allies were greater in number than they were.

When the battalion boarded thirty-two C-47 transport planes at Oran on February 8, it was a new experience. Until now they had traveled by foot, truck, train, and on ship. Altieri observed that the order to move out brought a dramatic change of Ranger morale from "moody indifference" to "zestful anticipation" of imminent action. From the Youks-les-Bains airport near Tebessa, they went by truck to Fredendall's headquarters. The following day, they moved to the small town of Gafsa. Held by French troops that were supported by the American artillery and tank-destroyer outfits, it was the southernmost anchor of the American front, about seven miles west of the enemy-held heights of El Guettar. In briefings by company commanders, the Rangers learned they were to conduct a series of raids against five positions guarding approaches to Sened Pass. The first, Sened Station, was a railway junction and supply depot about twelve miles from the pass. It was occupied by members of the Centauro Division of the Bersaglieri, regarded by the British as the best unit in the Italian army.

While Captain Roy Murray described the mission that was to be executed by A, E, and F companies and the Headquarters Company's mortar platoon, Altieri grimly remembered having been asked in Ireland if he would be able to stick a knife into an Italian soldier and twist it. Suddenly "face-to-face with the chilling reality" he had always hoped to avoid, he heard Murray explain, "We're gonna throw the Commando book at them—bayonets, knives, grenades—the works! Our orders are to terrorize and demoralize to our fullest capacities." Helmets were to be left behind. They would wear knitted caps. One C ration. One canteen of water. No entrenching tool. No extra ammunition bandolier. They would move at night, sleep during the day, and carry a shelter half to be used for camouflage. "We've got to leave our mark on these people," said Murray. "They've got to know that they've been worked over by Rangers. Every man uses his bayonet as much as he can—these are our orders."

After midnight on February 12, they traveled twenty miles by truck and jeep, dismounted at a French outpost, and moved in the long Ranger stride they had learned in Ireland and Scotland for eight miles of rugged terrain to arrive four miles from their objective at dawn. With skullcaps pulled down over ears and blackened faces, Altieri wrote, they "looked like zombies." Because Altieri's squad leader had been taken ill and was ordered to stay behind, Altieri was chosen to replace him. Aghast at being "saddled" with the responsibility for twelve men, including two of the "green" replacements, he told himself that to refuse to accept "at such a critical time would be the same as cowardice."

Warren Evans had been recently promoted from battalion sergeant major to second lieutenant and was in command of the second platoon of A Company. He recalled wearing the black cap, but didn't remember blackening his face. A former football player and a singer in Father Basil's worship services, he displayed a baritone voice that earned him the nickname "Bing," after Bing Crosby. "From our position," he wrote, "we eyeballed the enemy all through the next day. We used field glasses to study their every move and scope out the surrounding terrain."

Darby recalled, "Out came the shelter halves, and the men hid away in the mountains for the day, watching their objective like a cat ready to spring on its prey."

Around midnight, just before the setting of the moon, with the desert in darkness, Darby signaled the men to move. Describing the unfolding scene in *The Spearheaders*, Altieri wrote, "No weapons clanked, no leather creaked. Even our dog tags had been taped to prevent their clinking. The line of a hundred and eighty men led by Colonel Darby slithered ahead like a gigantic black snake. The pace started off mildly, then after three miles over open plain it picked up to a near run. A Company was in the lead, followed by Easy Company."

Without breaking pace, they climbed winding, steep draws clustered with rocks and boulders. The air became thinner, their breath shorter as they climbed gorges, crevices, and ravines. When a bluish gray dawn broke, they halted in a bowl-shaped saddle between a pair of towering cliffs and bivouacked for the day. At sunset, as the valley fell into shadows, with faces freshly coated with spit-soaked dirt and Darby and Dammer taking the lead, they appeared to Altieri like flitting ghouls as the column glided noiselessly down the mountainside and waited behind a low hill for the moon to go down. After a moment of alarm over the discovery of an enemy patrol that was quickly eliminated by a Company A scouting team's knives, the pace resumed. Because of the need for silence, Darby had devised a system of communicating between companies using hooded flashlights that blinked red or green.

Advancing abreast, Company A was on the left, E in the center, and F on the right flank. They crossed a valley to within 150 yards of the Italian position. As they marched closer and closer, Altieri found it incredible that the enemy was completely still and wondered if they were asleep. Based on experience, Bing Evans reasoned that if the Italians sensed that someone was out there, they would assume it was a patrol and, unable to see anything in the darkness, would fire high. Altieri expected at any moment to see the sky bathed in the light of a flare and to hear the chattering of machine guns, the pop of rifles, and the boom of cannon. He knew that to catch three companies of Rangers on an open plain in front of well-buttressed positions was a defender's dream. But there was only a mysterious silence.

The stillness was shattered with a long raking burst of machine-gun fire to the left of Evans's A Company. Altieri watched a chain of red and green tracer bullets as a dozen or more machine guns joined in a deadly chorus. He heard excited voices of Italians as they scurried to their positions. Almost at once, the entire hillside erupted with a terrific roar as thousands of hot, searing tracers whistled over heads and ricocheted into the rocks.

Seventeen years after finding himself reluctantly accepting the job of squad leader in a nighttime attack against a bastion of Italians in the mountains of a Tunisian desert, Altieri wrote that with no rocks to hide behind, no helmet to give the illusion of protection, and with nothing between the enemy's field of fire and the "crab-like forms" of crawling Rangers, he felt naked.

Rifles and machine guns "spewed" and cannon shells "swooshed" like freight trains. One of them took off PFC Elmer W. Garrison's head.

Newly minted Lieutenant Bing Evans gave this harrowing account:

> The next thing we knew we were in amongst them engaged in hand-to-hand combat and very fierce fighting. But we had the advantage. With the complete surprise, we had created real havoc. We were using Tommy guns, bayonets, knives and hand grenades. That's something that most infantry soldiers have never experienced.
>
> On this particular night, I had my knife in one hand and my .45 in the other and I was using both of them. Then the sky became as bright as day. Our opponents began to throw up flares so they could see all that was happening. At that point, they could see us and we could see them. All of a sudden, out of the dark came an enemy soldier. He was running toward me with a gun in his hand. He got very close. His eyes were big as saucers, frightened and wild. Looking into his eyes, I became paralyzed and found that I couldn't pull the trigger on my .45 piece. I couldn't do it! I knew he was ready to kill me, but I couldn't do it. Up until then I hadn't looked into the eyes of the one I was about to kill. But now I did.

At that moment, his runner, Tom Sullivan, was five steps away, to Evans's right and a little to the rear. "Being my runner, he was to stay with me at all times unless I sent him on a mission," Evans explained. "The runner is used as the main means of communication in case the walkie-talkies didn't work. A lot of times they didn't. Tommy sized up the situation and without hesitating, shot my attacker in the chest and killed him for me."

Of the Sened Station raid, Sullivan said in a letter to his younger brother Joe that the Rangers "wiped out gun positions and massacred the outpost" and that "seeing the flash of big guns going off in your face and expecting every moment to go flying through space" had been "quite an experience."

Darby reported that the Italians had "thought they were in an inaccessible place," but his Rangers had "rushed them with bayonets and knives and gave them everything they had" in "a good example of a sustained and coordinated night attack."

Altieri would write, "It was sickening, it was brutal, it was inhuman, but that was our job, and we were stuck with it."

Another Ranger said, "There was some pretty rough in-fighting there, but a man doesn't talk about what he does with a bayonet."

★ CHAPTER 9 ★

GOD HELP THE TANKS

"You can keep your promotion."

IN LESS THAN HALF AN HOUR AT SENED STATION, DARBY'S RANGERS had killed seventy-five men of Italy's Tenth Bersaglieri Regiment, captured eleven, destroyed a 50mm antitank gun, and silenced five machine guns. One Ranger was killed and twenty had been wounded.

"Now our only concern," James Altieri recalled, "was to get the hell out of there."

Faced with the dual challenges of the likelihood of a counterattack by German tanks and withdrawing battle-drained Rangers and their badly injured, Darby ordered Dammer to speed march the able-bodied men twelve miles over mountains and six of open plain to Gafsa. To carry casualties on stretchers made of shelter halves and assist the walking wounded, he called for volunteers for a second slow column that he would lead. Depicting an agonizing and harrowing forced march, and "thankful that the man who had organized and trained our outfit was with us," Altieri wrote, "Darby was magnificent. His very presence gave us amazing strength, both morally and physically. He took turns carrying stretchers. He did his best to cheer the wounded. Up and down the strung-out column he ranged, giving an encouraging word here, a reassuring pat there, a spirited challenge wherever and whenever needed."

The day after the return from Sened Station, General Fredendall awarded the Silver Star for gallantry in action to Sergeants Gerrit Rensink, Donald McCollam, and Mervin Heacock; T/5s Austin Low and Owen Sweasey; PFCs Edward Dean, Leslie Ferrier, and Joseph Dye; Lieutenant Leonard Dirks; Captains Max Schneider and Roy Murray; Major Herman Dammer; and Darby.

While the Rangers rested at Gafsa and basked in reports that the Italians had started calling the Americans who'd attacked them at Sened Station "Black Death," Darby was planning a second raid, scheduled for Sunday, February 14, against Djebel el Ank. The Allies were arrayed on a north-south line with the British in the north, the French Nineteenth Corps in the center, and Fredendall's Second Corps in the south. The challenge for Eisenhower was to keep Rommel's forces from linking with von Arnim, defeat both, and capture the Tunisian ports needed for an invasion of Europe across the Mediterranean. After a meeting with Eisenhower on February 13, General Fredendall's operations officer reported that Ike had judged the general disposition of the Allied forces "satisfactory."

Rommel, in reviewing the same map of Tunisia, discerned an extreme weakness in the American and French positions in the Eastern Dorsal passes of Fondouk, Faid, and Gafsa. If his panzers broke through, they could drive sixty to seventy miles to the American head-quarters at Tebessa and deep into Algeria, then turn east to destroy Montgomery's Eighth Army or force it to retreat. The German forces struck at dawn on Valentine's Day. Under strong air support, von Arnim's Tenth and Twenty-first Panzer Divisions hit the Americans at Faid Pass. Driving back units of the First Armored Division and inflicting heavy losses in men and tanks, they threatened to swiftly advance on Gafsa.

Ten days earlier, Fredendall had issued an order that in the event of a significant German attack in that region, the small force of American and French defenders was to withdraw in a delaying action and establish a defensive line on a ridge at Feriana. This plan required Rangers to form a rear guard and hold their position for four hours. Darby assigned the task to D and G companies and remained with them. As they were setting up a defense and putting out sentries, recalled Darby, they began to feel the chill of a darkened outpost in the desert.

When a forward observer reported noises that sounded as if three columns of tanks were approaching from the south, Darby sent D Company to meet them. He told everyone, "If tanks come, may God help the tanks."

The company moved forward, with instructions to fire only on Darby's orders. Noises grew louder and the scouts advanced stealthily in their direction. Grasping a walkie-talkie and expecting a report confirming that tanks were on the move, Darby heard, "Camels!" Instead of rows of panzers, they found hundreds of camels in a herd, "kicking rocks as they moved along."

Having encountered no Germans during their rearguard assignment at Feriana, Darby received orders to withdraw to Dernaia Pass. Followed by a column of six trucks and several jeeps, the "disgruntled" Rangers passed an airfield at Telepte and observed more than twenty Allied fighter planes on fire. Reaching the foot of a ridge at a junction of the road between Telepte and Kasserine, with one route branching west toward Tebessa and the other toward Dernaia Pass, four hundred Rangers spread out for two miles with orders to hold the area at all costs and delay the enemy from moving against French troops of the Constantine Division. To the Rangers' rear was an engineer battalion, a battalion of the Twenty-sixth Regimental Combat Team of the First Infantry Division, a battalion of American infantry, two French batteries, and the Seventh Regiment Tirailleurs Algerians with obsolete rifles.

While Darby and his men held their position, went out in scouting parties, captured the first men of Rommel's Afrika Korps, burned some enemy vehicles, and killed a few Italians, the forces gathering around them clashed in a titanic battle at Kasserine Pass. On February 22, he received a message from General Allen that began, "Dear Bill." The note from Terrible Terry cited "a hell of a mess on our front" and requested a reinforced company with "a hairy-chested company commander with big nuts." Darby sent Lieutenant James B. Lyle and C Company to the Sixth Infantry. A mobile reserve, they were the only Rangers at Kasserine and took no part in the fighting. They returned to the Rangers at the Kasserine-Feriana road outpost on February 24. Darby's after-action report noted that in the first real test of American troops in action against the Germans in North Africa, the Rangers had been "comparatively inactive." He said later, "By now we were becoming real veterans. Any greenness that may have previously clung to us had departed. To our soldiering ability we added experience in several kinds of warfare. We believed ourselves masters of any situation and were mentally prepared to accept any task."

Four days after the Americans suffered a terrible loss at Kasserine Pass that shook the confidence of their leadership from North Africa to Washington, D.C., the training of a second Rangers unit at Achnacarry ended with a ceremony attended by Lord Mountbatten and Major General Russell Hartle. They and a group in training at a

two-week course at Camp Forrest, Tennessee, would form the Second
Ranger Battalion and be assigned to the European theater.

On March 1, 1943, Darby's First Ranger Battalion moved to
Djebel Kouif as a reserve force. Five days later, wailing sirens of a
procession of staff cars and half-tracks signaled the arrival of a new
commander of Second Corps at a schoolhouse that had been Major
General Lloyd Fredendall's headquarters. Having concluded that Fredendall had become cautious and wary, Eisenhower had replaced him
with George S. Patton. On the day of the noisy arrival of "Old Blood
and Guts" that would come vividly alive for American moviegoers
three decades later in Franklin Schaffner's 1970 epic *Patton*, Darby
was in a hospital recovering from a flu-like illness that occasionally left
him delirious, leaving command of the Rangers to Dammer as plans
were being made for an Allied offensive to be launched on March 15.
The Rangers were to serve as auxiliary troops of the First Division.
Patton's orders were "Find 'em, attack 'em, destroy 'em."

Resuming command two days before D-day, Darby was not fully
recovered as Rangers rolled from Feriana to reoccupy Gafsa. Finding
it abandoned, they dug foxholes, set up pup tents, and posted sentries. As soldiers sprawled about, cleaning and oiling their rifles and
guns, Darby noted that nerves were taut. A few miles east, Germans
and Italians held a high, rocky mountain separating two sweeps of
flat land spreading east and south. At a place called El Guettar a road
forked south toward the town of Gabes and northward to Sfax and
a pass named Djebel el Ank. Before Terry Allen's First Division's offensive could begin, El Guettar had to be taken and the heights surrounding the Sfax and Gabes roads cleared. To determine the location
and strength of the enemy, Allen turned to the Rangers.

Never reticent in extolling the significance of the Rangers' assignments, James Altieri wrote of their task at El Guettar, "The entire
Tunisian war hinged on the outcome."

Darby was more modest. "We were given the task of determining what was there," he wrote, "so that General Allen could decide on his next move."

Describing a mission in which the odds were all in the enemy's favor and a job made to order for the First Ranger Battalion, Altieri recalled, "Darby knew a way must be found to get his Rangers up those mountains to the enemy's rear. It was a situation that demanded Indian-like craftiness, guile and great daring."

Darby provided this account:

> My soldiers got into the harness of their light packs and strode out past the First Division troops to the base of the mountain. Climbing up the slope, they found a gorge leading toward their objective. Below them they could hear troops digging foxholes and the buzz of truck tires on the macadam highway. Ammunition was going forward, telephone wires were being laid alongside the road, engineers were probing for enemy mines. It was dark, but the Rangers liked cover for our movements. In two hours we were approaching the town from the mountain side. Not a light showed in El Guettar that night of March 18. Nevertheless, we had been told the enemy troops numbered about two thousand; against that overwhelming force the Rangers' five hundred seemed puny. General Allen had instructed us that in taking German and Italian prisoners for identification, we were not to get committed to any fight from which we couldn't extricate ourselves.

When scouts slipped to the edge of the town and reported that El Guettar was empty, Darby advised Allen of the "good fortune" that the Germans had withdrawn and that Rangers held the town. This left them with the task of taking the pass at Djebel el Ank. Assisted by an engineer battalion, they were to be the spearhead for a battalion of the Twenty-sixth Regimental Combat Team. Leaving El Guettar after dark on March 20, they crossed gorges, rocky hills, and dry stream-beds and reached a spot slightly behind Italian positions at Djebel el Ank just as dawn broke. "As if from the balcony of an opera house," Darby wrote, "we looked out across the plain to the south at black dots, which were evidently vehicles of the First Division advancing to the east. The guns of the vehicles were firing, and their shells could be seen bursting on the enemy positions east of the plain. Now the German artillery opened up on us, and the explosions rocked the plateau where we lay. They were shooting at our command post, silhouetted sharply against the rocks." As Ranger groups pulled out of their plateau and ran down the mountain with rifles held high, zigzagging and ducking for cover behind rocks in a rush to knock out the Italian position, Darby radioed to C Company, "We need a little bayonet work. Give them some steel."

Shouting shrill Indian calls, skirmish lines of black-faced Rangers surged down on the sleeping Italians, who faced the plain. The attackers leapt from rock to rock and closed on the enemy with stunning surprise. The Italians never had a chance. Grenades, small-arms fire, and bayonet charges overwhelmed them.

By noon, Djebel el Ank was in Ranger hands, hundreds of Italians were captured, and scores of dead men of the Centauro Division were strewn over the mountainside. Darby radioed Allen, "The pass is cleared."

By speed, surprise, and ferocity of attack, Altieri proudly noted, the Rangers had taken an "impregnable pass" and for the next six days fought it out beside the First Division, supported by the First Armored Division and Ninth Infantry Division in a titanic clash. Known as the Battle of El Guettar, it signaled the inevitable end of the German and Italian occupation of North Africa, proved that American soldiers could fight and win, and cleared the way for an invasion of Sicily. Darby was "well satisfied" with the fighting the Rangers had done. They had been required to make a long march to Djebel el Ank and take it, then stave off a savage counterattack.

No one appeared to be more impressed with the Rangers and their leader than the new boss of Second Corps. Summoning Darby to its headquarters in Gafsa, General Patton offered him command of an infantry regiment in the rank of full colonel. Darby was reported to have replied, "Nothing doing. You can keep your promotion and I'll keep my Rangers."

The rebuff did not keep Patton from awarding Darby the Distinguished Service Cross for "extraordinary heroism in action" for the El Guettar action. When he and Darby stepped out onto a balcony at Second Corps headquarters, the general peered down at a figure wearing a Ranger patch on his sleeve and a green Commando beret. Startled and amazed that a soldier would dare disobey a Patton order that helmets be worn at all times, uniforms always be neat, and neckties worn even in battle, he exclaimed, "What the hell is that? Bring that officer to me at once. I'll kick his ass."

"No, you don't," Darby replied. "That is our British chaplain, sir, and you have no right to discipline him."

He explained that Father Basil had become a beloved figure not only among Rangers but to other Americans, who saw him as an interesting and kindly "Brit" who had adopted the GI uniform but clung to his green Commando beret. In the battle at Djebel al Ank, he had used his knowledge of Italian to persuade an Italian officer to surrender his unit. The British chaplain had become so much one of the guys, recalled Carl Lehmann, that many Catholic Rangers could not face him in the confessional. Basil responded by enlisting a French priest and furnishing him with a list of sins in French and English translations. When the priest ran a finger down the list, some young Rangers were so confused that they admitted to all of them.

Shortly after the Rangers returned to Gafsa from the El Guettar battles, Basil received a warning from London that if he did not return to England immediately he would be dismissed from His Majesty's Army. At his last service in an olive grove in Gafsa, he told the Rangers, "I can't tell you how sad I am to be leaving you. I will never forget you, and I hope you will remember me by never taking the Lord's name in vain."

With him went money collected throughout the battalion that he used to buy a silver chalice, on the base of which he had engraved "1st Ranger Battalion." When he turned and walked toward the British lorry that was waiting to take him back to his own army, Altieri said, "There wasn't a dry-eyed Ranger." The feisty, courageous priest had been with the Rangers in all kinds of combat in which they'd lost three killed and eighteen wounded, a casualty count that was fewer than the combined losses in training in Scotland and in the landing and battles in Algeria and Tunisia. Now, in mid-April of 1943, the men Altieri called "a pretty hot outfit" and Darby lauded as "all-around infantrymen" could only wait and wonder what the politicians and their generals who were running the war had in mind for them.

When they learned that Patton was returning to Casablanca and that the command of Second Corps had been given to Major General Omar N. Bradley, they greeted the change with hope that the "spit-and-polish" regime was over. They were surprised that the author of victory at El Guettar was gone, and wild speculation arose about what the top brass would tell Darby they expected the Rangers to do next.

As they pondered the future, they found themselves bivouacked at Nemours, Algeria. A seaport near the Moroccan frontier on the western side of the Gulf of Arzew, it was previously called Jamaa-el-Ghazuat (meaning "rendezvous of the pirates" in Arabic) and took its French name from Louis Charles Philippe Raphael, duc de Nemours. The second son of the duke of Orleans (later King Louis-Philippe of France), he had accompanied French army expeditions against the town of Constantine in 1836 and 1837. While the Rangers set up their tents around the historic locale, explored the town and swam in the Mediterranean in early May 1943, their commander was called to Eisenhower's headquarters in Algiers for briefings on the Rangers' role in a plan for the invasion of Sicily. Code-named Operation Husky, it had been conceived at the Casablanca Conference between Roosevelt and Churchill. The objectives were landings by Montgomery's Eighth Army on the southeastern coast, and General Bradley's Second Corps, including Patton's Seventh Army, to the west at Gela and Licata. Bradley and Patton's operations would be spearheaded by Rangers, with the goal of taking the cities of Palermo and Messina.

When asked how many battalions would be required to take out the coastal defenses at Gela, Darby answered, "Fifteen."

He was told that he would have to do it with the First Battalion and two new ones that were to be called "Ranger Force" and formed with volunteers from other units in North Africa. He was given six weeks to find and train them. "Since there was no alternative," he recorded, "I took a few assistants and made a recruiting drive around Oran. We circularized the town—putting up posters in recreation centers in an appeal to red-blooded Americans, made stump speeches, and 'impressed' soldiers found in the local hot spots."

A letter of May 17 titled "Volunteers for Ranger Battalions" sent by Headquarters, Atlantic Base Section, to all units specified that they be white (a policy of racial segregation of American forces would not be ended until 1947), at least five-feet-six, of normal weight, not over thirty-five years of age, in good physical shape, have excellent references as to character, have no record of trial by court-martial, and be no higher in rank than PFC. Infantry training was not a requirement, but desirable.

Captain Roy Murray established a training program at Nemours that was a replica of the Commando Depot in Scotland and included what the Rangers had learned in combat. The cadre for the new battalions were drawn from the First Battalion. While Darby was in command of the Ranger Force, he retained command of the First Battalion, consisting of C and D companies and new volunteers. The new Third Battalion had A and B companies as its cadre with Herman Dammer (now a major) in command. The Fourth Battalion cadre were Murray's E and F companies. Although the changes elevated James Altieri to F Company platoon staff sergeant, he regretted seeing his old F Company splintered off to feed the new companies. Finding this new structure strange, he wrote, "We were not a regiment, not a brigade, not even a combat team. We were now three separate battalions, each with its own commander, and yet we were all directly under the command of Colonel Darby."

Analyzing Darby's unique position as a battalion commander with duties approximating those of a leader of a regiment, the military biographer Michael J. King found it unfavorable for Darby because he had to think and act on two levels, battalion and regimental, but without an authorization for a regimental staff to assist him and no promotion to the regimental rank of full colonel. When he sought to shift the status of the "provisional" Ranger Force to the permanent status of regiment, with requisite promotion to colonel for himself, the War Department denied the request. Authorization for the Third and Fourth battalions also clung to the original concept that the Rangers would eventually return to parent units to train others in Commando tactics.

Preparation of the new men to be Rangers included daily speed marches and obstacle courses. Their courage was tested in a Nemours version of the Achnacarry cliff and castle climbs and by leaps in which a fully equipped would-be Ranger faced a six-hundred-foot slide down a nearly vertical precipice to a beach. Landings north of Nemours were opposed by machine guns that fired over the heads of the troops and explosions in the water and on the beaches. James Altieri gleefully noted, "Under a blistering hot African sun we gave these new Rangers the works. For six weeks we poured it on—all the Commandos had taught us in Scotland, all that Darby had taught us at Arzew, all we had learned the hard way in Tunisia. They learned fast, and they picked up the Ranger spirit."

On the last day of training, Darby inspected the three battalions, and after they marched in review he told them, "We are going into action soon. I know you will measure up to what the Army expects of you." The next day, the troops loaded onto transports and sailed along the Algerian coast. The First and Fourth landed at Algiers and marched twenty miles to the town of Zeralda to join Terry Allen's First Division. The Third went to Bizerte to link with Major General Lucian Truscott's Third Infantry Division. On June 19, 1943 (the anniversary of the formal creation of the First Ranger Battalion), the new battalions were officially activated.

★ Chapter 10 ★

GELA

"The sons of bitches just hit the whorehouses!"

AT THE AGE OF THIRTY-TWO, LIEUTENANT COLONEL WILLIAM OR-
lando Darby commanded a force that was the equivalent of an entire
regiment. He stood poised to cross the Mediterranean Sea and land
on an island that for centuries had been invaded by conquerors he
had read about as a schoolboy. Before his Rangers had come Alexander the Great, Phoenicians, Carthaginians, Romans, Vandals, Arabs, Normans, Crusaders, the French, Aragonese, Bourbons of Spain,
Mussolini's Legions, and the Nazis. Converging now would be troops
of the British Empire with scores to settle with the Germans that had

accumulated since 1939, along with Americans who had hoped to stay out of a world war that until December 7, 1941, seemed to be none of their business. Expecting to be sent to the Pacific to punish Japan for the attack on Pearl Harbor, he'd been sent to Northern Ireland and by chance—or the whim of fate—found himself pioneering a type of up-close war. The high school boy who had predicted that he would one day be great was now the leader of Rangers who had perfected the use of bayonets and knives in battle that was contrary to what President Theodore Roosevelt had called "supreme triumphs of war," in which soldiers showed "those stern and virile virtues which move men of stout heart and strong hand to uphold the honor of their flag in battle."

When Darby encountered the first son of the twenty-sixth president of the United States in the staging area at Zeralda, Brigadier General Ted Roosevelt of the First Division presented a dramatic contrast in appearance to the boss of the Rangers. In rumpled uniform, Roosevelt was a disheveled, grandfatherly figure whose appearance would have raised Patton's hackles. He was middle-aged and arthritic, and was preoccupied with worries about his own son. During the battle at Kasserine Pass, Second Lieutenant Quentin Roosevelt had been hit in the chest by a shell from a Messerschmitt as the plane strafed his unit during the German advance. With the bullet lodged in his liver, he was taken to three field hospitals before the ambulance driver found one that was not preparing to evacuate. He was so seriously wounded that he had been sent back to the United States with a Silver Star and the French Croix de Guerre for six weeks of treatment and recuperation. As the assistant commander of First Division, Ted was to land with his troops at Gela before daylight on D-day, July 10, after Darby's Rangers "Force X" destroyed, captured, or neutralized coastal defenses on high ground northwest of Gela. In advance of the landings, the U.S. Eighty-second Airborne and British paratroops were assigned to drop inland and Allied airpower would strike several airfields throughout Sicily.

On July 9 Rangers boarded U.S. and British ships to join an armada of 130 warships and 324 transports on a course through the Tunisian channel toward Sicily via Cape Bon. General Patton's order of the day to "soldiers of the Seventh Army" read as though it were a Ranger combat handbook. In landing operations, he asserted, "retreat is impossible." The troops were to attack "rapidly, ruthlessly, viciously and without rest." Calling the exhortation "Patton's Manifesto Number One," Sergeant James Altieri described it as "boldly etched in typical flamboyant Pattonese" and "a rousing clarion call to each soldier to do his utmost in the noblest tradition of the American soldier, etc."

On board the *Prince Charles*, a British troopship, Altieri and his buddies of D Company basked in the sun on the placid Mediterranean for four days. When the skies turned dark and the sea rough on the fifth day, the ship was wallowing in deep troughs, with raging winds roaring across her wave-washed decks. In crowded, ill-ventilated holds men whose mission was to storm and capture the heavily fortified coast citadel of Gela as part of the first-wave assault team threw up their suppers, rolled in their hammocks, and cursed fates that suddenly threatened to scatter the ships. Rumors soon spread that the invasion might be delayed and stirred bitter memories of the aborted raid on Galita.

In briefings on the geography of Gela by Darby's company commanders, the Rangers had been warned not to expect a repeat of the landings at Arzew. This time the enemy would not be listless, sleepy French clinging to a colony in Africa, but Italians defending their homeland. While Operation Torch had been a surprise, the Germans and Italians had been preparing for an invasion of Sicily for as long as the Allies. Compared to Gela, hitting the beach at Arzew would seem almost as easy as a stroll along the sands of a seaside resort. Gela's shore was a maze of wire obstacles and antipersonnel and antitank minefields. Behind it, to back up the 350,000 defenders against half a million Allies, stood the tanks of the powerful Hermann Goering Division. Unlike at Arzew, the Luftwaffe was poised to attack troops as they came ashore.

The Rangers had studied the layout of a town on a hill about a hundred and fifty feet above the coast, with a two-thousand-foot pier at its center. On the left flank (west of the town) stood a fort at a height of about two hundred feet. Darby's plan called for the First Battalion to take the beach to the left of the pier and the Fourth to go in on the right. The First would swing left to take the fort while the Fourth would move right against other coast defenses. The First Battalion, Thirty-ninth Engineers acting as infantry would take the center. The beach and town were defended by a battery of 77mm field artillery, two mortar companies, and twenty-five machine-gun emplacements in pillboxes that were camouflaged with vines and brush or concealed in huts. Intelligence reports noted that the pier had been rigged with explosives.

Shortly after midnight on July 10, Darby climbed down a rope ladder from his ship and into a U.S. Navy LCI (landing craft, infantry) equipped with twelve rockets in two launchers. Because of churning water whipped by forty-mile-an-hour winds, forty-eight LCIs bounced and pitched. In the planning for the assault, it was intended that they would be guided in by two boats flashing signal lights. Rough water briefly delayed their rendezvous. "Sorting out the landing craft," Darby noted with customary understatement, "was a difficult job."

Hard going in the bad weather had also interfered with the airborne drops. Buffeted by the winds and confused by a complex flight plan, inexperienced pilots became disoriented in the darkness and strayed from their courses. Of the 144 gliders bearing British paratroops to landing zones outside of Syracuse, only twelve landed on target. Sixty-nine crashed into the sea and the rest dispersed over a wide area. Colonel James Gavin's thirty-four hundred paratroopers of the Eighty-second were widely scattered twenty-five miles southeast of his intended drop zone. Nevertheless, they operated in small isolated groups and created confusion by attacking enemy patrols and cutting lines of communication. By midnight, the Italian commander General Albert Guzzoni was fully apprised of their presence. Axis air reconnaissance had also spotted Allied convoys moving toward Sicily earlier that day. Based on these reports, he surmised that the Allies intended to come ashore in the southeast and issued an alert nearly an hour before the first assault wave at Gela.

Looking ahead from the leading LCI at H hour (3:00 a.m.), Darby saw blue tracers fired by cannons cutting across the beach and thought nobody could possibly live through "the stuff" the Italians sprayed across the edge of the beach. When the LCI fired six rockets that shook the craft as if it had blown up, he watched with satisfaction as the missiles hit an ammunition dump, "blowing everything sky high" and knocking out defenses on that side of the beach and a block and a half of buildings. A moment later, the Italians detonated the explosives on the pier and blew away its center.

Altieri gazed forward at a frightful hell as his boat bucked toward the inferno on the beaches of Gela. For him each minute seemed an eternity of fear and morbid reality. At the front of the boat stood Lieutenant Walter Wojcik. For extraordinary courage at Sened Station and El Guettar, Darby had promoted the twenty-three-year-old sergeant to company commander. Altieri portrayed the curly haired, blond psychology major from Minneapolis, Minnesota, as built like a Roman gladiator, with a strong, forceful face and possessing a rare quality of character that imbued his men with intense loyalty. In the rear were Howard Andre and Randall Harris. The men sitting tensely, waiting for the boat to scrape bottom, had every reason to be confident of themselves. No company had been trained more thoroughly. Spurred by Wojcik, Andre, Harris, and others of the old F Company cadre, the new D Company's performance and spirit during training

132

had been outstanding, and for this reason they had been given the challenge of landing on one of the toughest areas of Beach Green.

So swift was the Ranger advance across the soft sand and so strong was the momentum of their surging bodies that when the first explosion of a buried land mine blew Lieutenant Wojcik into shredded bits, most of D Company had already entered the minefield. Four riflemen following Wojcik were also killed. The lieutenant leading the first platoon was blinded by shrapnel. Machine-gun fire cut down others. A blast that tossed Sergeant Randall several feet ripped open his abdomen. Covering the gaping gash with his cartridge belt, he struggled to his feet and led the remnants of the company up a steep embankment to a dirt road that ran parallel to a cliff topped by pillboxes and machine gunners. Without pause, Randall reached one pillbox, and flung in a hand grenade, silencing the cannon within. He raced down the road to join Andre. By leapfrogging between pillboxes they took out seven and killed twenty Italians. When the fighting was over, a lieutenant saw how seriously Randall had been wounded and called for men to take him to a first-aid station. "Hell no," Randall exclaimed, "I'm not helpless yet. Get me prisoners to guard, or something." For his heroic actions he was given a battlefield promotion to second lieutenant and the Distinguished Service Cross.

Ashore to the west of the wrecked pier, Companies D, E, and F secured their section of the beach and moved into the town from the northwest. Taking up positions along the stone walls of a warehouse, they came under machine-gun fire from the town's Cathedral Square. After an hour of blazing gunfire with Italians shooting from inside the cathedral and snipers firing down from its tower on Rangers ducking in and out of doorways, a D Company platoon reached the doors. Turning to Altieri, Lieutenant Nye said, "Okay, Al, clean 'em out."

Confronted with the prospect of spilling blood on consecrated ground, Altieri decided that "Rangers can't waste time on debating moral issues." He kicked open the door, threw in a hand grenade, waited for the explosion, and fired eight fast rounds into a corner of the cavernous cathedral. After a short firefight with two Italians holed up in the sacristy and three "die-hard Fascists of the Livorno Division" in the bell tower, Altieri knelt before the altar, crossed himself, and offered a silent prayer. He left the bloody cathedral and found the street as quiet as an American town on a Sunday morning.

While D Company was pacifying Cathedral Square, Darby and his bodyguard, Corporal Charles Riley, a former racetrack bookie, found a Ranger squad exchanging shots with Italians barricaded in a hotel. Darby had chosen Riley for the job from among the new recruits at Nemours in Tunisia because Riley spoke Italian, had an engaging manner and quick mind, and proved to be "an all-around good soldier, quick on the trigger, and indefatigable on the march or in bivouac." With a .45 automatic in hand and Riley armed with a Tommy gun, they led the squad into the hotel, and after a room-to-room battle punctuated by hand grenade blasts, emerged with what remained alive of thirty Italians.

When machine guns opened fire from a schoolhouse near Darby's headquarters at seven thirty, Darby noticed his jeep driver, Altieri's buddy Carlo Contrera, trembling. He asked Contrera, "What are you shaking for? Are you scared?"

Carlo replied, "No, sir. I'm just shaking with patriotism."

Touring the embattled town in the jeep with a machine gun mounted at the rear, Darby and Captain Charles "Chuck" Shunstrom rolled into Cathedral Square at nine thirty and learned that a column of light Italian tanks that appeared on the Niscemi-Gela road was nearing the cathedral. As Altieri put it, "They just kept rolling blithely along as if they were going to a Sunday church meeting." Noting that there was nothing the lightly armed Rangers could do but watch in amazement, his account continued, "It was incredible! A whole army supported by a mighty navy had thundered ashore and here before our eyes were sixteen black Renault tanks coming to pay their respects."

Apprised of the situation by Altieri, Darby said, "All right, we'll give them a fight. They won't get through, is that clear?"

"Yes, sir," replied Altieri. "They won't."

Admitting he was not worried what Germans and Italians would do if the tanks reached the beachhead, but fearful of "what Darby would do" to him if that happened, he recorded, "From our vantage points we could look down on the street at the intersection where the tanks would turn. We had all inserted armor-piercing clips in our weapons—fat chance they had of penetrating!—but it made us feel better. Strangely, aside from the unique excitement and sensation of being under a tank attack, none of the Rangers seemed nervous or edgy—just tense—waiting for the drama to unfold."

They didn't wait long.

A tank had just started to make the turn, with its machine guns and cannon blazing, splattering concrete and plaster off buildings. It halted as it was hit by a shower of grenades and rifle shots from the Rangers. Darby's jeep backed out of an alley far enough for Darby to swing the machine gun toward the tank. He fired until he emptied its ammunition belt. When the unscathed tank turned up a side street to avoid drawing abreast of Darby's position, Darby went in search of an antitank gun, found one, and hooked it to the jeep. Returning to the square, he wheeled the gun into position and on the third shot "saw the tank flame up."

Altieri wrote that "out of nowhere came a lone Engineer soldier, driving a jeep towing the most priceless object—a 37-millimeter antitank gun." Darby bellowed, "Hey there, soldier, swing that damned thing around here." The soldier did as he was told. Darby, "bareheaded, sleeves rolled up," and Shunstrom, "helmeted, bounded over and began setting up the gun for action." Before they could shoot, another tank clanked around the corner and came charging down on them. As it shot two rounds over their heads, Darby fired the antitank gun twice, hitting the tank with such force that it was "flung back for several feet and enveloped by a sheet of flame."

Declaring the action by Darby and Captain Shunstrom "one of the most outstanding and selfless acts of courage and daring," Altieri continued, "That was all the Rangers needed. The rest of the tanks did not pass. From alleyways and rooftops, Rangers, inspired by our valiant leader, waded in and made short work of the remaining tanks that had the temerity and misfortune to enter town."

When eighteen German Tiger tanks lumbered forth to counterattack around noon, Darby called for a barrage from the offshore cruiser *Shenandoah*. Its rounds, along with Darby's mortars and a captured Italian artillery piece fired by Shunstrom, knocked out twelve. Patton, standing at Darby's side, watched the Rangers wait until a battalion of attacking Italian infantry was two thousand yards away before laying down a devastating barrage of 4.2 mortar shells. In late afternoon Darby declared, "Gela quieted."

That night, said Altieri, every Ranger was "on his toes, weapons at the ready." They waited tensely for a counterattack. Enemy artillery beat a steady tattoo in and around the Ranger perimeter, where scouts had set up listening posts to detect troop and tank movements. As dawn broke on D-day plus one, July 11, Altieri saw clouds of black smoke rising over wheat fields on a plain surrounding Gela and heard the unmistakable sounds of many German tanks. After three artillery shells exploded nearby and smashed several buildings, a Ranger bellowed, "Oh, no! The sons of bitches just hit the whorehouses!"

Recalling the subsequent events in *The Spearheaders*, Altieri described himself as being "strangely mesmerized" by the fantastic scope and drama of the spectacle. He felt as though he was "hypnotized into a ludicrous belief" that he and the Rangers around him were privileged spectators, for whom two armies were about to clash with fury. The plain seemed to be a gigantic coliseum, and their shell-dented stone houses were the grandstands. The element of personal danger—the awareness that the tanks were out to destroy them—was missing in those first few moments in the early morning of July 11.

By noon, after hours of bombardment by U.S. Navy ships, fierce resistance from Rangers, and the timely arrival of five American tanks, the plain of Gela had been transformed into a grim graveyard of burning tank hulks and blackened bodies. When the battle was finished, the Italian Livorno Division had been crushed.

On July 12, Patton was again at Ranger headquarters. Telling Darby that the commander of the 180th Infantry Regiment had been relieved after a disappointing performance in capturing the town of Biscari, Patton said that the commanding general of the Forty-fifth Infantry Division had gotten permission from General Omar Bradley to request that Darby be named to replace him. Patton asked Darby if he would like to take over the regiment.

Darby replied, "You mean I get a choice, General? I'm not used to choices in the army."

"Take the regiment and I'll make you a full colonel in the morning," said Patton, "but I won't force your hand."

"Thanks anyhow," Darby answered, "but I think I'd better stick with my boys."

Speculating on the refusal, Michael J. King felt that Darby, as strong-willed as he was, wanted to be promoted on terms by which the War Department would create a Ranger regiment. Darby's officers and men believed that he did so out of loyalty to them. Whatever motivated him can never be known. He offered no explanation.

Of the Rangers' first days in Sicily, Darby recalled, "There were many local battles for towns and airdromes around Gela. Though dismissed with a sentence or two or unmentioned altogether in the communiqués, they were hard, bitter battles for us. One such engagement was a battle for the town of Butera."

Perched four thousand feet on a hill eight miles inland from Gela, it reminded Darby of an inverted ice cream cone. Altieri saw an impregnable medieval fortress. To another Ranger it was "a castle sitting up there." Darby gave the mission of assaulting the hilltop target at night to Captain Shunstrom's E Company. He told him, "We may take this place without a fight. We may walk into a trap."

In contact with Darby by radio, Shunstrom led two platoons of black-faced Rangers on a three-mile march to the mountain's base, then climbed for several hours. When scouts ran into Italian sentries, the battle was on. Seven Italians were killed. In a flanking movement that caught the main garrison by surprise, the Rangers moved in with bayonets. After fifteen minutes of hand-to-hand fighting, the Germans in the fortress fled and the Italians surrendered. Altieri noted in his diary, "We walk in like tourists."

While the First and Fourth Ranger battalions landed and battled at Gela, Major Herman Dammer's Third Battalion had come ashore several miles west of Gela near the town of Licata. Attached to General Truscott's Third Infantry Division (Reinforced), they met little resistance on landing, but as they moved into Licata they encountered machine-gun and rifle fire. After two days in the captured town, they went west to Favara to form the spearhead of a thrust by the Third Division to capture Agrigento. Around midnight, they ran into opposition at a crossroads on the Favara-Agrigento highway. After a sharp skirmish in which they suffered no casualties, they captured 165 Italians. With Agrigento in hand, the battalion advanced toward the hilltop town of Montaperto at the head of a valley that led south to Porto Empedocle. Once the site of a defensive tower built in the reign of the Holy Roman Emperor Charles V, it was first named Molo di Girgenti because of an artificial harbor that was built there in 1763. A century later, it was renamed for the Agrigentine philosopher Empedocles.

This movement westward by forces under Patton had not been in the original plan for the conquest of Sicily. The designers of Operation Husky put Patton's Seventh Army and Bradley's Second Corps on General Montgomery's left flank for a drive northward from Syracuse on Sicily's east coast to the key port city of Messina, just two miles from the Italian mainland. Displeased with a plan that gave Montgomery the lead role, Patton acted on his own and ordered Truscott to carry out "a reconnaissance in force" to capture Porto Empedocle as a stepping-stone toward taking Palermo. Of this bold maneuver Patton later said that had it failed, he would have been relieved of command. On July 17, when the overall commander of the Sicilian campaign, the British general Sir Harold Alexander, learned of the fall of Porto Empedocle, he permitted Patton to form a provisional corps to take Palermo, with the Third Ranger Battalion in the lead.

Although Darby was in official command of all the Ranger battalions, the effect was to place the Third out of his control. At the same time, he found himself given command of Task Force X. Of regimental proportions and consisting of the First and Fourth Ranger battalions and other units, it was assigned to move to the Belice River and attack across it "without delay" to seize Castelvetrano and a nearby airfield, then advance on Marsala on Sicily's western tip. As Force X crossed the Belice River on July 20, the Italians launched an attack. After what Darby called "a well-executed envelopment" by his men, the Italians surrendered. Castelvetrano fell almost as easily. Two days later, the task force arrived at Marsala. Joined by the Eighty-second Airborne, they took Trapani and San Giuseppe, south of Palermo.

Having achieved all its objectives, Darby's Force X now found itself halted forty miles from its base at Siacca on Sicily's southwest coast and burdened with 12,500 prisoners. Calling the Italians "a strange lot laden down with blankets and overcoats, not to mention each man's jealously guarded cache of pillaged souvenirs," Darby doubted that he had sufficient vehicles in all of Sicily to handle them and their huge bundles of possessions and equipment. "There was only an occasional truck," he wrote, "and like ants, fifty or sixty of them would clamber onto it, as many on the trailer, and even another ten standing on the hutch between truck and trailer. The few trucks were grossly overloaded, but they were able to go on."

Two days after Patton's forces entered and occupied Palermo,

Benito Mussolini's twenty-year reign as dictator of Italy ended. On July 25, 1943, his colleagues, including Count Galeazzo Ciano, the foreign minister and Mussolini's son-in-law, turned against him at a meeting of the Fascist Grand Council. King Vittorio Emanuele III called Mussolini to his palace and stripped him of his power. Upon leaving the palace, he was arrested and sent to Gran Sasso, a mountain resort in central Italy. He was replaced by General Pietro Badoglio, who immediately declared, "The war continues at the side of our Germanic allies."

On the same day, Task Force X was disbanded and the First and Fourth battalions went to the town of Corleone to bivouac, rest, refit, and await orders. At this time, the Third Battalion reverted to Darby's command. In the two weeks since landing in Sicily, his divided force had been in continuous combat across most of the island, helping to push the Germans north into a defensive stance around the port of Messina until they could withdraw to the Italian mainland.

While the British Eighth Army under Montgomery and General Omar Bradley's Seventh Army drove up the east coast, Patton's army moved east from Palermo in what became a race between them to take Messina. Separating the two forces, a mountain ridge (Monti Nebrodi) of three to four thousand feet restricted the American advance to a single coastal road. This forced Patton to employ amphibious maneuvers to bypass German resistance, resulting in pockets of enemy soldiers in the mountainous terrain to his rear. Ironically, the commander of the Rangers, who had trained primarily for amphibious assaults, found himself called upon by Patton to use them in a type of soldiering he learned as a captain of the Ninety-ninth Field Artillery based at Fort Hoyle, Maryland, in which the main means of conveyance of men and equipment was by pack animals. Referring to the assignment of fighting Germans in the mountains below Messina as warfare "à la mule," Darby recalled, "Mules had been requisitioned and sixty were received, along with eighteen horses. I offered to take over the mule transport and run the supplies, mainly because I was the only one in the area who had experience with mules. Looking for excitement and some fun, I rode proudly across northern Sicily on a rotund mule affectionately known as 'Rosebud.'" He added, "Although I admit that this mule was gentle, he still bit me in the seat every time I tried to mount him."

With Dammer in command of the Third Battalion and Captain Alex Worth in charge of a company tasked with handling a mule train carrying supplies and light howitzers, the men had the extraordinary experience of watching a lieutenant colonel working as if he were a private as he taught them how to break down the guns for loading onto the mules, then assisted them in a hard job that Darby described as being achieved after "much pushing, grunting, and explosive language." After nine days of rooting out pockets of Germans, the battalion arrived in the town of Sanbruca, about four miles west of Messina, at daylight on August 16.

Abandoned by the Germans, Messina was entered by Patton's troops on August 17, 1943. That night, the Rangers bivouacked and settled down to sleep in a hilltop cemetery. Shells fired across the Straits of Messina from Italy blasted burial vaults open and sent shattered caskets flying everywhere. "Skeletons were all around, and the smell of death curled the hairs of the Rangers' nostrils," Darby said of the macabre tableau, "but the exhausted Third Battalion slept on." The next day, Darby and Dammer's tired and dusty Rangers, with clothes in tatters, shoes worn thin, and most equipment ready for salvage, but with weapons in "tiptop shape," rejoined the First and Fourth at Corleone to be attached to Second Corps, receive replacements, and begin training for the invasion of Italy.

★ CHAPTER 11 ★

AVALANCHE

"We'll stay here till hell freezes over."

ON AUGUST 22, 1943, LIEUTENANT GENERAL GEORGE S. PATTON issued General Order Number Eighteen, addressed to "Soldiers of the Seventh Army." Cynically described by Sergeant Robert Dunn of the Rangers as "an enduring military classic, perhaps rivaling the best of Caesar's reports during the Gaul campaign," and labeled by Altieri as "Patton Manifesto Number Two," it began, "Born at sea, baptized in blood, and crowned in victory, in the course of thirty-eight days of incessant battle and unceasing labor, you have added a glorious chapter in the history of the war." For the record the message noted that the combined efforts of the U.S. Army and Navy had resulted in killing or capturing 113,350 enemy troops; destruction of 265 tanks, 2,324 other vehicles, and 1,162 large guns; and collection of "a mass of military booty running into hundreds of tons." Beyond the military victory, Patton said, they "destroyed the prestige of the enemy."

The cost of the Sicilian fighting to the Rangers had been substantial. When they settled into Corleone to regroup, refit, and train for the invasion of Italy, the First and Fourth battalions were about 60 percent of full strength and the Third at about 50 percent.

Before Patton issued the general order he had attached his name to a document of far more importance to Lieutenant Colonel William Darby. The effusive commander of the Seventh Army endorsed a letter from Darby to General Eisenhower. Dated August 10, 1943, on the topic "Status of Ranger Battalions," the communication reviewed the Rangers' organizational history and summarized their successes in North Africa and Sicily, then requested that the battalions be formed into a regiment under Darby's command. If this were not feasible, he continued, the Rangers should be disbanded and reformed into a reconnaissance regiment. Patton let it be known that if the Rangers were elevated to a regiment, he wanted them to become part of his Seventh Army. Despite the Rangers' record, Patton's endorsement, and Darby's reputation as a combat commander, Eisenhower disapproved the request. Although he did so on September 7, Darby would not learn of the refusal until mid-October.

In the meantime, the Ranger battalions encamped at Corleone, Sicily, were undergoing a significant transformation. Motivated by bitter memories of being inadequately armed against German tanks at Gela, Darby decided to expand his firepower by creating an anti-tank platoon within the First Ranger Battalion. Consisting of four M3 half-tracks equipped with 75mm guns, this "cannon company" was to be formed from former artillerymen drawn from all of the Ranger battalions and commanded by Captain Charles Shunstrom.

Of his efforts to recruit volunteers, Altieri wrote, "He got more than enough. [His] fame had spread (we lost count of his Silver Stars), and there were no small number of Rangers who actually were anxious to share [his] exciting adventures because he was known to be where the 'fighting was the hottest.' " The half-tracks were given names: *Ace of Diamonds, Ace of Hearts, Ace of Spades,* and *Ace of Clubs.* Shunstrom called his jeep *The Joker.*

While the cannon company formed, replacements were found to bring the battalions up to strength, and training continued. The Rangers found some respite in occasional entertainment by show-business troupes, including a visit by Bob Hope and members of the cast of his radio program. While Altieri credited Hope with "a terrific job," he was much more excited by the arrival of "exceptionally pretty" Red Cross "gals" who "descended" on Corleone for a week. He noted that the women served doughnuts and coffee "all day long and kept us on our toes in the personal appearance department." Rangers trimmed their beards and mustaches, put creases in their battle-worn trousers, patted down their hair, and "tried to smile their winningest when they passed by the sweet-scented girls."

Spirits suddenly sagged when Captain Ralph A. Coleby and PFC William Eger were killed in training. Then the camp was swept by an outbreak of malaria, jaundice, and dysentery. While half of the men were laid low with fevers and crowded latrines, a story spread through Ranger ranks that in visits to hospitals Patton had not only accused two soldiers of malingering, but slapped them and even threatened to shoot one of them for cowardice.

Of greater alarm to Darby's Rangers at this time was a decision by General Bradley to relieve Terry Allen and Ted Roosevelt from command of the First Infantry Division. Bradley said they were fired because the Big Red One's men had become increasingly temperamental and disdainful of both regulations and senior commands. He added that Allen had become too much of an individualist to submerge himself without friction in the group undertaking of war, and that under Allen's command the division had become "too full of self-pity and pride." He offered the explanation that he had acted to save Allen both from himself and from his brilliant record and to save the division from the heady effects of too much success.

But, as the historian and Allen biographer Gerald Astor wrote in *The Greatest War: Americans in Combat, 1941–1945*, the men of the First Division felt they had lost a fine leader, and the Rangers attached to the Big Red One agreed.

What the Rangers battling illnesses at Corleone did not know in mid-August of 1943 was that their collaboration with the First Division and Patton's Seventh Army was finished. For the invasion of Italy they would be assigned to the Fifth Army. Commanded by Lieutenant General Mark W. Clark, it would execute a three-part operation to land in Italy, take the port of Naples, and sweep up the boot-shaped peninsula to Rome. To learn the Rangers' role in the invasion plan, Darby and Dammer flew to a conference at Clark's headquarters in Algiers.

At age forty-seven, tall and lean Mark Wayne Clark had the distinction of having been the youngest officer to attain the rank of lieutenant general. A descendant of the Revolutionary War general George Rogers Clark and the son of a career army officer, he was born on May 1, 1896, at Madison Barracks, New York, and spent much of his youth in the Chicago suburb of Highland Park, near Fort Sheridan. With the assistance of an aunt, Zettie Marshall, the mother of George C. Marshall, he was appointed to West Point in 1913 and graduated 110th in a class of 139. Assigned to the infantry, he was promoted to captain in August 1917 and saw action with the Eleventh Infantry in France. Wounded and decorated for bravery, he returned to the United States in 1919 and later held posts in the Office of the Assistant Secretary of War (1929–33). He graduated from the Army Command and General Staff School at Fort Leavenworth,

Kansas, in 1935, then served as deputy chief of staff for the Civilian Conservation Corps, Seventh Corps area at Omaha, Nebraska. He graduated from the Army War College in 1937. In part because of his familial relationship with General Marshall and a longtime friendship with Eisenhower, he was named assistant chief of staff for operations of the General Headquarters, U.S. Army, in August 1941. A month after Pearl Harbor, he was appointed deputy chief of staff, Army Ground Forces, and less than six months later chief of staff. In October 1942, he became deputy commander in chief of the Allied Forces for the North African theater and subsequently planned Operation Torch. Prior to the invasion, he made a secret trip by way of a submarine to the North African coast to meet with friendly French officers. As deputy commander of Anglo-American invasion forces, he took into "protective custody" France's highest-ranking officer, Admiral Jean François Darlan, and induced him to renounce the Vichy government.

The plan for the invasion of Italy would begin on September 3 with the British Fifth and Canadian First divisions crossing the Strait of Messina and landing at Reggio di Calabria in an operation code-named Baytown to open the strait to Allied shipping. Operation Slapstick would entail the British First Airborne sailing from Bizerte and landing from ships at Taranto, where the heel of the boot joined the mainland. Operation Avalanche in the Gulf of Salerno, south of Naples, was to constitute the main assault and involve the British Tenth Corps on the left flank of Salerno and the U.S. Sixth Corps on the right. Under Lieutenant General Sir Richard McCreery would be the British Forty-sixth and Fifty-sixth divisions, Seventh Armored Division, Second and Forty-first Commandos, and Darby's First, Third, and Fourth Ranger battalions. This mixture of eight thousand British Commandos, U.S. Airborne, glider-carried artillery, tank units, engineers, and Shunstrom's "trusty" mortar battalion, Darby believed, was "as rugged a group as could be found among the Allied forces in Europe."

After securing the beaches, they were to move inland to the mountains and swing to the northwest toward Naples. In a zone extending nearly twenty-five miles from Maiori along the coast to the mouth of the Sele River, the immediate objectives were the port of Salerno, the Montecorvino airfield, an important rail and highway center at Battipaglia, and Ponte Sele on Highway 19. The left flank was entrusted to the Rangers and the Commando battalions.

The plan called for the Rangers to land at Maiori and advance north to seize the broad Nocera-Pagani pass between Salerno and Naples. Commandos were to land at Vietri sul Mare, turn east along the coastal road, and enter Salerno. The bulk of the Tenth Corps' assault forces would land on three beaches south of the Picentino River, with the Fifty-sixth Division leading the assault on the right flank and the Forty-sixth Division taking over the center. Between the Fifty-sixth Division and the beaches of Sixth Corps to the south was a gap of more than ten miles that had to be closed without delay as the two corps moved inland. The forces were to join at Ponte Sele. The U.S. Sixth Corps, commanded by Major General Ernest J. Dawley, was to operate on the right of the Tenth Corps and had the mission of establishing a beachhead south of the Sele River. Regimental combat teams of the Thirty-sixth Division (Reinforced), under Major General Fred L. Walker, were to launch simultaneous assaults on the Paestum beaches, advance inland to seize the high ground commanding the southern half of the Salerno plain, and prevent the movement of the enemy into the plain from the east and south.

Additional strength in the form of a floating reserve was to be provided by a reinforced regimental combat team of the Forty-fifth Division, commanded by Major General Troy H. Middleton, and a reinforced regimental combat team of the Eighty-second Airborne Division, under Major General Matthew B. Ridgway. Middleton's combat team was to be ready to land on D-day over any of the previously established beaches. Ridgway's troops were to be prepared to land with light equipment on beaches that had not been previously established. Follow-up troops were to include the balance of the Forty-fifth Division and Eighty-second Airborne, together with the Thirty-fourth Division, Third Division, Thirteenth Field Artillery Brigade, one armored division, one tank battalion, and supporting troops. A special naval force, placed under the command of Captain Charles L. Andrews, Jr., U.S.N., was to make a feint against beaches at the mouth of the Volturno River, northwest of Naples, to draw enemy forces there and divert them from the main assaults. The Fifth Army was to invade Italy with the equivalent of four divisions on D-day and double that strength with follow-up troops. Success depended on the ability of the British and American forces to establish a firm beachhead before the Germans could oppose them with units shifted from the east and south. D-day was September 9. H hour for the Rangers was 0300.

Envisioning the Sorrento Peninsula west of Salerno as a "scenic, mountainous area" that was "tailor-made for battle" and providing a "bird's-eye view" of the German forces in the plain of Naples, Darby left Clark's headquarters expecting to find his Rangers rubbing their hands in gleeful anticipation of "the chance to pull another stunt of forward observing as we had done in Sicily." Authorized by Clark to organize a staff to coordinate his plans, he formed a headquarters of this Ranger Force that included British officers. The mission was the destruction of defenses in the area of Capo d'Orso near the port of Maiori, clearing a road, seizing passes at Chiunzi and Nocera, and being prepared to "hang on in defense" and operate against the rear of any enemy that might delay the advance of the British Tenth Corps from its landing point south of Salerno.

"The entire job of the Rangers and accompanying units," he explained, "was to ease the way for British and American forces when they came rolling up through Salerno and Nocera."

In the plan he developed, the Fourth Battalion would be the first ashore to establish the beachhead, knock out the Capo d'Orso defenses, block the coastal road, and set up protection on the left flank of the following units. Fifteen minutes after H hour, the First Battalion would land and clear a portion of the coast road ten miles north of Maiori, occupy Mount St. Angelo di Cava, and set up a post to observe Route 18 between Maiori and Nocera. At H hour plus thirty, the Third Battalion would land and take the high ground on the First's left to Mount Chiunzi in preparation for an attack on Pagani. Taking this ground, Mount St. Angelo di Cava, and Mount Chiunzi would position the Rangers to threaten enemy movements against the British Tenth Corps as it drove north toward Nocera. Captain Charles Shunstrom's new cannon company would also land at H hour plus thirty and occupy a position near Mount St. Angelo di Cava, from which its guns could target German armor moving from the plain of Naples.

The Rangers would embark from Palermo on September 7 and cross the Tyrrhenian Sea to the Gulf of Salerno in three LSIs (landing ship, infantry). When a sergeant who had brought malaria patients to an abandoned schoolhouse-turned-hospital in Corleone told the fever-stricken Rangers that others were loading onto trucks bound for Palermo to be the spearhead of the invasion of Italy, many of the men of F Company were sick in bed.

"It was then," wrote Altieri, "that we discovered our Ranger fever was higher than our malaria fever. Some seventeen Rangers, on hearing this news, suddenly threw off their blankets, grabbed their belongings and hobbled out the doors over the protests of nurses and medical attendants. Into the truck we scrambled as a whistle blew somewhere summoning the MPs to stop the mass exodus. The truck slammed into gear and away we went down the road in a cloud of dust."

Twelve days before the Rangers converged on the Palermo docks, Tom Sullivan wrote to his younger brother Joe, "What a life for a soldier. On this campaign [Sicily] I was a clerk, corporal, supply sgt. rear guard and ice cream eater (when I can get it). The girls here, especially in the city, are very good-looking and remind me of home, as do the magnificent buildings I saw in one of the cities. Some parts of it did not look so swell. Most cities are old and dirty—often like Arab villages. Some are very modern."

· The letter of August 27, 1943, continued, "It's a prickly feeling you get on an invasion. I was very tense and kept gripping my rifle. As we were about to land I was raring to go—about that time a wave dashed over and cooled me off. We jumped into the water and ran ashore. Firing started and from there on it was *c'est la guerre*."

Looking back on his travels as a Ranger, Sully added, "I have ridden on ocean liners, ferryboats, riverboats, assault craft, a raider, a transport plane, rubber boats, donkey, truck, jeeps, and everything but a P38 [fighter plane] and submarine."

In planning the voyage to the Gulf of Salerno, Darby saw a logistical problem. Because the LCIs could float only one battalion at a time, they would have to shuttle the three battalions to the shore. They would be guided by a Hunter-class destroyer in the dark to a point at which the depth of the water required the destroyer to turn back, leaving the boats to go the rest of the way on their own. This presented a navigational problem. As Darby explained, "When thirty-five helmeted soldiers carrying rifles are aboard, and because troops never sit still, their constant movements cause the needle to deflect, so that the finest compass in the world swings back and forth." Darby's solution was a blinking light on the rear of the leading landing craft to signal the following boats and keep them on the course set by the destroyer. The boats were to line up in a double column, "very much like a mother duck and her brood."

After loading on September 7, the flotilla left Palermo early the next morning on a course to rendezvous with the full invasion convoy. In General Mark Clark's master invasion plan the Thirty-sixth Infantry Division departed from Oran, Algeria, and would join the U.S. Forty-fifth Infantry Division and the British Forty-sixth and Fifty-sixth divisions, with the American Third and Fourth infantry divisions and the British Seventh Armored following on. The Rangers were to arrive off Maiori well before H hour on D-day. Soon after sailing from Palermo, they were informed that Eisenhower had announced in a radio broadcast over Radio Algiers that the Italian government had surrendered unconditionally to the Allies. This startling news left many of the Rangers expecting a repeat of the aborted raid on Galita and that they would be turned back to Sicily. But this apprehension disappeared in the afternoon and well into the evening when the invasion convoy kept going under repeated attack by German planes.

When the landing ships drew within sight of land just after midnight, steep mountains of the Sorrento Peninsula formed a black silhouette beyond the one-thousand-yard, steeply sloped pebble beach on which the Rangers were to land. Darby thought of the target he had studied again and again on maps and in photographs as "beautiful in daylight," but like all the "perfect landing beaches" his Rangers had attacked it would have to be found in the dark. With Italy out of the war, the landings would be opposed by scores of Sixteenth Panzer Division tanks, seventeen thousand troops in four battalions of infantry, and three artillery battalions with thirty-six assault guns. As the landing ships halted to begin lowering assault craft, the shore batteries opened fire. The guns of the British Navy replied while landing craft were lowered and the Rangers' destroyer guide moved into position. With Darby in the leading boat, the destroyer's captain shouted from the bridge, "I say, are you there?"

Darby replied, "I'm here."

The captain answered, "Off we go."

True to Darby's imagery of swimming ducklings following their mother, the boatloads of taut, grim-faced Rangers headed toward the dark coast in lines of twos and into the pages of history as the first force of American soldiers to invade the mainland of Europe. Volunteers all, each with his own reason for wanting to become a Ranger, they had been selected by Darby for whatever traits of character or promise he'd discerned in them. From almost every region of the United States, they'd converged on small towns in Ireland and Scotland for testing and training by British Commandos while never forgetting—or letting their instructors forget—that they were Americans. They'd led the invasion of North Africa and contributed significantly to liberating it, spearheaded the landings in Sicily, and done their part in wresting the island from the Germans. Now they were descending on an Italian beach to begin the conquest of a continent that many of their parents or grandparents had left to find a better life in a country that, for the second time in less than thirty years, had rallied to save not only the people of Europe but Western civilization.

In the little boats were three battalions of young men who had put their personal lives on hold for as many reasons as their numbers. They'd left behind graves of men just like them in Scotland, Algeria, Tunisia, and Sicily. Each had been prayed over by a British Roman Catholic priest who acted like a character in a Charles Dickens story or Shakespearean drama.

With the Rangers as they trailed a Royal Navy destroyer went fond memories of little old ladies who put them up and fed them in quaint cottages, amorous recollections of the Scottish girls who'd entertained them and a few who married them, bawdy thoughts of lusty women in whorehouses along the way, and romantic fantasies of futures with idealized girls they'd left at home. Many, if not most, had written letters similar to one Tom Sullivan had sent his brother Joe from Tunisia. "I wonder how it will seem to be home again," he wrote. "It sure will be hard to settle down after all this bouncing about."

For the leader the Rangers had grown not only to admire and respect but love in the sixteen months since their conception at Carrickfergus in June 1942, the only thoughts were of the landing beach. Planning the assault, he'd reviewed the landings at Arzew and Gela.

In the first, a breakdown in communications had almost resulted in the Rangers being shelled by their own naval support. Gela had been marred by miscoordination in landing at the right spot. To be certain that neither situation was repeated, he had worked out potential problems in a conference with the captain of the British destroyer, assuring that shore-to-ship communication would be done over American radios. Finding the right place on the beach was assured by the arrangement in which the destroyer would guide the landing craft to a point a mile from shore.

After making a few slight changes of course, the destroyer reached the departure point. Leaning over the rail, the captain shouted to Darby, "You are now on course."

The ship swung away and the landing craft carrying the Fourth Battalion surged ahead, but Darby was unable to see the beach until they were about two hundred yards offshore.

"When the first assault craft hit the beach," he noted, "it was exactly in the center of the thousand-foot landing strip."

The time was 0310 hours, September 9, 1943.

Led by Roy Murray, the battalion discovered the beach had not only not been mined, but was not even defended, indicating that the Germans had not expected a landing on such a small strip of sand. Having carried out a surprise assault, Darby broke radio silence and informed the British ships that the battalion had hit the beach "on the nose," that the beachhead was established, and that the First and Third battalions could follow ashore and move inland on their mission to drive north up the coastal highway and into the mountains toward Chiunzi Pass.

A member of Altieri's F Company, nineteen-year-old Alan E. Merrill of Buffalo, New York, had tried to join the marines. Rejected because of color blindness, he was accepted into the army and found himself in Northern Ireland with the Thirty-fourth Division as Darby was recruiting Rangers. Briefly sidelined by pneumonia, he'd caught up with the Rangers in North Africa and fought there and in Sicily. Of the invasion of Italy he recalled, "Our landings had gone like clockwork. We had the total element of surprise. We started down the road while dawn's early light was in its earliest stages."

Darby recorded this account of the actions by the First and Third battalions:

> With scouts ahead, the men marched in single file on the edges of the road, advancing swiftly. It was pitch dark and the only sounds were the shuffle of combat shoes and the singing of crickets. An occasional toad jumped out on the road.
>
> Suddenly, the main party of Rangers came upon a parked car that the scouts had overlooked in the intense darkness. A not-unfriendly German voice hailed them. Guns whipped around, and after a few shots the enemy surrendered. A group of fourteen Germans had been laying mines on the road. Several of their number had gone off for a few hours, and when the Rangers approached, they thought their missing members were returning.

By 0800 in the morning they had established themselves in the high mountains on both sides of the Chiunzi Pass road. Dug in for defense, the First and Third battalions were on the right, or eastern, side of the road, and a parachute regiment was on the left at Mount Ceretto at a height of four thousand feet. The Rangers on the right held Mount St. Angelo di Cava, more than three thousand feet high, and Mount Chiunzi, about twenty-six hundred feet in elevation. Darby informed General Mark Clark by radio, "We have taken a position in the enemy's rear and we'll stay here till hell freezes over."

James Altieri remembered, "Astride these strategic heights the

Rangers dominated the enemy's main line of communication leading from Naples to Salerno."

Depicting the strategic value of the location held by the Rangers, Darby recorded that his guns were sited on Highway 18, denying it to the Germans and compelling them to use Highway 88, which swung eastward and southward toward Salerno. Holding their reserves in the Naples plain some five miles to the north, they could be observed clearly by the Rangers. While the First and Third Rangers were in position at the heights near Chiunzi Pass, they were able to employ naval gunfire to assist themselves and to harry the Germans in the Naples plain. Looking down to their rear in the Gulf of Salerno, the Rangers had the thrill of seeing the combined British and American battle fleet pulled in close toward Salerno to provide support.

To assist the gunners in targeting, Darby had placed a Ranger officer aboard the British battleship *Howe* with an American radio for communication with observation posts on Mount St. Angelo and Chiunzi Pass. His account of the bombardment continued, "The Germans were denied Chiunzi Pass simply because one observer was up there with a radio and could talk to the navy to direct their gunfire support. As the navy warmed to their task, they moved their ships right into the hollow of the coast near Amalfi."

Most of the ships elevated their guns in order to clear the mountain. Unable to raise its guns as high, the battleship used the pass at Chiunzi like a bowling alley. One Ranger heard the first fifteen-inch shells coming through the pass and thought it sounded like a freight train with the caboose wobbling from side to side.

A forward observer at a place nicknamed "Schuster's Mansion" (named for Captain Emil Schuster, a medical officer of the Third Battalion who set up his aid station in a stone house at that location) spotted Germans in a park near Nocera as they distributed ammunition. Calling in fire from the *Howe*, he watched with deep satisfaction as fifteen-inch shells touched off the ammo dump and obliterated the park in a series of deafening explosions.

Alan Merrill peered out to sea through binoculars at the invasion armada and heard the shell fire and the loud kaboom of the naval guns beginning the softening-up process. While on a scout patrol, he would be wounded by a German hand grenade, evacuated to North Africa, and returned to the Fourth Ranger Battalion, in time for the Rangers' fourth invasion. (In Operation Shingle he would be the first of thirty thousand men to land at Anzio.)

According to Clark's master plan for invading Italy, the Rangers were to hold the heights and delay Germans from sweeping through the Chiunzi Pass and down the northern roads while the main forces landed and swiftly drove inland toward Naples. This timetable required the two British Commando units, each the size of a Ranger battalion, to land between Maiori at Vietri sul Mare and Salerno with the objective of seizing and holding the Cava-Nocera Pass, clearing the way for the British Forty-sixth Division to rapidly advance toward Naples on D-day. As Darby noted ruefully, "It would have been a feasible mission [for the Rangers] *if the main Allied forces had arrived on schedule*" [emphasis added].

As a cadet at West Point and through his experiences in executing battle schemes from Algeria to Tunisia and Sicily, Darby had learned the military axiom that a master plan on paper was worthless in the reality of battle. While his Rangers had achieved their landing at Maiori with complete surprise and accomplished their mission to take and hold the heights of Chiunzi Pass, the bulk of the invasion forces had encountered fierce resistance. By nightfall on D-day, the Tenth Corps beachhead extended no more than three miles inland, the Forty-sixth Division had failed to take Salerno's port, and the Germans still held Montecorvino airport and the road and rail junction at Battipaglia.

Noting that the Rangers were left "out on a limb," Darby explained that because of the small number of men and the large area to defend, "we stretched ourselves thin, as we had done at Dernaia Pass in Tunisia. The terrain was in our favor. We quickly developed strong points, covering the gaps with machine-gun fire. Seven German counterattacks strongly supported by automatic weapons, mortars, and grenades were repelled during this period."

After an observer sent by General Clark to assess the situation at Chiunzi Pass on the afternoon of September 10 recommended augmenting the Rangers with motorized artillery and antitank units, Darby again found himself in command of a regimental-sized force that would total eighty-five hundred men and entitled him to the rank of full colonel. Having started his career in the artillery, he called taking charge of the additional firepower "an artilleryman's dream" and said that the enemy below him on the plain of Naples was "the most beautiful target" he'd ever seen.

On the afternoon of September 11, a small German patrol was driven back and an officer and enlisted man captured. Darby learned that they were members of the famed Hermann Goering Panzer Division. It was a crucial segment of German Field Marshal Albert Kesselring's plan to first blunt and then smash the Allied drive from Salerno to Naples.

By that evening, the Sixth Corps had made significant advances away from the Paestum beaches. The right flank was securely anchored on the hill positions in the Trentinara and Ogliastro areas gained by the 141st Regimental Combat Team. Around Roccad'aspide, the First Battalion, 142nd Infantry, held Hill 424, but the situation on the left flank was dangerous. The Second Battalion, 179th Infantry, had been unable to advance beyond the Calore crossing north of Hill 424, and enemy pressure had forced the battalion to fall back to La Cosa Creek during the night. An enemy counterattack had cut off the First and Third battalions from their support. In an effort to relieve the 179th Infantry from the effects of the enemy counterattack, the Fifth Army had thrown in the 157th Regimental Combat Team to attack a tobacco factory area west of the Sele River, but the attack had bogged down. At the end of the day the issue in the area from Bivio Cioffi east through the Sele-Calore corridor was "unsettled."

Farther east, the Forty-sixth Division had tightened its hold on the port of Salerno and attempted to drive north into the mountains, but made little progress. North of Sixth Corps, the Fifty-sixth had pushed patrols into Battipaglia before dawn on September 10. The Germans brought up tanks and two battalions of infantry, which drove advanced British elements out of the town. When the British managed to return and work their way into its streets by the evening of September 11, other units on the left of the Fifty-sixth Division line engaged in heavy fighting at a tobacco factory two miles west of Battipaglia and at Montecorvino airfield, which they finally secured. Meanwhile, the Fifth Army beachhead had been expanded along a thirty-five-to-fifty-mile coastline to an average depth of seven miles. Only in the center, in the Sele-Calore corridor, was the beachhead insecure.

To the north, the Tenth Corps had been meeting even more stubborn resistance and heavy German counterattacks. Although these thrusts had not penetrated the British lines, they had slowed the advance and stopped it in several sectors. On the far left of the Tenth Corps, the Rangers above Maiori held their lines overlooking the Nocera-Pagani valley. To ensure the retention of this valuable position, a nervous General Clark had sent Darby the reinforcements.

For Chuck Shunstrom the struggle to hold on to the Chiunzi heights had become a deadly game of "hit 'em and run." Standing in his jeep with field glasses, he searched for targets and directed half-track-mounted 75mm guns to advance and fire, then duck for cover as the artillery raked the surprised enemy. The Germans responded with artillery barrages. During one of these fierce retorts on September 16, twenty-four-year-old Sergeant Thomas Sullivan was killed. Recalling a "slight, genial, intelligent, enthusiastic and much-liked and admired man," Warren "Bing" Evans wrote, "That's the big problem of war—all of those people that I grew so close to and liked so much—well, here I am and they're dead."

"It was a long, hard fight, but the Rangers hung on," said Darby, "trusting that one day soon the American and British forces below Salerno would break out of their beachheads and drive north toward Naples. It was fortunate that the troops had had a rugged training course. We needed endurance, fighting without rest or relief and always short of food and water. Worse than that, there was the continuous threat that overwhelming forces might sweep aside our thinly held line and knock out the Allied left flank."

Twenty-one days after the Rangers landed at Maiori, the invasion forces broke out of the main beachhead south of Salerno. As they stormed up Highway 18 toward Naples, Darby led his Rangers down the mountains to Pagani and Castellammare on the western coast, leaving the tip of the Sorrento Peninsula, in Darby's colorful description, to "mountain goats and any Germans who wanted to act like them."

"Finally, on September 22, 1943," wrote Altieri, "after the bitterest fighting in Ranger history," the Rangers joined the big push to Naples, adding to their honors two more Presidential Citations. For "outstanding leadership and personal bravery" Darby was awarded another D.S.C.

A U.S. Army historian wrote, "Together with their British allies, Americans had again successfully stormed enemy-held beaches, this time on the coast of Europe. They had beaten off determined German counterattacks by a stubborn defense in which the infantry, the artillery, the engineers, and all the other arms had added new laurels to American battle records. When the enemy finally admitted failure and withdrew before the flanking threat of the Eighth Army, American and British divisions swept forward rapidly from the plains up into the mountains. Despite every obstacle of nature and the enemy, they had pushed on to their goal."

During the Salerno campaign and the taking of Naples, from September 9 to October 6, 727 American soldiers were killed in action, 2,720 were wounded, and 1,423 were reported missing, for a total of 4,870. Most of these casualties were within the Thirty-sixth and Forty-fifth divisions in the beachhead struggle. The British units in the Tenth Corps had a total of 6,847 killed, wounded, and missing. The Rangers counted 22 killed in action, 8 who died as a result of wounds, 73 wounded, and 9 missing in action.

While the Fifth Army stood poised for the next phase in the conquest of Italy, all of the territory south of the Volturno River lay in Allied hands. Supplies and men could now pour in through the port of Naples, and Allied bombers would soon carry out missions over Europe from Italian airfields. While absorbed in the Salerno campaign, the Germans were unable to send reinforcements to the islands of Sardinia and Corsica, which fell to a French expeditionary force. Recording that Allied control of the central Mediterranean was "nearly complete," a U.S. Army historian proclaimed that "the outer ramparts of Hitler's Fortress Europe were crumbling under the blows of two Allied armies in Italy."

Looking back on the role of the Rangers, Bing Evans mused that because they took the Chiunzi Pass and were able to direct artillery fire and naval gunfire on the main highway connecting the area to southern Italy, the Rangers could claim credit for the Salerno beachhead finally opening up. "Otherwise," he wrote, "I have no doubt the Allies would have been driven back into the sea."

★ CHAPTER 12 ★

A Year and a Day

"It was the same old hill story all over again."

Following the main Allied force into Naples by a few hours, the Rangers bivouacked in the city's botanical gardens. Darby described his battle-wearied men "lying down under palms and curling up in comfortable grassy plots." When an "enterprising Ranger" found a restaurant for the officers' mess and another for the enlisted ranks, Darby noted, there was for the first time since they'd taken Gela in Sicily "food and drink aplenty."

Deciding that his officer staff had earned a little rest and recreation, he and Dammer joined them for "a session of beer drinking

161

and enjoyment" that nearly ended in disaster. As Darby and Dammer boisterously sang old beer-garden songs that they had learned as West Pointers on weekend visits to the Yorkville section of New York, a neighborhood that had been settled by German immigrants, a group of American paratroopers burst through the door with Tommy guns poised, holding hand grenades and believing they had discovered a German army headquarters.

"I looked up at the intruders," Darby recalled, "and to my further disgust saw that the commander of the paratrooper battalion was an old familiar face from West Point, a man who had been overly serious and conscientious. The humor of the situation didn't appeal to this man and his paratroopers until long after everyone else in the room was bent over in loud guffaws. We, of course, invited our visitors in for a beer."

After a few days of leave in Naples, the Rangers moved south to San Lazzaro for a period of further rest, waiting for replacements, refitting, replenishment of supplies and equipment, and retraining. It was also a time for reflection. Darby recalled, "Behind us stretched almost a year of hard fighting: Arzew; then Gafsa, Sened Station, Dernaia Pass, El Guettar, Djebel el Ank, and Djebel Berda in Tunisia; Gela, Butera, Licata, Porto Empedocle, Castelvetrano, Marsala, and Messina in Sicily; and Sorrento's Chiunzi Pass in Italy. What lay ahead, we did not know. The road was long, and it was best to look only to the next bend. We could look forward only to fighting up the boot of Italy."

For that onslaught, General Mark Clark commanded the Sixth Corps, under Major General John P. Lucas, and the British Tenth Corps, commanded by Lieutenant General Sir Richard McCreery. The Sixth Corps was composed of three of the finest battle-tested divisions in the American army: the Third Division, under Major General Lucian Truscott; the Thirty-fourth Division, under Major General Charles W. Ryder; and the Forty-fifth Division, under Major General Troy H. Middleton. With their supporting units the two corps constituted a force of more than 100,000. To oppose the Allies, Field Marshal Kesselring had the Third and Fifteenth Panzer grenadier divisions, the Hermann Goering Division, and elements of the Twenty-sixth Panzer Division. Their purpose was to fight a delaying action in terrain and wintry weather that gave them the advantage.

Describing the situation, a U.S. Army historian recorded that the western part of the area from which the Fifth Army had to drive the enemy in order to reach the line of mountains designated as its objective was a broad stretch of level farmland fifteen to twenty miles wide extending northwest along the coast approximately thirty miles from Naples to the Mount Massico ridgeline. A fertile region of vineyards, olive groves, and carefully tilled fields, dotted with towns, this coastal plain was the zone of advance assigned by Clark to the Tenth Corps. The Volturno River, flowing west across it, provided the enemy with a strong defensive position. Clark ordered the Tenth Corps to drive to the Volturno, force a crossing of the river, and continue through the plain to seize the Mount Massico ridge.

The Sixth Corps was assigned the area of mountains and valleys stretching some thirty-five miles east from the coastal plain to include the eastern slopes of the massive Matese range, the watershed of the peninsula. This mountain country varied from low hills covered with olive orchards and terraced fields to barren rocky peaks about two thousand meters high. Villages of tightly crowded gray stone houses clung to the steep slopes. Crumbling ruins of ancient castles looked down on the green valleys below. The rugged mountains presented a formidable obstacle to the movement of troops. The Volturno and Calore rivers reinforced the barrier. Rising in the high mountains north of Venafro, the river followed an erratic course southeast to Amorosi, where it joined the Calore. Turning west, the river cut through a narrow gap in the mountains at Triflisco and flowed out into the coastal plain. The lower reaches of the Volturno and Calore

formed a continuous obstacle, almost sixty miles long, lying directly
in the path of any advance on Rome from the south. If the Fifth Army
breached the river defenses, the Germans would have to fall back to
the range of mountains behind Sessa Aurunca, Venafro, and Isernia.
This became known as the "Winter Line."

The German defense in the American sector was called the "Gustav Line." The objective of one Sixth Corps division was Benevento.
It was ordered to drive north and west twenty-two miles down the
Calore Valley to the Volturno River, turn northwest into the Volturno
Valley, and advance thirty miles to the mountains behind the small
town of Venafro. The two remaining divisions of the corps were to
cross the Volturno on a fifteen-mile front between the junction of the
rivers and the Triflisco Gap, and push northwest through hills lying
between the upper Volturno and the coastal plain to a mountain range
north of Sessa Aurunca. As part of this drive to cross the Volturno, the
Fourth Ranger Battalion, under the command of Roy Murray, was to
be assigned to the Third Division, Sixth Corps. Detached from the
Ranger camp at San Lazzaro on November 1, they passed through
Naples and climbed peaks of the Apennine Mountains that ranged
from two to four thousand feet.

After crossing the Volturno River early on the afternoon of November 3, the battalion ran into stiff German resistance the next
morning. Fighting in bitterly cold temperatures, rain, and sleet for
more than eighty hours with only lightweight tanker jackets, C rations for food, and little water, they held on until November 6. When
Murray requested of Sixth Corps headquarters that they be relieved,
the casualty count was seven dead, twenty-one wounded, and nine
missing.

As Murray's battered force withdrew to Sesto Campana, the First
and Third battalions loaded onto trucks for attachment to the Forty-
fifth Division with orders to relieve a regimental combat team in
mountains northwest of Venafro. The night of November 8, 1943,

Darby noted, was a year and a day since they had made their first assault landing at Arzew. Instead of the amphibious tactics for which the Rangers had been designed and trained, they found themselves again being used as ordinary infantry. These men who had eagerly signed up to be Rangers to demonstrate their individuality and had endured the rigors of Ranger training and had proved they were unique by spearheading invasions at Arzew, Gela, and Salerno resented that they were called upon for what they regarded as conventional fighting. The resulting disappointment and frustration was manifested in requests for transfers, and this attrition combined with the need for replacements after combat to dilute unit cohesion and lower morale among the remaining original Rangers.

Although Darby was acutely aware of the situation, it was not he who brought the matter to the attention of the chief of army ground forces. In an astonishingly frank letter to the high command in Washington, D.C., Major Roy Murray asserted that the point of creating a uniquely American Commando-style force was not being fully realized and requested issuance of "a clear-cut directive" recognizing the Rangers as a permanent, distinct force with its own headquarters, with Darby designated "senior Battalion Commander." Like previous requests from Darby for a Ranger regiment, Murray's proposal went unanswered.

"It was the same old hill story all over again," said Darby of the First Battalion's move to relieve various infantry companies of the Forty-fifth Division in the Venafro area. A small city tucked in the shadow of the San Croce and Corvo Mountains, it was in a corner of a triangular plain formed by the Volturno River. Southwest of the town, a narrow macadam road ran through the village of Ceppagna and the town of San Pietro Infine to join a highway leading north to Cassino. As the First Battalion moved into the heights on November 9, they were joined by the Eighty-third Mortar Battalion, Shunstrom's cannon unit, and the Fourth Ranger Battalion. With the Forty-fifth

Division occupying mountain foothills above Venafro, the Germans held the high ground overlooking roads and valleys against the towering backdrop of Mount Cassino.

The Rangers' task was to link the left flank of the Forty-fifth Division and right flank of the Third Division, and to prevent German forces from using the road to move around Mount Corvo and Mount Croce and toward Venafro. This required splitting the Rangers in two, with Darby's headquarters in a cave between the peaks. Darby saw this as an inadequate force for holding important observation posts that were the only ones overlooking the Volturno plain. To bolster the defense, he asked for and was given the 509th Parachute Battalion. Occupying a part of Mount Corvo, the Germans were dug in near a huge rock at the peak and separated from the Americans by a deep chasm. The only link was a narrow ridge at right angles to the opposing units. "Defended by both forces with obstacles, barbed wire, mines and guns laid to fire down its length," Darby recalled, "this ridge was practically impassable."

Determined to take it on November 11 and clear the opposite peak, designated Hill 670, Darby assigned the job to the 509th Parachute Battalion. Supported by the mortar battalion and Shunstrom's cannon company, they attacked at 0430 hours and engaged in more than seven hours of fighting, with one killed and three wounded. Five Germans were captured. After two counterattacks failed, the Germans dug in on the reverse slope and harassed the Rangers with sniper fire. With the ridge secured, Darby felt that his men were ready for any counterattacks and turned his attention to resupplying his force. Mules carried ammunition and food. Kitchens were moved from rear areas and the Rangers were served hot meals.

Like eagles, Darby's men peered down at the town of Conca Casale, observing Germans slink into doorways to dodge flying chunks of cement and wood blasted from buildings hit by American artillery shells. "Every day or so," Darby recorded, "we sent a night patrol down into the vicinity of the town." The usual result was one or more German prisoners and a running flow of information as to the numbers of Germans in the town and behind it. As the weather turned colder, with stretches of heavy rainfall, warfare that Darby termed static and nerve-racking was broken only by forays by patrols that reaped a few more prisoners.

"The mountains were miserable, and we heartily desired movement and new action," wrote Darby. "The enemy brought up heavier artillery, shelling the Rangers continually. Visibility got poorer; fog and waiting increased the tension. Clouds that covered the peaks were used by both sides as cover for moving in patrols for attacks."

While Darby compared the situation to naval actions in the Pacific where fleets moved forward and retreated under the protection of bad weather fronts, the plight of the Rangers was more like the bloody stalemate in France in World War I in which men died and the battlefield status was unchanged. Darby lamented, "The fighting continued to take its toll of my men."

Providing an even bleaker assessment of this stroke and counterstroke, Robert W. Black wrote in *Rangers in World War II*, "Each day the casualty list mounted. Darby's superiors had no understanding of the capabilities and limitations of a Ranger unit. The knowledge and experience of the Rangers was being shot to pieces in line combat."

Reflecting on the situation with his innate optimism, Darby wrote that Rangers were giving more than they received. Prisoners continued to be captured. Echoes of the Western Front are found in an account of a night patrol by Company F, Third Ranger Battalion, led by Bing Evans. Shrouded in the gray light of foggy dawn, they found themselves on one side of a ravine with Germans equally obscured on the other. Evans shouted across the gap, "Does anybody over there speak English?"

"Yes, I can," came the response. "I am the noncommissioned officer in charge."

Evans replied, "Let's declare a truce. I have a beautiful Red Cross girl over here who would like to meet you."

"No, thank you."

"Well, why don't you and your men come over and surrender," Evans said, "and we'll give you a steak dinner?"

The German laughed. "No, I couldn't do that."

"You speak English very well."

"I was educated at Michigan State, studying hotel management."

Over a few days of alternating shooting and lulls for conversation, Evans and his Rangers learned the German's name was Hans. His parents owned a hotel near Leipzig, and when he'd returned home to Germany on vacation from college, he'd been drafted into the army. When Evans was ordered to take the German position, the Rangers attacked at night from the rear and found Hans among the dead.

James Altieri recalled of the fighting at Venafro: "Each Ranger attack was followed by a German counterattack. Sometimes mountains would change hands several times in one day. Heavy enemy mortar and artillery barrages blistered the mountaintops and caused a great many Ranger casualties."

Late in the afternoon of November 19, two Ranger companies on Mount Corvo were attacked by several German companies, requiring Darby to call in fire by 4.2-inch and 60mm mortars. In a battle that raged through the night and the next day, the Germans remained in place. At dawn on November 21 an effort to dislodge Germans from a cave with Molotov cocktails was thwarted by artillery and machine guns. A daring exploit by an engineer (recorded by Darby as "aptly named Private Nervy") to dislodge Germans from a dugout with a pair of Bangalore torpedoes also failed. Repeated attempts against the dugout on November 22 proved futile.

The next day, the radio log of Darby's "Cave" headquarters noted these communications:

0925   Captain Shunstrom reports that E Company has cap-
       tured two prisoners, one of whom was shot trying to
       escape.

0958   Muleskinner killed by shellfire, and mule hit in leg—
       mule destroyed.

1002   Enemy small-arms fire heard.

1004   Company E suffered casualties by heavy shellfire, wound-
       ing four, one missing, one known dead.

1007   Enemy shot green flare on left flank: meaning enemy
       (the Rangers) has broken through, according to a pris-
       oner.

1008   Enemy shell has hit own position—a cave under a rock.

1015   Prisoner says they have had quite a few casualties in last
       few days. Is now carrying papers of lost comrades. New
       replacements coming in daily.

1023   Enemy machine-gun fire heard.

1024   Enemy attacking right flank of Company E. Call for
       mortar fire on forward slope.

1026   Section sent out on forward slope toward Company C's
       position in counterattack.

1028   Captain Shunstrom ordered Company D of the
       paratroopers to slide over to support our counter-
       counterattack.

1032   Captain Shunstrom moving Company D of paratroop-
       ers over to the pass and using half of them in attack.

1035   Running low on grenades.

1040   Water, grenades, and three cases of "frags" [fragmenta-
       tion bombs], one case of .30-caliber 8-round clips, and
       one case of offensive grenades required in addition to
       those sent at 0700.

1045   Our guns have started firing.

1047   Captain Shunstrom reported counterattack repelled momentarily. Moving back downhill to eight in front of OP [Outpost] No. 1. OP No. 1 alerted.

1057 Have 60mm fire concentrated in middle of enemy company.

1058 Emergency line [telephone] still out between Company C's CP [Command Post] and Force CP.

1059 Captain Shunstrom requests some concentration from fourteen guns as he had on previous day.

1104 Enemy machine gun heard.

1109 Colonel Darby returned. He is sending two [half]tracks to fire on enemy positions.

Ten minutes later, with the Germans attacking again, Darby ordered a counterattack by the paratroopers and Ranger Company D. Under the cover of artillery in Conca Casale and mortar fire, the Germans attempted to break through C Company's position, but were beaten back. Shunstrom advised Darby at 1135 that his cannon company was about into position and could commence firing five to ten minutes after ordered to do so. Darby sent a runner to tell his mortar units to cease firing when the paratroopers were sighted. They appeared at 1141.

A minute later, the log noted, "We are making attack. High-velocity and small-arms fire still coming in [from the Germans]."

To cover the attack, the Rangers' mortars began firing only smoke shells. At 1155, E Company reported paratroopers moving below their position. Five minutes later, the log noted, "Lieutenant Miller says, 'We knocked the hell of out of 'em. Dead Heinies all over the place.'"

At 1237, Darby left his cave headquarters to go up the hill. An hour later, he advised the assistant division commander, "We have received two heavy counterattacks today by about two hundred men following very close behind artillery screen. All were beaten off, but to do so we countered with our last reserve. We are not yet calling on a battalion of the 180th. We think the enemy are stopped, but situation is not good. Must have counterbattery fire."

The same message to the division commander added, "We've suffered heavy casualties. Another enemy attack in force will lose big hill for us. Artillery cannot be used until [our] wounded are out. If we could get a company of 180th to hold where we made attack from, it would save big hill. Forty-fifth Division's artillery alerted for counterbattery fire."

Subsequent messages noted that E Company had thirty-one men left, F had twenty-five, and B Company had five. After a weeklong battle, the incomplete official casualty record listed more than seventy Rangers killed and wounded. Summarizing the actions of the Rangers in the Allied offensive on the Winter Line, David W. Hogan, Jr., wrote in *U.S. Army Special Operations in World War II*, "By mid-December the continuous fighting and the cold, wet weather had taken a heavy toll. In one month of action, for example, the First Ranger Battalion lost 350 men, including nearly 200 casualties from exposure."

Darby, who had hoped to be assigned to Hawaii and fight the war across the Pacific, said about warfare in the wintry Italian mountains, "We were living through a period of constant attack and counterattack. There was rain and some snow, and the mountain was bitterly cold, particularly at night."

The day after the fighting recorded in the log of November 23, 1943, as German attacks continued in a manner Darby called thick and fast, he called back to his command post, "We are receiving heavy counterattack on left flank. Rush infantry company up to me immediately. I am at the 'Cave.' Get 4.2 and artillery busy . . . Hurry."

On the same day, November 24, an Italian girl visited the Rangers overlooking the town of Conca Casale to inform them there were no "Jerries" there and asked for the shelling to stop. "The report was obviously untrue," Darby wrote, "since the Germans were seen practically every hour of daylight running from doorway to doorway." On another occasion, the Germans raised a white flag in an attempt to throw the Rangers off guard before launching an attack. The next day, Darby recorded on the subject of Germans being "full of tricks" that the enemy attacked during a rainstorm, but was thrown back. Twice during another day, he wrote, the Germans used a bank of low clouds in the valley for cover to mount counterattacks. Another ruse was a call for help in the hope that a Ranger would suppose it came from a wounded Ranger. Some Germans put on women's clothes to lure a Ranger into the open and others disguised themselves as monks and nuns.

Darby noted that the Rangers had their own tricks for "getting at the enemy." One of these consisted of a booby-trapped ration box dropped from an airplane that exploded when it was investigated by a curious German. Another was to set up a loudspeaker at night close to a German position to blast music and either surround it with mines or place a team of snipers to lie in wait to kill anyone who ventured out to remove it.

On Thanksgiving Day, Darby and his Rangers celebrated with a noontime turkey dinner, then launched an attack that netted ten prisoners, all but one of them captured by Lieutenant Peer Buck. One of the captives stated that they had been in position for just four days and that under the Rangers' heavy mortar fire their unit strength had been reduced from eighty to forty men.

By the end of November the Ranger force had been in the mountains of Venafro for five weeks. A U.S. Army chronicle notes that the Allies had by then won an area twenty to sixty miles across the Italian peninsula. Within six weeks, Fifth Army troops had driven the Germans back to the Volturno, had executed a difficult river crossing in the face of a well-entrenched enemy, had gone on to cross the river a second and a third time, and had forced Kesselring's hard-pressed army back into a defensive position in the chain of mountains. Total battle casualties were 9,693. American units suffered 1,360 killed, 5,189 wounded, and 297 missing in action.

U.S. Army Staff Sergeant Robert J. Dewey described the struggle poetically:

"From Olive Groves Near Venafro"

Where ancient trees grow row on row
To surrounding mountains capped with snow—
How many died there?
We'll never know.

They traded the enemy shell for shell,
And took the place where comrades fell
Amidst the whistling, bursting shell—
How many died there?
We'll never know.

They are all brave both old and young
All are heroes, some unsung.
They gave their lives without regret—
These men, these men,
We'll ne'er forget.

★ CHAPTER 13 ★

FIELD ORDER NINETEEN

"Something was cooking."

ON DECEMBER 11, 1943, GENERAL MARK CLARK PROMOTED WILLIAM Darby to full colonel. Boosts in rank were also given to Roy Murray, who became lieutenant colonel, Walter Nye (major), and Howard Andre and James Altieri (lieutenant). Randall Harris was put in command of Fox Company. Relieved by the Third Battalion, 180th Infantry, two days later and detached from the Sixth Corps for return to the Fifth Army on December 14, the First Ranger Battalion moved to Lucrino Station near Naples to reunite with the Third and Fourth as the 6615th Ranger Force (Provisional) under Darby's direct command for the first time since Salerno. Herman Dammer became both executive officer and operations officer. A Darby classmate at West Point, Jack Dobson, took command of the First Battalion, Alvah Miller was put in charge of the Third, and Roy Murray remained in command of the Fourth.

Altieri noted that after four campaigns and thirteen major battles "the old-timers who had started back in Ireland were getting fewer and fewer." Nearly all had been wounded at least twice. Estimating the extent of killed or wounded at Venafro at 40 percent, Darby said, "We were weary and tired of the day-to-day patrols. Home-sickness overwhelmed the men, many of whom had been overseas for the better part of two years. With two assault landings, hard marching, and mountain fighting under their belts, the men of the three Ranger battalions had seen about everything in the fighting line. They were confident, experienced soldiers who had earned the right to cock their helmets over their ears, if they chose. Though in trim physical shape, their skin was drawn taut over cheeks and eyes were sunken."

Welcoming the respite from combat and anticipating basking in the warmth of the Mediterranean sun with Christmas approaching, the Rangers were surprised and delighted by the appearance at Lu-crino of their old friend Father Basil. Serving with the British Eighth Army, he "popped up," in the words of Altieri's happy account, to be greeted enthusiastically by the old-timers. He spent two days visiting all three battalions and conducted Christmas mass.

In green beret and attired in a complete Commando uniform, Darby recalled, the priest couldn't remain away from his adopted flock and sat up late into the night swapping tales of the doings of the Rangers and his own adventures since their parting in Tunisia. Unable to spend accumulated pay, Darby recorded, the men "poured out their goodwill in the collection plate." When Basil voiced concern about their generosity, Darby replied, "I know of nothing better they could do with their money. This is only an indication of what a walloping success you will make if you ever visit us in America."

Almost as popular a visitor as Basil was the Broadway, movie, and recording star Ella Logan. Born Ina Allan, in Dennistoun, Scotland, she began her career as a child star singing in music halls and by age seventeen was appearing in the West End of London. She had toured Europe in the early 1930s and claimed to have snubbed Adolf Hitler in a Cologne nightclub. Having married an American tap-dancer, she moved to the United States and began recording jazz records, followed by Hollywood stardom in films such as *52nd Street* and *The Goldwyn Follies*. Among her hit recordings were "I Was Doing All Right," "Love Is Here to Stay," "Oh Dear! What Can the Matter Be?," "Jingle (Bingle) Bells," "My Bonnie Lies Over the Ocean," "Come to the Fair," and "Two Sleepy People" (in a duet with Hoagy Carmichael). After she appeared on Broadway in late 1941 in "Sons o' Fun," a revue starring the comedy team of Olsen and Johnson, she moved to another revue, "Show Time," which ran 342 performances. When the tide of war turned toward the Allies in 1942 and it became possible for the stars of stage, screen, and recordings to travel to visit army camps, she joined the USO (United Service Organizations) and went to Africa, then followed the troops to Italy. Altieri recorded that when she told the Rangers they were her "favorite outfit," she was named a "Rangerette."

Recalling that the holidays were fun, Darby attributed much of the credit for the good times he and his officers enjoyed to his "irrepressible bodyguard." Corporal Charles Riley "put on his best smile and sallied out into the countryside to barter and bargain for chickens, whiskey and wine." Among the libations was "a green-tasting Scotch type" whisky that "had to be the result of a long search." A special treat for the officers cited by Rangers historian Robert W. Black was a "great party at a castle south of Naples" in the company of a bevy of nurses of the 225th Station Hospital. An observer reported seeing

Colonel Darby and the head nurse gazing at one another "like two eagles." Although there is scant information in recollections of Darby's
friends in Fort Smith, his West Point classmates, fellow officers, and
others regarding Darby's romantic life, marriage and divorce, he was
by all accounts a dashing figure who responded warmly and enthusiastically to girls and women who found him attractive and exciting.

Describing the strategic military situation in Italy as the Rangers
relaxed and romanced in early January 1944, Clayton D. Laurie wrote
in a narrative for the U.S. Army Center of Military History that Field
Marshal Albert Kesselring, whom Hitler had appointed as commander
of all German forces in Italy, promised to hold the Gustav Line to
prevent the Fifth Army from advancing into the Liri Valley, the most
logical and direct route to the major Allied objective of Rome. The
validity of this strategy was demonstrated repeatedly between October
1943 and January 1944 as the Allies launched costly attacks against
well-entrenched enemy forces. When it became obvious that the Germans were going to fight rather than pull back to northern Italy, the
Allied advance following the Salerno invasion was also slowed by bad
weather, rough terrain, and stiffening German resistance. After the
British conducted a successful amphibious operation at Termoli on
October 2 and 3, hopes were raised that a similar, larger assault south
of Rome could outflank the Gustav Line, facilitating a breakthrough
in the south that would cut the German lines of retreat, supply, and
communications.

On November 8, the British general Sir Harold Alexander, commander of the Fifteenth Army Group (consisting of the Fifth and
Eighth armies under Mark Clark and Bernard Law Montgomery),
directed Clark to formulate a plan for landing a single division at Anzio in an operation named Shingle as part of a three-pronged Allied
offensive with the objective of capturing Rome.

In order to devote himself fully to the planning for the invasion
of France (Operation Overlord) in the spring of 1944, General Eisen-

hower relinquished the command of the Allied forces in the Mediterranean to General Sir Henry M. Wilson in early January. Influenced by Prime Minister Churchill's desire to see Rome fall into Allied hands quickly, the British Chiefs of Staff decided that the key to the success of this strategy required a landing behind the Gustav Line.

"Anzio was selected," Laurie noted, "because it was considered the best site within striking distance of Rome but still within range of Allied aircraft operating from Naples."

Behind a beachhead that would be fifteen miles wide by seven miles deep, the terrain at Anzio consisted of rolling, often wooded farm country on a narrow coastal plain extending north from the town of Terracina to beyond the Tiber River. The entire region was part of an elaborate reclamation and resettlement project that had been undertaken by Mussolini to showcase Fascist agricultural improvements and was studded with water-pumping stations and farmhouses and crisscrossed by irrigation ditches and canals.

Twenty miles inland from Anzio on the approach to Rome were the Alban Hills. On their southwest side ran a major north-south route, Highway 7. To the southeast was the Velletri Gap, leading inland to Highway 6 at Valmontone. East of the Velletri Gap were the Lepini Mountains, along whose southeastern edge ran the Pontine Marshes extending to Terracina.

The proposed beachhead was bounded in the north by the Moletta and Incastro rivers, in the center by open fields leading to the villages of Padiglione and Aprilia along the Anzio-to-Albano road, and in the south by the villages of Cisterna di Littoria, a provincial capital, and the Mussolini Canal. The operations at Anzio were to be supported by a Fifteenth Army Group offensive. One week before the assault, the Fifth Army, consisting of the U.S. Second Corps, the British Tenth Corps, and the French Expeditionary Corps, would launch an offensive on the Gustav Line, cross the Garigliano and Rapido rivers, strike the German Tenth Army in the area of Cassino, breach

the enemy line, push up the Liri Valley, and link up with the forces at
Anzio for the drive on Rome. Meanwhile, Allied, British, and Com-
monwealth forces of the Eighth Army were ordered to break through
on the Adriatic front or at least tie down German forces to prevent
their transfer to the Anzio area.

General Clark designated Major General John P. Lucas, commander of the Fifth Army's Sixth Corps, to lead the invasion. They
were to first divert enemy strength from the south and then prepare
defensive positions. The second portion of Lucas's orders directed him
to move toward the Alban Hills and points east for the linkup with
the remainder of the Fifth Army on D-day plus seven. The date for
the invasion was to be January 22.

After a conference, with General Alexander presiding, on January
9, with staff members of the Fifteenth Army Group, the Fifth Army,
and the Sixth Corps in attendance, Lucas had doubts about the plan.
He confided to his diary, "Apparently Shingle has become the most
important operation in the present scheme of things. Sir Harold
started the conference by stating that the operation would take place
on January 22 with the troops as scheduled and that there would
be no more discussion of these points. He quoted Mr. Churchill
as saying, 'It will astonish the world,' and added, 'It will certainly
frighten Kesselring.' I felt like a lamb being led to the slaughter but
thought I was entitled to one bleat so I registered a protest against
the target date as it gave me too little time for rehearsal. This is vital
to the success of anything as terribly complicated as this. I was ruled
down, as I knew I would be, many reasons being advanced as to the
necessity for this speed. The real reasons cannot be military. I have
the bare minimum of ships and craft. The ones that are sunk cannot
be replaced. The force that can be gotten ashore in a hurry is weak
and I haven't sufficient artillery to hold me over but, on the other
hand, I will have more air support than any similar operation ever
had before."

Following the conference Alexander told Lucas, "We have every confidence in you. That is why you were picked."

For the initial assault Clark selected a combined Anglo-American force then gathering in Naples. Because the Allies wanted to land the largest possible contingent that the number of amphibious assault shipping allowed, the invasion force consisted of the U.S. Third Infantry Division; the British First Infantry Division and Forty-sixth Royal Tank Regiment; the U.S. 751st Tank Battalion, the 504th Parachute Infantry Regiment of the 82nd Airborne Division, and the 509th Parachute Infantry Battalion; two British Commando battalions; and Darby's Rangers.

Although the plan, Field Order Nineteen, was published on January 15 and called for the First, Third, and Fourth battalions to land at 0200 on a beach designated "Yellow," Darby and his officers had been alerted to the prospects of making an amphibious assault while they were still fighting at Venafro. Viewing the Anzio landing as "an end run," Darby decided that the Rangers' part of the operation was "simple and similar to those which had gone before" and "not a big chunk of enemy territory to bite off." Satisfied that his men were sufficiently rested after the Christmas respite, and with replacements for those he'd lost at Venafro, he commenced a period of intense training to prepare them for an assault similar to Arzew and Gela, in which they would land directly in front of Anzio, burst into the town, and sweep out to occupy a half moon of beachhead.

The site for rehearsals on the night of January 17, in conjunction with the Third Infantry Division and the U.S. Navy, was a beach just west of Naples at the ancient maritime town of Pozzuoli. To move, protect, and assist the assault forces, the planners assembled a naval flotilla from six nations. Called Task Force Eighty-one, it was commanded by U.S. Rear Admiral Frank Lowry and contained more than 250 combat-loaded vessels and amphibious assault craft of all sizes and descriptions, including 74 vessels of Task Force X-Ray, assigned to get American forces safely ashore and support the beachhead operations. To ensure that everything would go well between sailors and Rangers, Darby invited the naval officers to a meal. He recalled, "We ate in my mess and got to know each other by the first name and had dinner together and a drink or two."

When Darby described their difficulties with guide craft at Gela, the naval officer, a Captain Lewis, pledged, "This time you are going to have the guide boats there. I will have a man sitting off the end of the dock waving you in."

Because of a shortage of landing-craft production in the United States to meet the needs of both the Anzio landing and the preparations for Operation Overlord, Darby learned that there would not be enough boats to float his entire force ashore at the same time and that the mortar battalion would have to come in on a later landing. He wrote, "That's a tricky thing in war. It is all right to turn for supplies and supporting troops, but it is a comforting thing to have the initial assault troops all afloat at the same time. We had to take a chance that we would not need artillery support during the initial phase of the battle."

His plan called for the Ranger Force landing two battalions abreast. The First would be on the left and the Fourth on the right, with boats returning to bring ashore in following waves the Third Battalion, the mortar battalion, the 509th Parachute Infantry Battalion, the Thirty-sixth Engineer Combat Regiment, and a detachment of the 163rd Signal Photography Company. The objectives would be seizing the port and protecting it from sabotage, destruction of defensive batteries, clearing the beach area between Anzio and Nettuno, and making contact with the First Infantry Division on the left, the Third Infantry on the right, and the 504th Parachute Infantry Regiment in the north.

The Ranger Force would then be attached to the Third Infantry Division and under command of the officer who since the founding of the Rangers in 1942 had been their godfather figure, General Lucian Truscott.

Darby depicted Anzio as strung out along the coast and running down to a harbor at the end of a peninsula. The built-up portion of the town was barely more than two blocks wide. A railroad ran through a cut with several overpasses and footbridges that paralleled the road to Rome. Less than a mile south of Anzio was Nettuno. Between them stood the estate of a scion of the aristocratic Borghese family, which included Pope Paul V, a husband of the sister of Napoleon (Pauline), and the bold young organizer of a famous 1907 automobile race from China via the Gobi Desert to Paris and later a daring commander of a submarine force in the Italian navy. The home of Prince Borghese had sheer cliffs that dropped down to a sea littered with rocks. South of the harbor and directly in front of Anzio lay a beach about forty yards deep and covered with rough sand. Designated "Yellow Beach," it was backed by a seawall that varied from three to six feet in height and was flanked by jetties. At the center of the beach stood a large white casino that Darby described as "showy." He told Captain Lewis that when he ran out of the landing craft, "I'll be going so fast that I want to make sure that when I hit the beach and start running, that I will run right through the front door."

When the Rangers assembled on the docks of Baia on Pozzuoli Bay, north of Naples, on January 20, James Altieri and the veterans of Arzew found that among the three ships that were to transport them to Anzio was the ex–Glasgow ferryboat—HMS *Royal Ulsterman*—that had taken them to North Africa. Darby considered this "an omen of good fortune." Anchored with it were the *Princess Beatrix*, the *Winchester Castle*, and LCTs (landing craft, tanks) 410 and 542. The flotilla also consisted of craft fitted with rocket launchers and DUKWs. Called "ducks" and "swimming trucks," they were landing boats equipped with wheels that became trucks on land and were armed with either 4.2-inch mortars or 57mm antitank guns. The loading of men was done, Darby noted, "with an old familiarity."

Having learned in the Sorrento landing operation the importance of taking along extra supplies, the Rangers stowed every corner of the ships and boats with bandoliers of rifle ammunition, grenades, and mortar shells. The armada slipped out of Pozzuoli Bay at midnight, January 21, 1944. Unnoticed by the enemy during the voyage, the ships arrived off Anzio twenty-four hours later.

Called Task Force Peter, the fifty-two ships were under command of Admiral Thomas H. Troubridge, Royal Navy. To obtain surprise, the Allied planners had decided to dispense with a long preliminary naval bombardment and employ a short and intense ten-minute barrage by two British assault vessels equipped with fifteen hundred five-inch rockets.

Darby observed as LCAs swung on davits and were lowered into the sea to be boarded by his troops. When the men were aboard, the boats churned around in darkness, awaiting the arrival of guide boats. Of the Anzio landings, he wrote, "We were under way quickly with the two LCIs moving forward with us for about one mile. Ashore, lights weaved in and out, evidently those of automobiles following the main road. After picking up the first guide light [of the escort craft], the first wave of the Rangers continued ahead toward the next light. Then we spied the Anzio pier and, near it, a guide boat bobbing up and down. Its crew waved the Rangers to shore."

About ten minutes before the Rangers hit the sand at Anzio, a ship loaded with hundreds of rockets the size of six-inch shells was supposed to fire for one single minute. On the way in, the whoosh of rockets on the Third Division beaches could be heard, but for some reason the Rangers' rocket ship failed to follow suit. The Rangers held their breath while they were off the pier at Anzio, wondering why their ship had not fired. When the first group touched land at 0200 in an unopposed landing, they were exactly on schedule. In Ranger style, the troops ran aggressively across the beach, moving inland to gain their initial beachhead, where they could reorganize.

183

When Darby hit the beach, he found his expectation that Captain Lewis's guides would take him to the front door of the casino had been met within a few feet. Although he had worried about the lack of rocket fire, he found that the failure had assisted in making the landing a complete surprise. Recording that two Germans who appeared on the beach to challenge the Rangers were shot quickly, Darby noted with relief, "We met no further resistance until we were in the center of Anzio."

As the Rangers surged into the town, engineer detachments cleared the beach of mines and disposed of demolition charges the Germans had placed on the pier. A delighted General Lucas wrote in his diary, "I sent the Rangers in on Yellow Beach to save that harbor. Everything was prepared by the enemy for its demolition, great holes dug in the mole and in the sides of all the buildings, all filled with explosives, but they had time to blow very few of them."

James Altieri reported, "Storming ashore on the cold, black night of January 22, 1944, the three Ranger battalions made a perfect, silent landing directly in the harbor at Anzio. Surprisingly, the enemy was caught completely off guard. Within three hours the entire port of Anzio was secured as Rangers struck out to enlarge the beachhead. Three armored cars, two machine-gun nests and a battery of 100-millimeter coast guns were bagged and forty Germans killed. The landing was the most successful in Ranger history."

Allied air forces flew twelve hundred sorties against targets in and around the beachhead. On the beach itself, the U.S. Thirty-sixth Engineer Combat Regiment bulldozed exits, laid corduroy roads, cleared mines, and readied the port to receive its first amphibious assault boat and a supply ship.

Setting up his headquarters in the casino, Darby established communications with the *Ulster Monarch* to keep apprised of the unloading of equipment and supplies and the activities of his men. By 0700 the entire Ranger Force was ashore and the First, Third, and Fourth

Photo courtesy of U.S. Army Signal Corps

Less than a month after being decorated for heroism by the British in northern Italy in April 1945, Colonel William O. Darby was hit in the chest by shrapnel from an artillery round fired by retreating Germans, and died just days before VE Day.

Rangers trained on the "bullet and bayonet" course at the British Commando Depot in Achnacarry, Scotland, in April 1942.

In the early stages of training, Rangers wore helmets and used rifles dating back to World War I. They were trained by veteran Commandos of Britain's Special Services Brigade.

Photo courtesy of U.S. Army Signal Corps

Rangers, coached by Commandos in the techniques of "unarmed combat," learned how to silently attack and kill enemy sentries.

Photo courtesy of U.S. Army Signal Corps

Observing as a Commando shows Americans how to take down an enemy are Brigadier General Lucian K. Truscott, Jr. (in riding boots), and Colonel William O. Darby (second from Truscott's left). Truscott was chosen by U.S. Army chief of staff George C. Marshall to set up an American-style Commando unit that Truscott named Rangers and Darby led in combat from 1942 to 1944.

Photo courtesy of U.S. Army Signal Corps

Training at the Commando Depot in Scotland was based on the British "me and my pal" policy of the Commandos, in which the soldiers ran obstacle courses in pairs.

Photo courtesy of U.S. Army Signal Corps

Teams of Rangers lifted and tossed logs in a training exercise adapted from an ancient Scottish sport.

Darby required every Ranger officer to take Commando training. In this cliff-climbing exercise, it's chief medical officer First Lieutenant William Jarrett, formerly a surgeon at Columbia University Medical School.

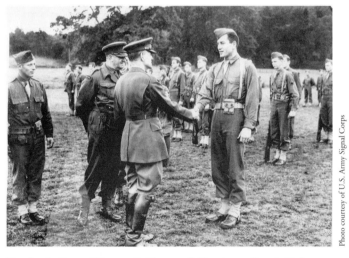

Ex–football star Warren E. Evans of Aberdeen, South Dakota, is welcomed to the Rangers by Brigadier General Lucian K. Truscott, Jr., in August 1942. With a professional-style singing voice, Evans was nicknamed Bing after Bing Crosby. To Truscott's left stands Colonel Charles Vaughan, commander of Britain's Special Services Brigade (Commandos) and designer of the Rangers' training course in Scotland. Sergeant Evans later received a battlefield commission in North Africa.

Photo courtesy of U.S. Army Signal Corps

Rehearsing invasion techniques in Scotland, Rangers practiced "opposed landings" from small boats while British Commandos sprayed machine-gun fire over their heads.

Photo courtesy of U.S. Army Signal Corps

Rangers got a preview of combat as they dashed onto a beach in Scotland while under fire from British artillery. One Ranger commented on the realism by exclaiming, "I think those damned Brits are actually trying to kill us!"

Two months after leading Rangers in capturing the port of Arzew in Algeria in French North Africa, Lieutenant Colonel Darby joined his troops on the pacified beach in a "speed march," which was the keystone of Ranger training.

Photo courtesy of U.S. Army Signal Corps

Resting with the men of the First Ranger Battalion after chow on the beach at Arzew on December 12, 1942, Darby was soon to be in command of two more battalions (3rd and 4th) for the invasions of Sicily and Italy.

While on road march in Arzew, Rangers were amused to be passing a French warehouse for tents, ropes, and camping gear.

With machine guns shouldered, Corporal Chester Fisher of Clinton, Iowa, and PFC Edward T. Calhoun of Campbellsville, Kentucky, step off in a speed march at Arzew.

In taking Arzew, the Rangers took out two French artillery forts and captured the port of Arzew's industrial sites.

By taking Arzew, the Rangers secured the waterfront so the docks could be used to land reinforcements and equipment.

Although the government of French North Africa was allied with Germany, the French forces at Arzew put up only token resistance to "save their honor." The native people, such as this local man passing marching Rangers on his way to market, welcomed Americans as liberators.

Photo courtesy of U.S. Army Signal Corps

While sailing to North Africa on Irish ferryboats that were converted to troopships, the Rangers practiced loading into landing craft for the invasion.

Photo courtesy of U.S. Army Signal Corps

On November 8, 1942, the First Ranger Battalion boarded landing craft to assault the port of Arzew in two places, knock out coast-artillery fortifications, and clear the way for the full invasion force.

After a nighttime attack on a French coastal-artillery site called Batterie du Nord, Companies C, D, E, and F under Colonel Darby silenced the big guns while Companies A and B under Major Herman Dammer captured a second gun emplacement and the port of Arzew.

After finding a suspicious-looking building in Arzew, Rangers used techniques learned in training in Scotland to kick open the door and prepare to toss in hand grenades.

Photo courtesy of U.S. Army Signal Corps

To keep in touch with his troops, Darby used a motorcycle, which became as identified with him as ivory-grip pistols were with General George S. Patton and a long-stemmed corncob pipe with General Douglas MacArthur.

After a skirmish in the Santa Maria sector in Italy on January 16, 1944, Rangers medical corpsman Sergeant Thomas Prudhomme of Natchez, Louisiana, treats 3rd Ranger Battalion PFC John Brady of Fairmount, Virginia, for a leg wound.

Rangers boarded landing craft near Naples, Italy, for an invasion at Anzio. During an attack on the nearby town of Cisterna on January 30, 1944, the three Ranger battalions were trapped in a huge German counterattack. The battalions were virtually destroyed and more than seven hundred Rangers were taken prisoner.

On a return visit to his hometown of Fort Smith, Arkansas, in April 1944, Colonel William Orlando Darby was given a hero's welcome with a parade, a ceremony on the steps of the courthouse, and the "Outstanding Young Man of the Year" award, presented by Fort Smith's Junior Chamber of Commerce president V. O. Reeves, Jr. Almost exactly one year later, Darby was commander of the 179th Infantry, 45th Division, and killed in action in northern Italy.

Darby's boyhood home in Fort Smith has been preserved as a museum with everything inside maintained as it was on the day his parents were informed he had been killed.

Promoted to brigadier general by President Truman after his death, Darby is buried at Fort Smith National Cemetery.

battalions had reached and were holding their objectives. At 0815 he ordered the 509th Parachute Infantry Battalion to advance on Nettuno. Less than an hour later, they had moved two-thirds of the way. At 1015, the town was in their hands and the Rangers' right flank was secured.

By midnight, the Sixth Corps had landed 36,000 men and 3,200 vehicles while capturing 227 Germans at a cost of 13 killed, 97 wounded, and 44 missing. The British First Division had landed north of Anzio and taken control of a strategic road. The U.S. Third Infantry Division had come ashore to the south and occupied the territory beyond the Mussolini Canal. The invasion had been so successful, and resistance so slight, that even Lieutenant Altieri believed that the way to Rome was wide open. "But Rome wasn't included in our battle plan," he recalled. "Our mission was to establish the beachhead with the British Tenth Corps on our left and the Truscott-led Third Division on our right and then hold."

Informed of the landings an hour after they began and surmising their objective, Field Marshal Kesselring responded by ordering the Fourth Parachute Division to move from Rome and directed the Hermann Goering Panzer Division to block roads between Anzio and the Alban Hills. Additional forces were drawn from the Gustav Line, northern Italy, France, Germany, and Yugoslavia. The result of these actions was that when the commander of the Fourteenth Army, Generaloberst Eberhard von Mackensen, took over German forces at Anzio, he had elements of eight divisions deployed and five more on the way. His orders were not to defend but to attack.

Military historians have written volumes analyzing the decisions and errors of the American commanders at Anzio, particularly of General Lucas's failure to exploit the success of the invasion. James Altieri encapsulated the result in this paragraph in *The Spearheaders*: "Within seven days, while we were digging in and strengthening our beachhead forward lines, the Germans had ringed our seven-by-eleven-mile toehold with major elements of ten divisions. Some were flown in by air from Yugoslavia, some moved in by train from northern Italy and others wheeled in from nearby reserve concentration points. Without withdrawing from their [forces holding the Gustav Line at Cassino], the Germans contained the [Anzio] beachhead with a ring of steel."

To Darby, the territory held by his Rangers resembled a billiard table. Calling the area "uncommonly flat and bare for some distance inland," he depicted roads flanked by little groups of houses of stucco or stone construction. Fifteen miles inland lay the Naples-to-Rome road—the historic Appian Way—and the Colli Laziali mountain ridge of the Alban Hills backed by other ranges that rose two to four thousand feet. Entrenched in these heights, the Germans were able to observe, Darby noted, every move of the Rangers in the plain, and their dug-in artillery "fired downhill against our foxholes, seeming to look into every one of them."

Accustomed to the reverse, in which his Rangers were positioned on the high ground, he could only observe with frustration as enemy patrols "scurried around" while others laid mines under the cover of artillery from the hills. When he received a report on the night of January 24 of German paratroops dropping in the Rangers' sector, he mounted his motorcycle, raced to the location, and found that the parachutists were the crew of a German plane that had been shot down. Returning to his command post, he learned that a landing craft carrying Companies C and D of the Eighty-third Chemical [mortar] Battalion had hit a mine and blown up and that when survivors were transferred to another ship, it also struck a mine. The death toll was almost three hundred.

Now operating with the Third Division, the Rangers were under Truscott's command and Darby had orders to protect the left flank of the British First Division in an attack on the town of Carroceto at daylight on January 25. He gave the assignment to the Fourth Battalion, the 509th Paratroop Battalion, and a mortar unit, with the First and Third held in reserve in a pine woods several miles to the rear. From positions in a network of drainage ditches near the Padiglione Woods about nine miles inland from Anzio, they launched an attack and threw back a counterthrust. Although Truscott recommended an all-out attack by the Third Division to seize the strategically important town and road junction of Cisterna di Littoria, General Lucas chose to wait until the arrival onshore at Anzio of armored units. Meanwhile, the port and the beachhead came under almost constant attack by German planes and artillery fire.

Noting that between January 25 and 28 the Rangers held their ground near Carroceto, Altieri wrote that heavy fighting raged day and night. While the Germans launched probing attacks trying to push through Ranger positions, the Rangers sent out night patrols to raid and harass the enemy.

Describing one of these, Darby wrote, "A group led by Sergeant Egan crawled toward one of the farmhouses carrying light machine guns and 60mm infantry mortars. Machine pistol and gunfire caught several of his men, but the patrol—whittled down to four men—took the house. Under cover of the fire of the group's weapons, a Ranger ran forward to the shadow of the roof, where he faded against the walls. Cautiously he threw grenades in the windows and door to clear the building."

With German resistance getting stronger, and a German counterattack against the British at Carroceto spilling over into the Fourth Ranger Battalion's area, the Rangers held firm on a line of resistance that included mines and barbed wire between there and the town and Padiglione. As the Rangers moved forward in a skirmish line at dawn on January 27 to a road running eastward from Carroceto, the Germans fired from foxholes and houses and German artillery shelled the British from a factory area. In an attack by the Third and Fourth

Ranger battalions and the 509th Paratroopers against a strongly defended road junction, with Germans in thick-walled stone houses, Lieutenant Randall Harris and executive officer Howard Andre led their F Company in a charge. Met by fierce fire, Andre was killed and Harris was seriously wounded, for the third time. By noon, the objective had been achieved.

With Harris evacuated to a hospital ship, James Altieri found himself in command of F Company. Recording that Andre had been at Dieppe and in every Ranger action since, and that he was killed less than a month after having received his field commission, Altieri wrote, "The inexorable law of averages was catching up with the old Rangers."

The Ranger front ran along a dirt road from Carroceto to the small town of Spaccasassi, with an outpost line of Third and Fourth battalion patrols placed forward to warn of enemy attacks. To the rear was the First Battalion, forming a line of resistance among drainage ditches. Recording that between that line and the Anzio beach there were about seven to ten miles of flat countryside, Darby wrote, "That was to be the extent of the Anzio beachhead for the following four months."

On the afternoon of January 28, Darby was informed by Third Division headquarters that the Rangers were to be relieved during the night by the British First Reconnaissance Regiment and moved south and east behind the Third Division front. As the Rangers said farewell to their comrades in the 509th Parachute Battalion, picked up all the equipment that could be carried by marching men, and swung into the Ranger stride toward an assembly point at Nettuno, Darby contemplated the status of the Anzio invasion. "As veteran soldiers," he wrote, "we knew that the situation in the beachhead wasn't duck soup. Enemy resistance was developing according to pattern, and their artillery was sticking airbursts where they wanted them above the billiard-table battle area. Enemy patrols were increasing their activity. They also were appearing in the houses near the front line and were operating a considerable number of armored vehicles on the roads northeast of Carroceto."

With his Rangers ordered to move, Darby concluded, "Something was cooking."

★ CHAPTER 14 ★

DOWN OUR ALLEY

"Jerryland."

FOR MORE THAN TWO YEARS, THE AMERICAN PEOPLE HAD FOUND heartening stories in their newspapers, on radio, and in the newsreels of how the United States had rebounded from a series of defeats since December 7, 1941, to gain a string of victories on the battlefronts of the Pacific, against German submarines in the Atlantic, and in the Mediterranean theater. They had learned a wartime geography and military jargon to speak with the authority of generals. They discussed U-boats, destroyers, aircraft carriers, P-40 fighter planes, B-17 heavy bombers, and Mitchell B-25s, like those flown by Colonel Jimmy

Doolittle's raiders, who bombed Tokyo in payback for Pearl Harbor. They talked of George Patton, Ike, General MacArthur, Admiral Bull Halsey, FDR, and Churchill as if they were next-door neighbors. Through accounts by war correspondents on radio and stories in the daily papers by reporters such as Ernie Pyle, in Movietone and Pathe newsreels, and through photographs taken by combat cameramen such as Phil Stern, mothers, fathers, wives, brothers, and sisters of GIs, marines, sailors, and airmen had been carried closer to the reality of war than at any time in history. They were able to proudly reel off details of triumphs in faraway places named Guadalcanal, New Guinea, the Solomons, Arzew, El Guettar, Gela, Palermo, Messina, and Salerno.

Then, suddenly and alarmingly in late January 1944, things had gone terribly wrong at a place somewhere in Italy.

"Few geographical names relating to military operations in World War II became known to more people than the name 'Anzio,' and few operations in World War II have become more controversial," wrote Lieutenant General Lucian K. Truscott a decade later in *Command Missions*.

For more than sixty years, historians have been searching for the answers to the questions asked in late January 1944 by puzzled and worried Americans: What went wrong at Anzio? Why had a surprise invasion that seemed to have caught the Germans flatfooted abruptly stalled? When would the Allies break out from the beachhead, drive inland, and sweep north to Rome?

The historian Robert W. Black noted in *Rangers in World War II* that while General Lucas "has been much criticized for being overly cautious and slow in moving inland from the beaches of Anzio," both his seniors, Alexander and Clark, "visited Anzio after the troops were onshore, and neither general expressed dissatisfaction," leaving Lucas "under the impression his [force] dispositions were approved."

Michael D. Hull wrote in "Rangers' Rendezvous with Destiny," in the magazine *WWII History* (July 2004), that Lucas was "a cautious officer, more interested in putting the harbor into operation and building up strength than in breaking out and mounting an offensive."

In *William Orlando Darby: A Military History*, Michael J. King cited Lucas's "timidity" and hesitation in making a "decisive thrust inland" that left the Germans to "gather strength."

Darby stated his belief that "if everyone had moved forward" from their positions after the invasion "instead of taking their time to regroup," a drive inland would have been successful.

Truscott opined, "I suppose that armchair strategists will always labor under the delusion that there was a 'fleeting opportunity' at Anzio during which some Napoleonic figure would have charged over the Colli Laziali [Alban Hills], played havoc with the German line of communications, and galloped on into Rome. Any such concept betrays lack of comprehension of the military problem involved. It was necessary to occupy the [Sixth] Corps Beachhead line to prevent the enemy from interfering with the beaches. Otherwise, enemy artillery and armored detachments, operating against the flanks, could have cut us off from the beach and prevented the unloading of troops, supplies, and equipment."

Under such conditions, Truscott explained, "any reckless drive [inland] with means then available in the beachhead could only have ended in disaster and might well have resulted in destruction of the entire force."

In a thesis titled *The Ranger Force at the Battle of Cisterna*, presented to the faculty of the U.S. Command and General Staff College at Fort Leavenworth, Kansas, in 2004, Major Jeff R. Stewart proposed an analysis that was not only sympathetic to Lucas but appreciative of the "tenacity" of the Germans to stop the Allied breakout. He wrote:

> After the successful Allied invasion of Salerno, the
> German High Command decided to make the Allies

pay for every inch of European soil. Field Marshal Albert Kesselring took command of Army Group C in November 1943 and immediately demonstrated his determination to defend as far forward as possible. Army Group C was composed of the German Tenth Army, with nine divisions, charged with the defense of the southern portion of the Italian peninsula while the Fourteenth Army, with nine divisions which were not at full strength, occupied the north.

The invading Allies consisted of the Fifteenth Army Group under Alexander, which was split in two sectors, with the U.S. Fifth Army attacking in the west and the British Eighth Army attacking in the east. After the Salerno invasion, the going had proved slow. Brutal weather, unforgiving terrain, and German tenacity impeded the Allied advance until it stalled at the Gustav Line, resulting in bloody battles and leaving the Rangers holding out alone for weeks. To break this stalemate, the Allies conceived the amphibious end run by means of the landing at Anzio-Nettuno on January 22, 1944, by the Sixth Corps, led by the Rangers. With the beachhead secured, Lucas chose to solidify his strength in preparation for an offensive.

Since D-day at Anzio, the Allies had off-loaded twenty-one cargo ships and landed 6,350 tons of matériel. On February 1, the port was in full operation. The air defenses had downed ninety-seven attacking Luftwaffe aircraft, but the Germans had succeeded in sinking one destroyer and a hospital ship, as well as destroying significant stocks of supplies piled on beaches. Mindful of the need for reinforcements, Lucas ordered ashore the last of the Forty-fifth Infantry Division and the final portions of the First Armored Division allotted to the operation, raising the total of Allied soldiers on the beachhead to 61,332.

Noting that the German commanders reacted to the delay in the Allied attack "skillfully and swiftly," Stewart's analysis continued:

They diverted the northern sector's reserve to the Anzio area and immediately began preparations to stabilize the southern front while planning a counterattack to throw the Allied landing force into the sea. The Germans used their peculiar ability to cobble effective combat groups out of disparate units to begin building an effective defense to blunt Allied expansion from the beachhead. They encircled the beachhead with a series of interlocked defensive strong points concentrated on villages and farmhouses. Effective use was made of surviving structures, irrigation ditches, and railroad embankments to establish interlocking defenses and "kill zones" upon the open plains.

In making these preparations, the Germans gave particular attention to the buildup of key areas a few miles inland from Anzio, including the villages of Campoleone and a small but important railroad center named Cisterna di Littoria. Passing through the village was Highway 7. Famous in Roman history as the Appian Way, it ran northeast to Velletri at the foothills of the Colli Laziali (Alban Hills) and on to Rome. Darby's Rangers named the area "Jerryland."

Confident that Cisterna could be taken "if arrangements were made to employ the whole [Third Division]," Truscott proposed to Lucas on January 26, 1944, that the 179th Regimental Combat Team and elements of the Fourth Infantry Division be used to release the Fourth for an all-out attack, after which the Fourth would resume defense and the First would seize the town of Campoleone. But, according to Truscott, Lucas "was not yet ready."

Under pressure from Alexander, whose British forces were engaged in a bloody fight at Cassino, and an increasingly impatient Clark, Lucas met with Truscott and other commanders to plan a two-pronged attack on Cisterna and Campoleone by the British First Infantry Division, and the newly arrived American Combat Command A (under Major General E. N. Harmon), the U.S. First Armored Division, Truscott's Third Division, and the Rangers.

The First, Third, and Fourth battalions arrived at a staging area near the town of San Antonio after an all-night march on January 29. Darby called his officers together and revealed hastily drawn-up battle plans. Close to their right, two miles away, lay the Mussolini Canal, running along the west side of the Pontine Marshes, with Nettuno and Anzio to their left rear and barely visible in the distance. Directly north beyond Cisterna were the first ridges of Colli Laziali, which for Darby evoked memories of the bloody mountains of Venafro. During the day, the Rangers "lay at ease in our bivouac," Darby recalled, "cleaning our bayonets and knives and inspecting our rifles and automatic weapons." While the men shaved beards and got haircuts, Darby and his officers studied the plan of attack. They discussed how to infiltrate enemy lines, get into Cisterna and occupy it, "capturing or killing any enemy," while awaiting reinforcements from the Third Division late in the afternoon of January 30.

Of the opposition, Truscott recalled, the Hermann Goering Panzer Division facing the Third Infantry Division was extended over a wide front that it held with organized strongpoints supported by mobile armored detachments. He and Darby believed two of the Ranger battalions could "infiltrate between these strongpoints under cover of darkness and enter the town of Cisterna. Trained for such night infiltration and for street fighting, they could be expected to cause much confusion in the German lines."

Altieri recalled that the First and Third battalions were assigned "the daring mission" of infiltrating the enemy forward lines at night by marching six miles and storming the town by dawn. They were to "bypass all enemy forces en route to their objective." Sentries and outpost guards were to be killed "noiselessly by knife or bayonet."

If the First Battalion met resistance, it was to "creep off toward the objective" and the Third was to engage. Altieri's Fourth Battalion was to follow an hour later and clear the main road to Cisterna for a rush by reinforcements, with the Fifteenth Infantry Regiment and Third Division following.

In the overall scheme, the First and Third Ranger battalions were to spearhead the assault by infiltrating the German lines and seizing and holding Cisterna until the Fourth Rangers and Fifteenth Infantry, Third Division, arrived via the Conca-Cisterna road. At 0200 on January 30, the Seventh Infantry, Third Division, was to push on the left flank to a point above Cisterna and cut Highway 7. The Fifteenth Infantry would pass to the right of Cisterna and cut the highway south of town. As a diversion, the 504th Parachute Infantry would attack along the Mussolini Canal.

Darby noted that intelligence sources (G2) reported that the Germans showed no intent to counterattack and no signs of enemy concentrations had been observed. A January 29 report had stated, "The enemy's attitude on our front is entirely defensive." It described the fighting quality of the non-German troops that had been rushed from outside Italy after the Salerno invasion as poor and German positions at Cisterna as an "outpost line of resistance" (OPR). The main line of resistance (MLR), it stated, "will undoubtedly be found on the high ground" east and west of Velletri, about five miles beyond Cisterna. Declaring the enemy's immediate situation with respect to tanks and artillery "not good," the estimate stated that the mission of the reserves "is to prepare and man defenses on the MLR rather than to be used in a counterattack."

For these reasons, the intelligence survey concluded, "our own actions, if carried through with particular vigor and firmness, whether in attacking or defending, may enable us to attain success which would not have been possible against old-type, all-German formations."

This estimate of the German unreadiness on the eve of the Cisterna-

Campoleone attack appeared to validate a Fifth Army G2 estimate of January 16, prior to the Anzio landings, that confidently stated:

> Within the past few days there have been increasing indications that enemy strength on the front of the Fifth Army is ebbing due to casualties, exhaustion, and possibly lowering of morale. One of the causes of this condition, no doubt, has been the recent, continuous Allied attacks. From this it can be deduced that he has no fresh reserves and very few tired ones. His entire strength will probably be needed to defend his organized defensive positions.
>
> In view of the weakening of enemy strength on the front as indicated above, it would appear doubtful if the enemy can hold the organized defensive line through Cassino against a coordinated enemy attack. Since this attack [by the Allies breaking out from Salerno] is to be launched before Shingle [the Anzio invasion] it is considered likely that this additional threat will cause him to withdraw from his defensive position once he has appreciated the magnitude of that operation.

Based on these estimates, the offensive against Cisterna-Campoleone designed at the meeting of commanders on January 29 assigned the Seventh Infantry Regiment a zone of attack to the west with a final objective astride Highway 7 northeast of Cisterna. The Fifteenth Infantry Regiment would have a similar attack zone to the east, with Highway 7 as its objective. Both were to infiltrate an infantry battalion at 0200 hours followed by armor and infantry attacks prior to dawn. The Thirtieth Infantry Regiment was to hold the line and act as reserve.

In the center, the Ranger Force was to take Cisterna. Truscott's field order, dated January 28, required crossing the line of departure at 0100 on January 30, moving out rapidly to infiltrate Cisterna, seizing and holding it until relieved. At a meeting at 1800 on January 29, Darby and Dammer studied the field order and issued their own force order. Darby again described the area as resembling "a billiard table," but "crisscrossed by roads, streams, and canals." In the plan, the Fourth Battalion was to move up a secondary road bearing northwest toward Cisterna. Farther to the east was a similar road approaching Cisterna with a slight inclination to the west. The Rangers were to operate in this triangle, with the Fourth Battalion moving through the villages of Femina Morta and Isola Bella. To the right, the First and Third battalions were to infiltrate the area between the roads. The First was under the command of Major Jack Dobson. The Third was led by Major Alvah Miller. The Fourth's leader was Colonel Roy Murray.

"The mission of our battalion—the Fourth," recalled Lieutenant James Altieri, "was to follow an hour later and clear the main road leading to Cisterna so that reinforcements could be rushed into the town to assist the First and Third. The Fifteenth Infantry Regiment of the Third Division was to follow us. At dawn, the famous hard-hitting 504th Parachute Regiment was to support our drive with a furious attack on the right. The Seventh Infantry Regiment was to attack on the left, and link up with the Ranger Force in Cisterna."

Although there are no indications in Darby's accounts of the preparations for the attack that he had reservations about its efficacy, Robert W. Black's chronicle of the hours prior to the operation cites observers who discerned that Darby "was not in favor of the plan." His driver, Carlo Contrera, is quoted as having told friends later that Darby was angry at the orders and remarked, "The men are too tired for another raid." According to Black in *Rangers in World War II*, a communications officer of the Fourth Battalion told fellow Rangers that he had heard Darby asking for more time to conduct reconnaissance. Another Ranger reportedly heard Darby say, "It's not my plan." But Michael J. King in *William Orlando Darby: A Military Biography* attributes to Colonel William S. Hutchinson, Jr., an account of Darby stating that the mission was acceptable to Darby, "who did not believe that an attack the size of that about to be mounted could fail." Darby wrote of the Rangers' assignment, "The plan itself was not a usual one for my Rangers. In fact it was right down our alley and one that would have delighted the heart of Major Rogers in pre-Revolutionary days."

Concerning intelligence estimates of weaknesses in German defenses, King states that a notation in the Ranger Force's daily journal indicated a belief at Darby's headquarters that the enemy opposition at Cisterna might be "considerable." On the topic of pre-attack intelligence in *The Ranger Force at the Battle of Cisterna*, Major Jeff R. Stewart noted that in carrying out the attack plan Darby worried about using "previously reconnoitered routes" and that Darby noted, "There was no opportunity to send our [Ranger] reconnaissance patrols since we were to attack after dark on the same day" [that they arrived at the point of departure for the attack].

Although Major Dobson permitted Company A of the First Battalion the mission of patrolling for the first two miles of the infiltration route (only half of the distance to Cisterna), the unit was instructed to avoid engagement except in self-defense. The result, said Stewart, was that the Rangers "would be moving over strange terrain, during limited visibility, to conduct their attack. An infiltration under such conditions was possible, if the enemy positions were only scattered strongpoints manned by weary German units, as the intelligence summary indicated."

As always, Lieutenant James Altieri of the Fourth Ranger Division was optimistic. "It was a tough mission, but we felt confident that we could accomplish it as we had every other mission," he recalled. "We had met and defeated Germans before. We could do it again."

Toward evening on January 29, 1944, Rangers who had been lolling on pine branches in the bivouac area rolled up their barracks bags and left them in a pile in the care of cooks and truck drivers. Pockets were stuffed with hand grenades. Shoulders bore bandoliers of extra ammo. The mortar crews of the Eighty-third Chemical Battalion toted extra rounds. Ahead was a seven-mile hike that, compared to the speed marches of Scotland, seemed like a leisurely stroll.

The Italian night was just the kind the Rangers loved—cold and moonless.

★ CHAPTER 15 ★

A GOOD DEAL OF TROUBLE

"You couldn't do anything about it."

THE RANGERS COMPLETED A SEVEN-MILE MARCH FROM THEIR ASSEM-
bly area to the designated line of departure (LD) by midnight. Darby
convened a conference with his officers in a stone house at a road
junction about four miles from Cisterna. Reviewing the plan, Darby
stressed that radio silence was to be observed until the troops had
crossed a line running east through Isola Bella, less than two miles
from Cisterna. In the advance on the right of the line, the First Battalion had orders that "under no circumstances were they to stay and

fight." The Third would engage in battle only if forced to do so in order to permit the First to continue.

Because the area's network of roads and the flat terrain offered the Germans "ideal tank country," the Rangers were accompanied by a tank-destroyer outfit, their own cannon company, and the Eighty-third Chemical (mortar) Battalion. The Rangers also carried "a plentiful supply of sticky grenades" and numerous antitank rocket launchers. Darby's officers reported that the men were "in good spirits." Although the night was dark, Darby noted that the troops were "at ease" because "night operations were second nature to us." The First Battalion would cross the LD at 0100, followed by the Third at 0115.

With blackened faces and equipment muffled, the Rangers crept forward in the shadows of the banks of the west branch of the Mussolini Canal and Pantano ditch to the right side of the Conca-Cisterna road. As Corporal Ben Mosier of Ashtabula, Ohio, passed two German artillery batteries, he heard the voices of the crews. "We could have wiped them out," he reported, "but we weren't showing our hand." Sergeant Thomas Fergen of Parkston, South Dakota, related later, "We could see their sentries, but they didn't see us. We had to keep quiet."

In his headquarters with the Fourth Battalion in an isolated house near the LD to the right of the Conca-Cisterna road, and "hooked in by wire and radio with the Third Division," Darby registered that the Germans "showed no hostile intent and gave no signs that they knew we were sifting through their defenses." With the infiltration apparently off to a good start, the Fourth crossed the LD at 0200 according to the plan and advanced north along the road. Moving in an "approach march formation," the order of companies was C and D, Headquarters, A, B, E, and F. After twenty minutes, they had moved five hundred yards to the right flank and parallel to the road.

At 0248, in what the historian Michael J. King termed "the first of several events that did not augur well for the success of the mission," four radio operators who were to have accompanied the Third Battalion reported that they had gotten lost. To have key radiomen lose their way, Darby grumbled, was "the god-damnedest thing" he had ever heard of. The second problem was loss of contact with the First Battalion halfway into the operation.

At approximately 0300, Company C came under machine-gun fire from the front and deployed to the left flank while D Company shifted to the right. In the middle of it, Lieutenant James Altieri found that "out of the black night, coming from the fields on both sides of the road, machine-gun tracers suddenly magnified into a wall of flaming steel."

With "determined resistance from houses, farm buildings, and dug-in emplacements less than a half mile north of the road junction where the Ranger conference had been held," Darby recorded, this was "the first intimation that all was not well."

Rather than falling back into a defensive line in the high ground beyond Cisterna while Lucas built up his troops at Anzio, as the intelligence reports had contemplated, Kesselring had chosen to place his force on the flat terrain around Cisterna and launch a counterattack. Instead of the inexperienced soldiers G2 had forecast, he had at his disposal the best of Germany's tank and infantry forces in Italy, including the Hermann Goering Division, the Fourth Parachute Division, three divisions of the Fourteenth Army, and the 114th and 715th divisions. By January 29, 1944, German strength had reached seventy thousand. The result was that as the Rangers' infiltration mission began they faced roughly three to four times the forecast German strength and a force that was not aligned in defense, but ready to launch a massive counterattack. To support it, Kesselring had thirty-two 15-centimeter guns, forty-two 10.5-centimeter guns, and three 10-centimeter guns, plus thirty-one 2-centimeter antiaircraft guns. Placed around the approach to Cisterna were rifle pits dug at ten-yard intervals and machine-gun nests every hundred yards with interlocking fields at a height of one foot.

Having gone less than half a mile along the Conca-Cisterna road, the leading company of the Fourth Battalion responded to the German machine-gun fire with an attack that Altieri called "at close quarters with grenades and bayonets." They knocked out two machine-gun nests, but "others in depth continued firing." After two ferocious assaults that failed to penetrate the line, Lieutenant George Nunnelly and most of his C Company were killed, while the remainder were forced to hole up in a shallow ditch. Every inch of ground, Altieri recalled, "was covered by deadly grazing fire and enemy shells were now landing on the road."

When Colonel Roy Murray led an assault by A and B companies on the right flank, it was stopped by a "perfect system of crossfire" and "selected lanes of fire." Two more company commanders were killed and numerous men were badly wounded. Altieri recorded, "We had met solid, strong, determined opposition—and worse, we weren't getting ahead."

As dawn approached, the leading company of the First Ranger Battalion found itself in the middle of a German bivouac area. The Rangers fired Tommy guns at point-blank range and attacked with bayonets. Attached to the Headquarters Company and carrying demolitions, Carl Lehmann remembered the camp with "no tents, just men lying under blankets." He saw astonished Germans "rising all around, running away with hands in the air" and crying *Kamarad* while he ran through them, "shooting from the hip." By the time he'd expended the clip from his M1, he had run completely through the camp and reached a shallow hedgerow parallel to a ditch. At this point he heard the "clatter" of a German motorized artillery piece and saw it on a low ridge about a hundred yards to his left.

Although Lehmann did not know it at the time, the weapon, known as a "flak wagon," was part of the newly arrived Second Parachute *Lehr* Battalion (a unit regularly used to reinforce a threatened sector at the front) and was equipped with the *Nebelwerfer*. Developed in the early 1930s, the weapon consisted of six barrels on a mobile carriage adapted from the 37mm antitank gun. The six rockets were electrically fired over a period of ten seconds. Designed to saturate a target with spin-stabilized smoke, explosive, or gas rockers, the weapon was first used in the German attack on the Soviet Union in 1941.

"Dawn was just breaking, and the flak wagon was silhouetted against the lightening sky," Lehmann later recalled. "I dropped, reloaded, and commenced firing at the soldiers who were trying to unlimber a brace of automatic guns in the open body of the truck. They were in plain sight and easy targets, and beat a hasty retreat to the far side of the ridge. It was then that I became aware that a line of Rangers had followed me up the ditch, many doing the same as I. We had quite a successful shoot for several minutes at Germans whose heads we could see, but who could see only our muzzle flashes. All of the metal of my M1 was hot and the wood was smoking."

Lehmann's account of the battle continued:

> After some little time shooting one clip after another, I heard Sergeant Perry Bills shouting my name; after I replied he directed me to come in his direction (in an open field toward the ditch). I jumped up and ran to join those in the field, and the others in the hedgerow did the same, to the accompaniment of small-arms fire, still inaccurate because of the dark. When I reached Bills's general area, I became aware of a large number of men flattened out in the field with no cover at all, and the small-arms fire was building. I attempted to light a British phosphorus contact grenade, but it failed to detonate. A wounded officer nearby, seeing what I attempted, tossed me an American one with which I was successful in producing a cloud of smoke. However, I had had to toss it quite

close to me because of the surrounding men, and perceiving the danger of falling tendrils overhead, I again began running, not stopping until I ran into a firefight between First Battalion men and some Kraut infantry. I am not sure how this ended but after it did, I commenced looking for C Company.

There was a tall barn nearby and I climbed to its second floor, which had a door looking south the way we had come, as well as another window higher up and facing west, which I attempted to gain for a better look with a handy ladder. No sooner had I started up the ladder when I heard the ungodly clatter of an armored vehicle outside. I abandoned the ladder and stole a peek through the door, which revealed a self-propelled gun with a driver and a four-man crew in the back, working about the gun, directly under me. I dropped a grenade in it and hit the ground running on the other side of the barn before it exploded. I did not inspect the results.

Describing running here and there like a scared rabbit while looking for his company, Lehmann noted that he could see scurrying German vehicles on the road on their right—out of rifle range—and all of the action was now going on to the north and west of him.

The First and Third battalions, Jim Altieri recorded, were in the middle of the goriest, costliest battle in Ranger history. Ground-grazing machine-gun fire covered every ditch and their mortars crashed all around him. In one attack he lost one of his platoon lieutenants and four key noncoms as well as ten men badly wounded. "We were desperate," he said. "We knew we had to crack through to save the First and Third—but each attack in broad daylight over open ground brought frightening casualties."

About two miles from Cisterna, the two battalions lost contact with one another. Three of the First's companies moved forward and three halted. Taking over their command, Shunstrom sent a runner to the rear to locate the Third. When he returned, he reported that Major Alvah Miller had been killed by a shell from a German tank that had appeared from around a bend. The company was able to fight off two tanks and a half-track with grenades and bazookas. With the Third Battalion "strung out" to the east and to the rear, First Battalion commander Jack Dobson broke radio silence to report to Darby at 0700 that Miller was dead and that Dobson had been wounded. The First was in an open field about eight hundred yards short of Cisterna and three German self-propelled guns were giving him "a good deal of trouble."

With the battalions arrayed defensively in a crescent-shaped area to the north along the road and Third Battalion's B, C, and D companies providing security to the south, German tanks and self-propelled guns roamed freely, blasting the Ranger positions, and withdrawing to reload. If Rangers exposed themselves to attack the armored units, they were raked by machine-gun and sniper fire. Sergeant Tom Fergen recalled, "One tank came out of a driveway behind a house ahead of us. One of my squad [Sergeant Frank Mattivi] climbed on board it while it was moving and dropped an incendiary grenade into the open turret. At the same time a bazooka gunner hit it head-on, and I was up beside it with a sticky grenade. The grenade exploded while I was getting away. I ducked in time to see the tank blow up and start burning. One of the crew got out and tried to get under the tank, but I shot him." When the bazooka round hit, Mattivi was bounced into the air, but landed unscathed.

Corporal Mosier related a harrowing account of another episode at sunrise in which the Rangers observed a tank at their rear. Thinking it was American, they cheered. "Then it opened up on us," Mosier said. Responding with a sticky grenade and a bazooka, the Rangers knocked it out and killed the crew, but ten more tanks appeared, followed by German infantry armed with automatic weapons.

When a German infantry attack formed in the south near Third Battalion's Company B and maneuvered against the Rangers in the north, the action blocked the Rangers from orderly withdrawal and any chance of linking up with the Fourth Battalion. In an effort to assist the First and Third, Darby ordered two half-tracks and two tank destroyers to rush to the area.

Having replaced Shunstrom in command of the cannon company, Lieutenant Otis Davey asked for volunteers and led the attack in an M10 tank destroyer, followed by Sergeant Joe Cain in the *Ace of Diamonds* half-track with a 75mm cannon. When they came to a halt three hundred yards from the enemy, they encountered two German tanks hidden in bushes on the opposite side of the road. As one of the tanks began moving, with its cannon swinging in the direction of the Rangers' positions, two Rangers armed with rocket launchers slid forward. Firing at almost point-blank range, they knocked out both German tanks. Unfortunately, the American vehicles maneuvered into a minefield and two of them were lost, including the *Ace of Diamonds*. As the First and Third battalions fought for their lives and the Fourth Battalion attempted to batter its way into Isola Bella, communications between E, F, and Headquarters companies and A, B, C, and D companies were either intermittent or impossible, but the desperate nature of the battle was revealed in part of a telephone conversation that was picked up at division headquarters: "The machine-gun fire is terrific from both flanks. The shells are landing all over the place. [They] look like 170s. Fourth Battalion is the boy that is in the jam."

Killed in the shelling of the Fourth's command post were intelligence officer Major William Martin and Darby's clerk, Corporal Presley Stroud.

Darby recorded, "When the sun came up, the two Ranger battalions at Cisterna were surrounded. Between sunrise and 0700, when radio silence was broken, we came to the realization that the battle was lost."

Corporal Mosier recalled, "The sun was up when they let loose with their artillery. We were in the woods, not much of a woods, and they were firing into us. After the first volley, you felt naked. You knew they could see you, and you couldn't do anything about it."

Sergeant Fergen said, "The tanks caused most of the trouble. I was in a field with the rest of my men when the tanks moved in. They came from Highway 7, swinging into the field, racing after us. You could run about twenty yards and then hit the ground. If you waited longer, they got you. They got three next to me with a direct hit."

Darby grimly recorded, "All around Cisterna the Germans, who had shown no sign of strength twenty-four hours before, had moved in large numbers of soldiers. Their artillery sent its blistering fire into our attackers. Houses, once invitingly empty, were now nests for snipers and machine guns. The Germans had reinforced their lines on the exact day the Allies had selected for attack."

★ CHAPTER 16 ★

Finest Hour

"Colonel, we are awfully sorry."

Through a combination of luck, fortuitous timing, and the ambition that had profoundly impressed boyhood friends and teachers in Fort Smith and his superiors as a young army officer, William Orlando Darby had become the organizer and leader of a unique outfit known as the Rangers. He had led them in four invasions and numerous battles in which they had performed not as spearheaders but as infantry. Arzew had been followed by La Macta and St. Cloud. Gela became a fight against attacking armor. Salerno became the long holdout at the Chiunzi Pass. In each of these, he had relied on his training and experience as an artillery officer and employed a weapon he had come to appreciate in prewar maneuvers in Puerto Rico—the mortar.

The war correspondent Richard Tregaskis, in his book *Invasion Diary*, described Captain Chuck Shunstrom directing mortar fire at Venafro as a wild man fiddling with a 60mm mortar tube, preparing to add a few shells to the torrent of explosives falling on the German positions atop Mount Corvo. "Here's the way to shoot one of these things," he announced.

Demonstrating his firing system, Shunstrom wrapped the bare tube in an old glove, which would insulate the heat of the barrel, seized the tube with his left hand, aimed it, and dropped the mortar shell down the mouth with his right hand. The first burst sprang up less than fifty feet from the top of the white rock at the peak of Mount Corvo. A second blew up on the rock itself. Of ten or eleven shells, three landed on the stone. When one slammed close to the cave where the Germans had dug in, Shunstrom gave a grunt of satisfaction. At the same time, heavy mortars hammered the far slope of Corvo and set fire to trees. Shunstrom said, "Great fun, as long as we're dishing it out and not taking it."

Now, after Anzio, with the Rangers battling for their lives at Cisterna, Darby hoped to use mortars and cannons to again prove the maxim attributed to Napoleon that "God is on the side with the best artillery." Unfortunately, when the Rangers called for an artillery concentration on the northern and western sections of the town, they had no forward observers to direct the fire, and the 4.2 mortar battalion was unable to help because the base plates of the heavy weapons sank into the mud and couldn't be fired with accuracy.

Recording that the Germans had no such difficulty, Darby noted that the enemy artillery was ranged in the defense area, and self-propelled guns were roaming outside the circle, "much like the Indians around a desert caravan drawn up in a bivouac," that the fighting was similar to that encountered by the plainsmen of the Old West, and that the snipers were the same as in past wars, except in the weaponry.

"There was no idea of giving up," Darby wrote. "Their plan was to hold on to what they had until help came. The calls for assistance to the First Battalion radio came through clearly to my headquarters, which was bogged down and sweating out at Femina Morta."

A sergeant of the First Battalion whom Darby identified as a husky, top-grade fighting man from Brooklyn who had been a Ranger from their beginning said tearfully via his radio, "Some of the fellows are giving up. Colonel, we are awfully sorry. They can't help it, because we are running out of ammunition. But I ain't surrendering. They are coming into the building now." The radio went dead.

With the Third Division and other Allied units engaged in fierce fighting of their own, the First and Third Ranger battalions were pinned down by Germans in trees, houses, foxholes, and dug-in emplacements while enemy tanks roamed freely on advantageous terrain from both flanks in a viselike attack. Again and again, Fourth Battalion companies swept across the fields, capturing strongpoints and farmhouses. But each avenue cost dearly. German paratroops were entrenched in depth in well-camouflaged ground-level dugouts.

"The action was so close," Darby said, "it was like sitting in a movie house and watching a newsreel."

Sergeant Tom Fergen reported, "I saw a man whose face was cut up. He said he didn't want to be taken prisoner and asked me to shoot him."

Fergen replied, "Are you crazy?"

The desperate Ranger answered, "We're finished and I don't want them to get me."

Fergen refused, but he wrote later, "He wasn't so crazy. He knew what it was. Out there in the field, the tanks were chasing us and then from the houses around the field, the snipers tried to pick us off. They were using machine guns, machine pistols, and rifles, and they were shooting straight."

Darby noted, "The sand in the hourglass was running out. The Rangers knew it, as did the Germans." Corporal Mosier reported that his company commander, described by Darby as "a tall, bespectacled West Pointer," told his men to flee. "I hate to do this, but it's too late now," he said as he pointed south. "Take out and God bless you."

"There were eight of us together," Mosier recalled. "The lieutenant [the only platoon leader left and who stayed behind] told me that he wouldn't be captured and showed me his two bandoliers of ammunition. He was loaded up and firing to cover us when we set off. We headed for the ditch. All this time the tracers were flying close enough to stop them with your hand. Along the ditch there were snipers all the way."

When the group had passed through the German lines, only Fergen and machine gunner T/5 Joseph Vytrachik were left.

In an attempt to assist the trapped battalions in the afternoon, Darby ordered the cannon company to swing around Femina Morta toward Cisterna. Led by a young captain, described by Darby as "aquiver with excitement about his task," the four half-tracks made four attempts. After the last try, the captain returned and wept at having failed. After making his report, he left the Ranger command post "in the depths of despair" and was shot through the head by a sniper.

When Sergeant Major Robert Ehalt of the Third Battalion reported to Darby by radio at noon that he and nine others were holed up in a farmhouse and running out of ammunition, Darby said, "Get the men together and lam for it." A blacksmith in civilian life, Ehalt had been with the Rangers from the beginning. After fighting another half hour, he reported to Darby that the battle was lost and that he was destroying the radio.

Darby replied, "I leave everything in your hands. Tell the men I'm with them to the end."

Ehalt said, "So long, Colonel. Maybe when it's all over I'll see you again."

He would later say of Cisterna, "If we only would have had one more hour of darkness."

Darby asked his staff to leave him. Alone in the farmhouse, he wept.

Carlo Contrera said that when he emerged a few moments later with reddened eyes, his shoulders were "straight and his chin thrust forward defiantly." Picking up the field telephone, he informed General Mike O'Daniel at Third Division headquarters of the loss of the First and Third Ranger battalions.

"It was heartbreaking," wrote Altieri. "Two of the finest and most spirited outfits in the army were ground to bits by an awesome mailed fist—and all the while hoped vainly for help that never came. They fought tenaciously, they went down fighting, although hopelessly outnumbered. Their stand was the Rangers' finest hour."

In two days of fighting at Cisterna, the Fourth Battalion suffered thirty killed and fifty-eight wounded. The First and Third had twelve killed and thirty-six wounded. But the greatest toll was in the number of Rangers taken prisoner. Unable to fight on because they had run out of ammunition or found themselves vastly outnumbered and overrun, some Rangers calmly buried or disassembled their weapons and scattered the parts. Many continued to fight as they fled, only to be caught while they attempted to find cover. Of the 767 men who infiltrated Cisterna, only six made their way back to friendly lines.

Carl Lehmann was captured after dropping the grenade from the window of the barn onto the self-propelled gun. Searching for his company, he'd encountered the remains of Lieutenant Rip Reed's platoon. Because Reed was wounded, the platoon had been taken over by Sergeant Perry Bills. Dug in on the extreme right of the battlefield, they could see Germans on their right, but out of rifle range. After taking an occasional shot, mostly long-range, at vehicles on the road,

Lehmann dozed off from exhaustion, but was soon awakened by Bills shouting, "Them bastards is giving up!" Looking forward, Lehmann saw bare-headed Rangers with their hands clasped over their heads being marched ahead of Germans toward Ranger positions.

"We jumped to our feet as one and started running in the opposite direction," Lehmann wrote, "but not one of us tried to shoot through the prisoners."

On another part of the battlefield, a German tank infantry team advancing toward the remnants of Jack Dobson's First Battalion had also pulled Rangers from ditches and forced them to move in front of the column as human shields. If Dobson's men were able to get a clear shot around a Ranger, they opened fire. The Germans responded by shooting or bayoneting some of their captives and herding the others forward.

In describing the capture of the medical officer of the Third Battalion in *Rangers in World War II*, the historian Robert W. Black states that when the doctor refused to stop aiding wounded Rangers and join a group of prisoners, a German officer raised his pistol and shot him in the face, killing him. In Darby's account, the battalion doctor, a big man with a lantern jaw and a long record of Ranger combat, protested the order to leave the wounded, seized the German's pistol, and shot him. As he tried to return to his wounded, he was killed.

Noting that there were numerous occurrences of individual heroism by Rangers trying to avoid capture, Black wrote, "There were also reports that some of those newly arrived and ill-trained troops promptly surrendered." In *Rangers: Selected Combat Operations in World War II*, Michael J. King opined that however much or little this may have contributed to the outcome at Cisterna, the decline in the Rangers' combat skills was an unfortunate result of misusing the Rangers. From North Africa through Italy, the Rangers had been too frequently used as conventional infantry, and most of their casualties were suffered in those actions. As Ranger casualties were replaced with less-well-trained men, Ranger Force's quality became diluted, the level of its combat skills declined, and unit cohesion weakened. This deterioration was evident throughout the Cisterna battle. But in *The Ranger Force at the Battle of Cisterna*, Jeff Stewart found no reason to fault the behavior of replacements. He wrote, "Eyewitness accounts credit the lightly armed Rangers with destroying at least fifteen armored vehicles during the engagement. Even their enemies paid homage to the ferocity of the battle. . . . One German soldier poetically remembered Cisterna as 'Blood soaked field and harvests of steel.' There can be no question of the fighting abilities of the Ranger Force during their final battle."

Although the Rangers failed to accomplish their mission at Cisterna, their determined fight against overwhelming odds succeeded in thwarting a German counterattack toward Anzio. A recent U.S. Army history notes that the Anzio campaign continues to be controversial, just as it was during its planning and implementation stages, and that the operation clearly failed in its immediate objectives of outflanking the Gustav Line, restoring mobility to the Italian campaign, and speeding the capture of Rome. Allied forces were quickly pinned down and contained within a small beachhead, and they were effectively rendered incapable of conducting any sort of major offensive action for four months pending the advance of Fifth Army forces to the south. Anzio failed to be the panacea the Allies sought. As General Lucas repeatedly stated before the landing, which he had always considered a gamble, the allotments of men and supplies to the action were not commensurate with the high goals sought by British planners. He maintained that under the circumstances the small Anzio force had accomplished all that could have been realistically expected. But Lucas's critics charged that a more aggressive and imaginative commander, such as a Patton or Truscott, could have obtained the desired goals by an immediate, bold offensive from the beachhead. Lucas was overly cautious, expended valuable time digging in, and allowed the Germans to prepare countermeasures to ensure that an operation conceived as a daring Allied offensive behind enemy lines became a long, costly campaign of attrition.

Yet analyses show that the campaign did accomplish several goals. The presence of a significant Allied force behind the German main line of resistance, uncomfortably close to Rome, represented a constant threat. The Germans could not ignore Anzio and were forced into a response, thereby surrendering the initiative in Italy to the Allies. The 135,000 troops of the German Fourteenth Army surrounding Anzio could not be moved elsewhere, nor could they be used to make the already formidable Gustav Line virtually impregnable. The Anzio beachhead thereby guaranteed that the drain of scarce German troop reserves, equipment, and matériel continued unabated, ultimately enabling the Allied Fifteenth Army Group to break through in the south.

"Had the attack on Cisterna not taken place and had the Germans been able to counterattack earlier," wrote King, "the outcome might have been different." James Altieri said, "The sudden attack behind the enemy's lines had completely disorganized the German offensive before it began and helped save the Anzio beachhead at its most crucial period."

Darby reflected, "There was something to be proud of in the grim story—something that welled up in the heart of every soldier who heard the Ranger story. They had done their duty, had fought to the limit of human endurance, and almost inevitably—as with other groups of soldiers in history who had taken the long chance by raiding into enemy-held territory—they had met their fate. . . . There was a pioneer American savor to the story. How often in our early days had other groups of fighting men—selected, hard fighting, experienced men—found themselves in the Rangers' position on that fateful 29 January at Cisterna. In this fight were elements of Custer's last stand, of the Alamo, even of Major Rogers's Rangers in the French and Indian War. The gallant Rogers band had fought and died in raids into enemy country. They made raid after raid, but the sands of time ran against them. They were too few, too courageous, too well versed in the art of warfare, not to have realized that time and fate were holding the high cards."

★ CHAPTER 17 ★

QUITE A FLAP

"The Rangers are somewhat misunderstood young men."

OF THE GRIM DUTY OF HAVING TO RELAY DARBY'S REPORT ON THE annihilation of the First and Third Ranger battalions by telephone to General Mark Clark on the night of January 30, 1944, Lucian Truscott wrote in *Command Missions*, "It was a sad blow to all of us, and particularly to Colonel Darby and me. He had organized the First Ranger Battalion under my direction in North Ireland, and had fought with them in North Africa, Tunisia, Sicily and southern Italy."

Truscott had endured a difficult week. Already plagued by laryngitis that had reduced his voice to little more than whisper, he had been injured on January 24 when a German bomb exploded beside his foot during an air raid. Had it not been for the cavalry boots he always wore during battle, the wound would have been far more serious. With the leg encased in an adhesive cast, he attended a conference on January 27 with Lucas to discuss the plans for the coordinated attack from the Anzio beachhead that Clark was urging Lucas to mount.

Noting that a key part of the plan required Darby's Rangers to infiltrate German lines under cover of darkness and enter the town of Cisterna, Truscott explained, "Trained for such night infiltration and for street fighting, they could be expected to cause much confusion in the German lines. Meanwhile, the Fifteenth Infantry and the remaining Ranger Battalion [Fourth] would attack one hour later to break through the German defenses and support the Rangers."

Analyzing this plan in which the Rangers would be employed as infantry and to which Darby voiced no objections, Major Jeff R. Stewart wrote in *The Ranger Force at the Battle of Cisterna* that Darby was not a maverick or a specialist in unconventional operations, but a West Pointer and an artillery officer and brilliant tactician who saw his Rangers as a highly trained infantry fighting force and not necessarily as specialists reserved for unique situations.

Describing the Rangers as an average group of Americans who had asked only for the opportunity to fight, Darby said, "Some people think of the Rangers as supermen. They are not. They don't think of themselves as home run hitters or star quarterbacks. They are just garden-variety infantry soldiers, every one of them, young and willing to do a job. They train for weeks on one particular mission until they can do it blindfolded. Then they go out and do it at night against a real enemy. Weapons they knew intimately. Battle preparedness was their continuing study and practice. They learned the tricks of modern warfare: improving ruses, how to stalk a sentry, how to blow up a pillbox. When tanks and heavier weapons were brought against them, they fought them with their infantry weapons—with rocket launchers and sticky grenades thrown from up close. The name Rangers was aptly chosen. My men lived up to it with the full measure of their willingness and spirit. They were proud soldiers, confident warriors, and evidence that the spirit of battling against any odds still lives among the American nation."

After El Guettar, the war correspondent Ralph Ingersoll had written, "The Rangers are somewhat misunderstood young men. They are thought of as American Commandos. And, as the term Commando is popularly thought of, that would make them specialists in raiding enemy coastal defenses. Actually they are either more or less than that, depending on the point of view. They are simply trained infantrymen, the specialness of their training being its rigorousness. There is nothing that a Commando or a Ranger can do that an infantryman should not be able to do or which many infantrymen are not able to do. But the Ranger can simply do more of it and do it harder."

Yet, because of battle stories provided by reporters of the Rangers in North Africa and Sicily, newsreels, and wide dissemination of pictures by combat cameramen, the Rangers had been embraced by the American public as the very supermen that their publicity encouraged. Although reporters and photographers had been on the front lines of American wars since the Civil War, it was General Eisenhower who told a meeting of U.S. newspaper editors, "Public opinion wins wars." That Darby also appreciated the value of the press is evidenced by the enthusiasm with which he welcomed Phil Stern to Ranger ranks. Correspondents covering them from Dieppe and North Africa to Sicily and Italy not only found good copy in them, but in their dashing, handsome, and appealing young leader.

Consequently, when Darby informed Truscott that the First and Third Ranger battalions had been decimated at Cisterna, Truscott faced the terrible prospect of passing on the bad news of the loss of the famous and popularly acclaimed band of soldiers to a proud commander who possessed as keen an appreciation of the value of publicity as Eisenhower.

War reporters first heard about Mark Wayne Clark as the tall and slender officer who had been smuggled into French North Africa on a submarine in a daring cloak-and-dagger mission to persuade the Vichy forces not to resist Operation Torch, then became a heroic figure in the invasion at Casablanca. They knew that Clark was a West Pointer who early in his career had become a close friend of Eisenhower and of Chief of Staff George C. Marshall, resulting in Ike naming him commander of the Fifth Army. As a result, the overall commander in Italy, the British general Alexander, came to know Clark as a difficult subordinate who, for political reasons, must be afforded respect and consideration that Alexander would never have shown a British officer under his command. Observers felt that Clark was keenly aware of this and became arrogant. One historian wrote that Clark's egotism and hunger for publicity made him resentful of his British superiors and suspicious of their intentions.

It was also widely understood that Clark was obsessed with a belief that his Fifth Army was destined to capture the Italian capital. Clark wanted to enter the Eternal City like an ancient Roman general, at the head of the triumphal parade. His strategy for achieving this had resulted in the "end run" around the Gustav Line by means of the landings at Anzio, with General Lucas in command. Under pressure from Clark and Alexander to break out from the beachhead, Lucas had presented Clark and Truscott with a plan to take the key objective, the town of Cisterna, with the Rangers in the lead, a plan that Truscott and Darby approved.

Recalling the disastrous result, Truscott wrote in *Command Missions* that there was "quite a flap" when he reported to General Clark by telephone that night that the Rangers had been destroyed as a fighting force. "He came to see me the next morning," wrote Truscott, "and implied that they were unsuitable for such a mission.

I reminded him that I had been responsible for organizing the original Ranger battalion and that Colonel Darby and I perhaps understood their capabilities better than other American officers. He said no more. However, General Clark feared unfavorable publicity, for he ordered an investigation to fix the responsibility. This was wholly unnecessary for the responsibility was entirely my own, since both Colonel Darby and I considered the mission a proper one, which should have been well within the capabilities of these fine soldiers. That ended the matter."

It was not the last of the affair. An argument over placing the blame for the loss of the Rangers continues to rage among military scholars and World War II historians. Michael J. King notes that the debate started immediately. He wrote, "While Darby was recovering from losing most of his command, his superiors were already beginning to avoid or obscure responsibility for the debacle."

Clark entered in his diary that he was distressed to find that the attack began with the Ranger Force in the attack on Cisterna, calling the decision a definite error in judgment because the Rangers did not have the support weapons to overcome the resistance indicated.

On this crucial point King wrote, "Out of fairness to Clark, he had not been involved in the detailed planning of the attack on Cisterna and did not know that the Rangers had been chosen to lead the way. Indeed, he would have been violating the chain of command had he bypassed Sixth Corps' headquarters to tell a division commander how to plan an attack."

Critical analyses of the disaster that befell the Rangers are based on four theories:

1. They were used improperly.
2. The quality of Darby's force was degraded.
3. The Germans knew the Rangers were coming and ambushed them.

4. The Rangers were destroyed because Allied intelligence had failed to correctly gauge German strength.

WERE THE RANGERS MISUSED?

When the Rangers set out for Cisterna on the night of January 29, 1944, they were not the organization that Darby had forged in Northern Ireland and Scotland in the summer of 1942 as the First Ranger Battalion. The Third and Fourth had been created at Nemours, Algeria, in 1943. But between the landing at Arzew in November 1942 and the formation of the Third and Fourth, the First Battalion had spent only eight days in true Ranger operations. Immediately after Arzew, they were employed as regular infantry at La Macta and St. Cloud, then went into a long period of training. Following the landing at Gela, Sicily, they were again used as infantry. Salerno was followed by the defense of Chiunzi Pass. The result was that they were engaged in conventional combat four times as many days as in Ranger operations.

Therefore, Michael J. King argues, in view of the critical situation that developed after the Anzio landing, and because of the effective use of Rangers conventionally in Algeria, Sicily, and at Salerno, it would have been wasteful of manpower for the commanders responsible to have held the Rangers in reserve. When Clark was asked in an interview by King why Clark did not employ the Rangers' special skills against the Winter Line, Clark replied that although he believed in the Ranger concept, he was chronically short of manpower and could not take them off the line for special operations.

In examining the conventional use of Rangers, King places part of the responsibility on Darby. He recalled that the Rangers were not Darby's idea. By good fortune and ambition he had been chosen to realize an American-style Commando unit that originated in the mind of George C. Marshall and had been promoted by Truscott. While

Darby might be expected to take a personal interest in the Rangers, King noted in his Darby biography, there was no reason to believe that he had any strong convictions regarding their proper or improper use. Indeed, he had expanded the Rangers from a lightly armed battalion to three battalions with a cannon company.

Exploring this thesis in *The Ranger Force at the Battle of Cisterna*, Major Jeff Stewart found that while Darby was aware of the special characteristics of the Rangers, he continued to think of them as a conventional force with additional training and skills and offered no protest that in the Lucas attack plan the Rangers were being misused.

THE QUALITY OF DARBY'S RANGERS WAS DEGRADED.

This explanation for the calamity of Cisterna rests on the fact that new Rangers brought in to replace casualties in the African and Sicilian campaigns were not afforded the same level of training as the original Rangers. The historian John Lock states in *To Fight With Intrepidity* that the combined First and Third Ranger battalions at Cisterna suffered excessively heavy losses as a result of having to commit untrained and unseasoned replacements before they were ready.

The difficulties in finding new Rangers that had confronted Darby after the Arzew battles were compounded with the creation of the Third and Fourth battalions. "We had new outfits on paper," observed James Altieri, "but we had to get volunteers to fill the ranks. And six weeks were all we had to whip the three new battalions into fighting shape for another invasion we knew we would again lead. . . . Our own lives, as well as theirs, depended on how thoroughly we trained them, and we were determined to eliminate as many of the weak ones as we could."

Darby estimated that after the Sicilian campaign the First and Third battalions were about 40 percent under strength and the Fourth was about half its usual size, requiring yet another effort to find and train replacements as quickly as possible. Lacking a system to ensure a flow of specially trained replacements, each battalion detached an officer and a few enlisted men to remain in the rear and select and train volunteers for Ranger duty, but this arrangement gave only a limited amount of time in which to train recruits. The quality of the battalions declined as veteran casualties were replaced by enthusiastic but inadequately trained personnel.

Citing the loss of experience that was bled out of the Rangers in North Africa, Sicily, and Salerno as a contributing factor in the Cisterna disaster, the historian Robert W. Black wrote that this loss may have harmed the Rangers in the infiltration phase and that some of the untested men quickly surrendering during the battle "points up the lack of proper training."

Michael King concluded that the conventional fighting to which the Rangers had too often been committed had cost them dearly in the lives of trained and experienced men and that replacements, though highly motivated, had received nothing equal to the time and training that had been lavished on their predecessors. This led to a dilution of the Ranger battalions with less-well-trained men and to a decline in their unit cohesion.

Were the Rangers Ambushed?

The most disturbing and offensive explanation of the Rangers' defeat was that they were tricked into falling into a German ambush. Analysts agree that the genesis of this theory was a statement by a Polish prisoner to Sixth Corps interrogators that the infiltration by the First and Third battalions had been detected as soon as it began and that German commanders had ordered their frontline troops to let the Rangers walk into a trap. According to the young Polish private, he had seen the plan in which German defenders had been told to "withdraw hurriedly through the town, as though they were forced to give ground." They were to fire all weapons including antitank guns to make it look as real as possible, then move to both flanks of the town and await orders to counterattack with the purpose of cutting off all troops.

This account gained some credence in a report filed by Captain Charles Shunstrom on July 10, 1944. Following his escape from captivity after the battle, he stated that because those who attacked the center met no opposition until they reached a position approximately eight hundred yards short of the objective, and the Rangers on the flanks encountered stiff resistance, the Germans had prepared an ambush.

While these statements appeared at the time to validate the ambush explanation, later analysts of the statements given by Shunstrom and the Polish prisoner, coupled with the German reports on the battle for Cisterna, found both statements to be questionable. The main reason to doubt the prisoner rests on the unlikelihood of a Polish private being shown the German plan to spring a trap. Regarding Shunstrom, it was noted that because he had been attempting to restore the communications between the First and Third battalions at the outset of the attack, he had not been in a position to observe that in the initial contact between the Rangers and the German line the Rangers encountered no opposition. When he was able to work his way to forward positions, the battle had become too significantly developed and confusing for him to discern that they had been led into a trap.

The most persuasive evidence that there was no ambush is found in the German battle report and in German intelligence summaries. The latter makes no mention of Rangers until three days after the battle. The battle order from Fourteenth Army headquarters stated that only a position based on a system of strongpoints, supplemented by a system of defense, was capable of breaking up a large-scale attack by the enemy. The order asserted that penetrations "cannot be avoided, but a breakthrough must be prevented." Accordingly, the German defense resulted in a thirty-five-hundred-meter gap exactly at the point where the Rangers executed their infiltration and where the Germans set up their main line of resistance through Cisterna. This placed the lightly armed Rangers, advancing with no support by tanks, in the unfortunate position of fighting in daylight against dug-in positions with interlocking fields of fire.

The after-battle report of a German squad leader noted, "We had no details about the direction of the [Ranger] thrust, as the operation was primarily aimed at keeping the enemy from outflanking us." A German commander said, "To check a force of Rangers who had thrust into the positions held by a neighboring company, I launched a counterattack at one of their flanks, thus cutting off a large number of Americans from their unit. About four to five hundred fell into our hands. However, others had escaped and entrenched themselves in surrounding farms. They surrendered after a heroic stand."

Regarding Shunstrom's report, Major Jeff R. Stewart wrote in *The Ranger Force at the Battle of Cisterna*, "His description of the 'ambush' all too accurately describes the plight of a force caught in front of a meticulously prepared defensive position."

Ranger Ken Markham vehemently declared, "There is no one who can make me believe the Germans let us slip by. We could have killed them at any time. I think we did an excellent job of bypassing the enemy without their knowledge." Carl Lehmann said, "I reject the assertions of half a dozen historians—most of whom were in swaddling when our ramps went down—that it was an ambush."

Writes Robert W. Black correctly, "The Germans won the battle honors that day, but they do not deserve the credit of having knowingly set a trap for the Rangers." It would have been out of character of them to hope that the Americans would fall into a trap.

Was There a Failure of Intelligence?

When Darby left a meeting of regimental and other commanders at Truscott's command post on the afternoon of January 29, 1944, he had the assurance of Third Division intelligence officers in their "Estimate of the Situation" that an infiltration to Cisterna by Rangers supported by a combined arms attack had "a high probability of success." The G2 report identified units facing the Third Infantry Division as the Hermann Goering Division, augmented by a scattering of units from larger formations in a line of outposts southwest of Cisterna. Specifying an Outpost Defensive Line along a railroad track and in Cisterna, it said that the main line of defense would undoubtedly be found on true high ground to both the west and east for the purpose of keeping any attack from reaching the hills beyond Cisterna and taking Highway 6.

The German attitude was predicted to be entirely defensive and the immediate situation with respect to tanks and artillery "is not too good." German counterattacks were expected to be by small units, including two or three tanks, but there was the possibility that elements of the 356th Division and the Twenty-ninth and Twenty-sixth Panzer Grenadier divisions might be fed into the line in a piecemeal fashion. Should they respond en masse, stated the estimate, it was likely that they would be discovered by air reconnaissance or other methods before the counterattack could be delivered. The estimate also noted the possibility of the appearance of a newly formed German parachute division, but it said its most likely mission would be to prepare and man the defenses and not be used in a counterattack.

Depicting the quality of Germans troops as deteriorated, particularly at squad and platoon level, and noting that the enemy force included Polish troops, the estimate described the German mind-set as defensive rather than offensive. The G2 view was that "our own actions, if carried through with particular vigor and firmness, whether in attacking or defending, may enable us to attain success which would not have been possible against old-type, all-German formations."

The intelligence estimate conclusion was that it did not seem probable that the enemy was prepared to deliver a major counterattack involving units of division size, but that it would "probably resort to delaying action coupled with small-scale counterattacks in an effort to grind us to a standstill."

This estimation was based on a belief that the maximum German strength would amount to four divisions. In fact, there was evidence that the enemy was rapidly adding to its forces in response to orders to Kesselring from Hitler himself to remove what Hitler termed "the abscess" south of Rome. A report of Allied surveillance of the Cisterna region described movements of motorized units, new artillery locations, and increased activity on the northwest flank of the beachhead that indicated a view to future offensive action. Another report noted the rail yards at Rome were full, indicating that the enemy was definitely bringing reserves into the area from the north to oppose the Anzio front. As early as January 27 patrols detected Germans digging in along the railway west of Cisterna, and enemy strongpoints were observed along the main roads.

For reasons never explained, this information either was not passed up to those with the responsibility for presenting the intelligence estimate or was not properly interpreted by them. The result was one of the gravest Allied miscalculations of the Second World War.

While there is some plausibility in explaining the destruction of the Rangers in the battle to take Cisterna as an example of their continual misuse (with Darby's assent) and a result of their degraded fighting quality, but no evidence that they were ambushed, military analysts and historians agree that it was the failure to correctly judge German troop strength and a mistaken assessment of enemy intent that led to their commitment to a plan of action that inadvertently marked them for doom.

"The battle of Cisterna and the destruction of the Ranger Force," wrote Major Jeff R. Stewart in his analysis of the calamity, "serve as a dramatic demonstration of what can happen when units are poorly used against a thinking, aggressive enemy. A lack of coherent doctrine combined with an inaccurate intelligence picture resulted in the loss of one of the most effective combat units in the Mediterranean theater."

Michael J. King wrote, "Uninspired generalship and poor intelligence on the American side all but guaranteed that the attack on Cisterna would fail. The new Rangers' relatively poor state of training did not cause the disaster, nor could Darby's presence with the lead battalions have prevented it. Ranger Force's failure was a consequence of failure by division and corps. While none of Darby's superiors assumed responsibility for the disaster, none of them thought to blame Darby."

Because so many of the participants in the Cisterna raid were dead or taken prisoner, the investigation that had been ordered by Clark stated that so many factors contributed to the failure of the operation that it could be ascribed only to chance. Darby felt the same. He wrote, "The Rangers blamed no one for their losses. The infantry troops had run into the same reinforced enemy defense, had jumped off, hit something solid, and recoiled. Slipping through enemy lines, my raiders had met the same strengthened enemy and were surrounded."

★ CHAPTER 18 ★

THE HOUDINI RANGERS

"Don't do it again."

WITHIN HOURS OF THE REALIZATION THAT MORE THAN SEVEN HUN-dred Rangers were captured at Cisterna, Darby learned that the Germans had rushed them to Rome and staged a public display of famous captives that was deliberately reminiscent of spectacles that honored conquests of the legions of the Caesars. "Assembled with other Allied prisoners," recalled Sergeant Carl Lehmann, "we were marched past the Colosseum in Rome for the benefit of propaganda cameras. It was one of the worst days of my life."

Sergeant Frank "Joey" Mattivi remembered marching "through

the damned streets" and spectators "spitting at us" and people on balconies "jeering at us, cussing in Italian." An original Ranger, he had joined the National Guard in Excelsior Springs, Missouri, while employed by the Civilian Conservation Corps and had been one of the first sent overseas when the United States entered the war. Stationed in Northern Ireland, he volunteered for the Rangers "mainly to escape the boredom." Reviewing the circumstances prior to his capture with Fox Company of the First Battalion, he stated, "About ten or eleven that morning, three tanks started moving toward the house that Ray Sadowski was at the top of. I don't know what made me do it—I guess it was just part of the job—anyway, I jumped up on the side of a tank and dropped a phosphorus grenade in it. I didn't know that one of our men on the other side had a bazooka, and he fired and hit it just below the turret, and the concussion knocked me off the tank. We knocked out two tanks."

Eventually out of ammunition and surrounded, Mattivi had no choice but to surrender. "We walked around with our hands in the air for an hour or so," he recalls in an account of what happened next, as recorded in Patrick K. O'Donnell's collection of oral histories, *Beyond Valor: World War II's Rangers and Airborne Veterans Reveal the Heart of Combat.* "They marched us down in a ravine. There were guards in front of us and guards behind us. When we got down there we noticed the guards behind us got out in front. The guy next to me said, 'Well, I think maybe we've had it.' We thought maybe they were going to take us down there and shoot us. About that time there were two motorcycles coming down, and these officers came down there, and I heard one of them say, 'Nix, nix.' They were talking there for maybe fifteen, ten minutes, and so I think maybe they had something to do with us not getting killed."

Loaded into trucks, they were conveyed to a holding area that Mattivi described as "just a temporary stockade." After a day or so, they were again put into trucks and taken to "a castle up the line," where they were kept all night. At some point, the location was bombed by Allied planes. "The raid shook the castle a little bit," Mattivi noted, but no one was killed. The next day, they were trucked to Rome and marched "through the damned streets."

While some Italians among the crowds spat at the prisoners and others who had been provided with garbage or rotten vegetables dutifully threw them, Chuck Shunstrom reported that the February 1 victory show did not prove as successful as the German planners had desired. He stated, "The Italians were supposed to boo us and cheer the master race as we marched five abreast through the streets. Instead, the Italian women cried and the men flashed surreptitious V-for-victory signs. They would stroke their hair or brush off a sleeve with fingers shaped to a V. When a dumb German guard wanted to know what the V sign meant, none of us knew a thing about it. We marched along singing 'God Bless America.' "

Among the Rangers flaunted for the benefit of German cameras on the streets of Rome, Kenneth Morgan Markham of the First Battalion found the exploitation and taunts from civilians that the Rangers were finished "humiliating." Twenty-two years of age and born and raised in the hill country of Daniel Boone and Davy Crockett's Tennessee, he had been a scout in Major Jack Dobson's First Battalion. Crawling forward beside the lead scout, Frank Mattivi, they left the cover of the Pantano ditch and reached a road parallel to Cisterna.

"I was the first man across," he recalled. "There was an olive orchard over there. It was a bivouac area for what seemed to be a whole division that pulled into that area to counterattack. Major Dobson and I and Frank Mattivi got in there and we started to open up because that's all we could do. He [Dobson] told me to cross the road and try to get back to Major [Alvah] Miller [commander of the Third Battalion]. I got back there and you just couldn't believe how much firefighting was going on. Everybody was all confused."

When Markham located Major Miller's position, he was informed that Miller had been killed by a mortar shell that "hit his head and blew him all to pieces." Returning to the olive grove, he encountered "a mass of fire" that prevented him from crossing the road.

As he crawled into a ditch he found about a dozen dead Rangers, but two captains, Chuck Shunstrom and Frederic Saam, were alive and hunkering down. Their plan was to hold out until help came. To advance any farther would be suicide. Surrounded by an enemy with superiority in firepower and occupying commanding positions, they received a report that some Americans were seen with their hands in the air at a position about two hundred yards to the rear. They had been captured by German paratroop infantry supported by two armored personnel carriers. When the Germans found themselves under sporadic small-arms fire, two of the guards were seen to fall. Immediately, two Germans bayoneted two of the Americans. The Germans then formed the prisoners into ranks and marched them toward a position held by Bing Evans's company. When they ambushed the guards, killing two more, the Germans retaliated by bayoneting two prisoners in the back. Running out of ammunition, Evans had no choice but to surrender.

The Germans by now had about eighty American prisoners in a column of fours and immediately started to march them toward the center of Shunstrom's position. With Evans forced to lead the column up the road, the Germans shouted, "Surrender or we will shoot the prisoners."

Shunstrom recalled, "All the time small-arms fire was coming into our positions from the enemy to our front and flanks, keeping us well pinned down. The oncoming column came to a position about one hundred fifty yards from the command post and halted. The orders for our ambush were not to fire until given the order, but someone fired a shot into the oncoming column and killed one of our own men. This one shot started everybody else in the ambush firing, and the result was that two or three of our own men were killed in the column plus one or two of the German guards. The Germans immediately backed off and took cover and started to spray our column of prisoners with automatic fire from submachine guns. The men that had set up in ambush immediately ceased firing, and a few who were evidently new in combat got hysterical and started to leave their positions and surrender. All attempts to stop this obedience of orders failed. Even an attempt to stop them by shooting them failed."

Observing the surrendering Rangers in the company of Scotty Munro, Larry Hurst, C. J. Hodal, and about twenty others, and deciding that his own capture was "inevitable," Carl Lehmann buried his knife, wristwatch, and a captured German Luger he'd carried since Algeria, but forgot that in his shirt pocket was a collection of epaulets he'd taken from the tunics of Germans he'd found dead in a bunker. Captured a few minutes later, he and others were herded to a farmyard to be searched. When the wing-shaped souvenirs he called "scalps" were discovered by a "little Kraut" who "looked to be about fifteen," and the German directed him to move away from the other prisoners, he feared that he was about to reap his "final reward."

When the young guard took the scalps to the officer (*Feldwebel*) in charge, "begging him for permission to shoot me," Lehmann recalled, the officer shook his head and said *"Nein."* As "the little bastard kept it up," he drew more head shakes and quiet *Neins*. Before this played out, Lehmann said, "I was blessing the *Feldwebel*'s obviously sainted mother for having birthed him. Before we were marched out of the farmyard to the rear areas, the *Feldwebel* came close and smiled at me. 'You haff a Churman name, Carl.' That and what went before was worth the snappy salute I delivered and which he returned."

After the propaganda extravaganza in Rome, Lehmann's group of captives arrived at a POW camp named Stalag II-B. Located a mile and a half west of Hammerstein in West Prussia, it sprawled over twenty-five acres and was surrounded by two barbed-wire fences and divided into compounds and subcompounds. Ten thousand Russians lived in the East Compound, while sixteen thousand French, sixteen hundred Serbs, nine hundred Belgians, and numerous Americans were segregated by nationalities in the North Compound. In the American enclosure were a playing field, workshops and a dispensary, showers and a delousing chamber. Lehmann provided this account of his arrival by train a few days after the parade in Rome: "As we debarked from the boxcars (40 & 8s [forty men or eight horses]) we were informed that we were to be deloused, and directed to put our clothing on hangers for transport through a gas chamber to kill the fleas and lice, while we went into a communal shower."

According to German and American records, at times more than six hundred men were quartered in each of the three single-story barracks that were fifteen yards wide and sixty yards long. While this resulted in extremely crowded conditions, it contrasted well with the barracks of Russians, which held as many as a thousand men each. Barracks were divided by a center washroom that had twenty taps. Bunks were triple-decked with excelsior mattresses and one German blanket (plus two from the Red Cross) for each man. In the front and rear of a barracks was a urinal to be used only at night. Three stoves furnished what heat there was.

Except for housekeeping chores, no work was performed in the stalag. All men fit to work were sent out to "Kommandos" consisting of groups of twenty men taken under guard to a huge farm. Americans were billeted in a section of a large brick-floored barn. Adjoining sections were occupied by pigs, cows, and grain. The men slept on double bunks. Guards lived in a small room opening onto the Americans' quarters. Each day the men rose at 0600 and breakfasted on Red Cross food and potato soup, bread, and hot water (for coffee), which they drew from the farm kitchen. At 0630 they washed their spoons and enameled bowls and cleaned their barracks. They shaved and washed themselves in three large wash pans filled from a single spigot that gave only cold water. At 0700 they rode out to potato fields in horse-drawn wagons driven by German farmhands. Under the armed guards, they dug potatoes until 1130, when they rode back to the farm for the noon meal. This consisted of Red Cross food augmented by German vegetable soup.

Boarding wagons at 1300, they worked until 1630. The evening meal at 1700 consisted of Red Cross food and soup, potatoes and gravy. After this meal they could sit outdoors in a fenced-in pen (thirty by eight feet) until 1830, when the guard locked them in their section for the night. On Sundays the guard permitted them to lounge or walk in the "yard" all day, but they spent a good deal of their time scrubbing the barracks and washing clothes. Their Sunday dinner from the farm was usually a meat pudding and cheese. Once a month each POW received a large Red Cross food box containing four Red Cross parcels. These were taken to distant Kommandos by rail and to nearby units by trucks. Parcels were stored in the guards' room until issued. A POW who did no work got no pay. Workers received seventy pfennigs a day.

Carl Lehmann was assigned to a farm party of twenty-two Americans at a huge former feudal estate named Fairszein that he described as "complete with a mansion, extensive farm buildings, a dairy with hundreds of cattle, a schnapps factory and a group of residence buildings for the peasant workers." POWs were housed in a small two-story building surrounded by barbed wire, with a kitchen containing the bread oven for the estate and two sleeping rooms for the prisoners on the first floor. A pair of German guards occupied the second floor.

While Lehmann and original members of the First Ranger Battalion had been enjoying their reunion with Father Basil at Lucrino during Christmas week, nineteen-year-old PFC Donald Silas Green had been a Ranger less than three months. Known to his new buddies, his family, and his civilian friends as "Jiggs," he reported in a letter to his parents on Christmas Eve, "We are back from the front lines now for a period of rest and it seems plenty good. Don't worry about me.

I was always a lucky little cuss. Our colonel once said that he guessed by some of the jobs we got that the generals figured we were a cross of a General Sherman tank and a mountain goat."

Born on March 23, 1924, in Groton, Massachusetts, Green had enlisted in the army and had been assigned to the Air Force Service Command. Sent to Italy, he learned that the Rangers were seeking volunteers and put in for a transfer. Assigned to the Third Battalion, he reported in a letter on November 11, 1943, "I am fine and happy. This Ranger outfit is a swell outfit but plenty tough." After landing at Anzio, he wrote to his mother, "I have seen enough action to last me forever but still can't complain. I am fine and right in the groove."

The next communication his family received was a War Department telegram in March stating that he had been missing in action since January 30, 1944. When they heard from him directly in June, he was a prisoner of war at Stalag VII-A, somewhere in Germany. Subsequent letters were sent from Stalag II-B.

Among the prisoners was a Ranger who had been captured in Algeria. Twenty years old, Steve Kretzer had lied about his age and joined the army in 1940 at age sixteen to escape the turmoil of his parents divorcing. Trained as a scout and taught to ride and repair motorcycles, he was assigned to a reconnaissance company of the First Armored Regiment, First Armored Division and shipped to Carrickfergus, Northern Ireland, in 1942 to continue training and prepare for invading Europe. When the call went out for volunteers to learn British Commando tactics, he volunteered, passed the initial interviews and tests to become a Ranger, and was sent to train at Achnacarry.

Following the landings at Arzew, he went AWOL "to see the coastline." Upon his return, he noted, Darby "busted" him to private and confined him in Arzew's "old world dungeon." While temporarily reattached to the First Armored Regiment reconnaissance company, he and a buddy riding in the motorcycle's sidecar were behind enemy lines near Faid Pass when Germans started their push toward Kasserine Pass. Strafed by a German fighter, they managed to escape. As they tried to get back to the American line, the Germans machine-gunned them, killing his buddy, and seriously wounding Kretzer's left leg. Captured on February 14, 1943, he was found wearing a leather bomber jacket with lieutenant colonel oak leaves that had been given to him by a bomber pilot whom Kretzer had rescued and taken back to Allied lines a few days before. Noting that the Germans assumed he was an officer, Kretzer said that he gave his correct name, rank, and serial number, but they refused to believe him. Consequently, he was given special treatment and flown in a German Junker to Naples. Shortly thereafter, the Germans discovered through the Red Cross that he was a private and not an officer. Thrown in with the enlisted POWs, he was soon taken to Stalag II-B. Soon after his capture, German doctors had wanted to amputate his left leg. He refused, but he allowed the doctors to experiment on him by laying in a bone graft. The left leg was a bit shorter than the right. At Stalag II-B he learned to act and play the bass fiddle. He escaped three times, once staying free for a month, but was recaptured. Warned that if he tried again he would be killed, he made no more attempts.

When John Thomas Brown of Huntsville, Alabama, left his job at the Redstone Arsenal to join the army, he said he did so because all his friends were wearing the uniform and "if they could feel honored wearing it, I figured I could wear one myself." A PFC in the First Ranger Battalion, he and a sergeant had found themselves in a shell hole at Cisterna and being ordered to surrender by a group of Germans pointing guns at several Ranger prisoners.

"They were yelling for us to stop firing or else they would be shot," Brown recalled. "The sergeant asked me, 'What are we going to do?' I told him, 'I don't think we have much of a choice. You heard what the man said. If you shoot one more time, they're going to blow those guys away."

Before surrendering, Brown and the sergeant removed their

Ranger insignia from their uniforms and buried them. "The Germans had made a vow to never take a Ranger alive," he explained, "so we knew we had to rip our patches off. They would have shot us like a rabbit if they saw that tab on our shoulder, so the patch had to go."

In the form of an upward-curving scroll, the narrow black shoulder patch had "Ranger" and the battalion number in white and framed by thin red stripes. A distinctive emblem had been suggested by Captain Roy Murray after the Dieppe raid. As explained by William D. Linn II in *History of the Ranger Scroll*, American soldiers in England, attempting to capitalize on reports of the sensational raid, bragged in pubs that they were Rangers in order to win favor with local women. This resulted in fights with such frequency between Rangers and the impostors that something had to be done. When Roy Murray proposed a distinctive Ranger emblem, Darby requested approval from Truscott and General Mark Clark on August 28, 1942. When it was granted on October 8, Darby declared a battalion-wide contest, with a prize for the winning design. It went to Sergeant Anthony Rada of Flint, Michigan. Although his scroll had a blue background, a shortage of blue dye dictated that the field be black. Because the Rangers had been promised in radio broadcasts by a female propagandist named "Axis Sally" via Radio Berlin that if a soldier wearing the Ranger patch were captured, he would be executed on sight, most of those who were forced to surrender at Cisterna drew their fighting knives and cut off the identifying scrolls.

Of the stress of being a POW, Brown recalled, "Some of our guys couldn't handle it and committed suicide. I just tried to keep positive thoughts in my head. I thought about home, family members and hope. There were many nights I didn't sleep. They would put us in groups of ten and if one man was missing during inspection for accountability, the other nine were shot. No questions asked."

Carl Lehmann cited a "blond, handsome Aryan with severe combat wounds and a very bad attitude" who had guarded Lehmann on

241

the train to Rummelsberg and displayed a dislike for Lehmann. Perhaps the German sensed that Lehmann was likely to attempt to escape. If so, his intuition was astute. Soon after arriving at Stalag II-B, he slipped away from a work gang, but he was caught and returned to the stalag.

Although there was an escape committee in the camp, Lehmann discovered that it had "never helped any escape." It declined to assist him because he didn't speak German, but after he threatened to report them when the war was over, the committee reluctantly provided him with identity papers as a paroled French POW, a document purporting to give him permission to travel to the next town, money, a map, the location of a safe house in Berlin, and a compass. Having been given upon his return to prison camp a "spanking new" olive drab U.S. Army uniform by the Red Cross, he dyed it "an attractive reddish brown," that with a change of the buttons and topped with a beret made him "one of the best-dressed Froggies [Frenchmen] in German captivity." With the escape documents stuffed in his underwear and shoes, he was assigned to a street work detail in a nearby town. Quartered for the night in a house, he squeezed through a narrow transom and between strands of barbed wire and out into the streets.

The following is his account of the escape:

> After one and a half night's traveling, mostly through woods, I got to the town with the railroad station where I was to entrain for Berlin and the safe house nearby. I walked to the station in broad daylight, bathed in admiring glances from Frauleins unaccustomed to such finery on a Froggie or anyone else, for that matter. Unchallenged, I approached the ticket window, presented my "credentials" and requested a ticket. I immediately saw, from the expression on the face of the old man at the window and

from his haste to get to the telephone, that a large stack of shit was about to hit the fan. I sprinted for the door, out of town and into a deep wood again, where I kept going until nightfall. A change of plan was in order—North and the Baltic beckoned.

After a few days, though, skulking through the night countryside, subsisting on raw potatoes and carrots dug from storage trenches in the fields, I became hopelessly sick with the malarial chills and fever again. I have no memory of how I got to a doctor's office and then back to Stalag II-B, but was told soldiers had found me at roadside. After convalescence I went before the Commandant and was sentenced to two weeks in the Cooler. He inquired as to my surprised expression and I answered that I expected more than three weeks, because that is what my sentence was the last time I escaped. He smiled and said, "It is soldier's duty to escape—but don't do it again, understand?"

Held in a temporary prison camp for five days after the parade of Rangers in Rome, Ken Markham found himself crammed with other Rangers in a boxcar and shipped to Florence with only bread for meals. About ten miles past the city, he saw a chance to attempt an escape by means of two small barbed-wire-covered windows on each side of the boxcar. After working the wire loose, he used a blanket to push it open wide enough for him to crawl out headfirst.

"I guess the train was going thirty-five to forty miles an hour," he said, "so I pushed out the window and just rolled and rolled and rolled. I must have rolled a hundred yards. I was banged up pretty good. There was another guy who followed me out. Germans were shooting at us. He [the other escapee] was going to meet me at a little bridge that we saw as we passed, so I worked my way back down there, waiting for him, and I heard more fire. I met him at the place. The next thing I remember is that we ran into a guy who was riding a bicycle. It was four in the morning. I thought to myself, "Maybe this guy was with the Underground or something." I asked him for something to eat because we were really hungry. Luckily, he took us into his apartment and the next day we got in touch with the Underground."

Markham stayed with the Italian partisans in an apartment in Florence for nearly a month, along with other Allied prisoners. When a British soldier ventured out one night, he was followed back to the hiding place by members of the Gestapo.

With the house surrounded, Markham crawled onto the roof but was caught and put in a civilian prison in Florence. He was held for about thirty days in a kind of dungeon with five men in the cell until the Red Cross demanded that they be moved into a regular POW camp, Stalag VII-A.

Ranger officers were held at Hammelburg in Lower Franconia, Bavaria, about twenty-five kilometers west of Schweinfurt. Among the prisoners were British veterans of Dunkirk who had been held since 1940 and a large number of Australians and New Zealanders who had been captured in Greece and Crete in 1941. The barrack blocks were rectangular in shape with a vat in the center that was used to boil water for tea or coffee. There were three-tiered bunks and tables with wooden benches on one side of the room. There was no hot water for washing and showers. The toilet was a "forty holer" at the end of the compound. Lights were turned out at 9:30 p.m. Guards patrolled the compound with dogs. Whether a POW lived depended on the whims or moods of guards. Clarence Meltesen reported that the shooting of Lieutenant John Weeks was cold-blooded murder by a guard at a gate. Muttering to the men as they passed him, the guard lifted his rifle, steadied it on a strand of barbed wire, and shot Weeks in the back of his head. An explanation was offered that the guard had recently lost his wife in an air raid.

Bing Evans recorded that after a second escape attempt he was in solitary confinement "because they figured I'd do something"; he was thrown naked into a heat cell with radiators all along one wall. Every now and then a German would come in and offer him a cigarette and turn the heat off, then give him a beating. When they decided this was worthless, he was sentenced to be shot as a spy and put into a Russian compound. He recalled, "[The Russians] were really starving to death. I remember they brought the bones of an old dead horse by and tossed those bones over to us; and I remember we fought like cats and dogs to get a bone. I got a big bone so you could eat the marrow out of it. Then I sat back and looked at myself and thought, 'What kind of a human being am I who can stand there and fight like an animal for the bones of an old dead horse?' I began crying, and still wake up crying."

Charles Shunstrom had already secured a unique place in Ranger history as the second lieutenant in command of men from Company C in the Dieppe Raid. He had assisted Darby in knocking out a German tank at Gela, and his skills with a mortar and as leader of the cannon company had become the stuff from which legends are born. He was taken to a POW camp at La Turina. Among the prisoners he met was U.S. Army Air Corps lieutenant Michael Mauritz. Forced to make a landing in German territory, Mauritz executed it so perfectly on marshy ground that his plane was barely damaged. Captured almost immediately and paraded through the streets of Rome with the Rangers, he found Italians who were forced to watch very quiet and interpreted this as their silent statement that "they supported us."

After nine days in the prison camp, Shunstrom and Mauritz plotted an escape. Although Shunstrom had naturally dark eyes and hair, Mauritz's hair was fair. In the hope of passing as an Italian, he slathered it with black shoe polish. According to Mauritz in an interview he gave to the author Francine Costello for a book she was planning on Mauritz's wartime exploits, the first person the two met after escaping was an Italian standing in the fields of the no-man's-land surrounding the camp. Mauritz asked him for a cigarette and was given tobacco and rolling papers. Later, a sympathetic but frightened woman gave them sausage and bread, then urged them to leave. Of others who assisted their escape, Mauritz said, "We experienced nothing but kindness from the Italians. We were never refused food from anyone, anywhere."

Recording that on a few occasions they were denied shelter by scared Italians, Mauritz said that almost everywhere they were allowed to sleep in first-floor stables, but with the clear understanding that if they were discovered and the Italians were accused of sheltering American *scapati* (escapees), the Italians would claim they were unaware that Americans had hidden in the stables.

Shunstrom and Mauritz's goal was to walk from La Turina in Tuscany to the Adriatic Coast at Ancona, where they had been told that British submarines on patrol regularly surfaced to look for escapees. During the five months that it took them to make the journey, they met and joined groups of Italian partisans in sabotaging German communications lines and carrying out Ranger-like raids on German installations.

Citing Shunstrom, Lieutenant William Newman, Sergeant Scotty Monroe, and others who had joined and organized the partisans into hard-hitting guerrilla raiders, Altieri credited them with making "slashing raids against enemy supply points, communications lines and arsenals" that played an important part in the Italian campaign by demoralizing the enemy and seriously disrupting and hampering the German war effort.

The approximately 10 percent of the Rangers captured at Cisterna who succeeded in escaping from German prison camps eventually held reunions and proudly named themselves the "Ranger Houdini Club."

★ CHAPTER 19 ★

HOME IS THE HERO

"Fort Smith's foremost citizen and soldier."

OBSERVING THE ANGUISH ON DARBY'S FACE IN THE HOURS AFTER HE informed Truscott of the destruction of the First and Third Ranger battalions at Cisterna, Major William S. Hutchinson, the executive officer of the Eighty-third Chemical (mortar) Battalion, believed Darby felt that if he had been with them, rather than behind the line at the Fourth's command post, the outcome of the battle would have been different.

As Hutchinson watched him become increasingly "despondent," he recalled a fateful day in Algeria in March 1942 when Darby ran into Lieutenant Colonel Kenneth A. Cunin on a street in Oran. The commanding officer of the Eighty-third Chemical Battalion, Cunin had been a friend since they served together in the Eighty-second Field Artillery at Fort Bliss in 1935. The result of the chance meeting in Algeria seven years later was Darby's request that Cunin's mortar outfit be attached to the Rangers for the invasion of Sicily. It was a decision that changed the character of the Rangers by adding firepower that was later augmented by Darby's creation of the cannon company. As Cunin's executive officer, Hutchinson witnessed several occasions that provided insight into Darby's leadership style and character. In a dramatic instance while Hutchinson was flat on his belly in the middle of a German barrage and directing return fire, Darby had walked up and stood next to him to carry on a conversation in view of the enemy. Hutchinson concluded from this that Darby "was deathly afraid that his troops would show fear," and that Darby "had to show courage in front of his men to inspire them to act bravely."

A decade earlier in Fort Smith, Darby had pledged to Virginia Gardner, "I will never be in back of my men." In a story that Rangers liked to tell, a staff officer looking for Darby went to the Salerno beach shortly after the landing. After stopping several men wearing the Ranger patch, he approached another asking for the commander. The Ranger replied, "You'll never find him this far back." Recalling Darby's attack on the German tank at Gela, James Altieri wrote, "Our Ranger chief and his tough right-hand man, Captain Shunstrom, had just performed one of the war's most outstanding and selfless acts of courage and daring. That was all the Rangers needed." Rangers who had been at El Guettar would never forget Darby's battle cry, "Onward we stagger, and if the tanks come, may God help the tanks."

Now, after two bitter days of fighting at Cisterna, Darby faced the grim reality that the First and Third battalions had been decimated and that the Fourth, in its attempt to break through and rescue the First and Third, had suffered severe losses, including five company commanders. The Rangers had lost more men at Cisterna than in their campaigns in North Africa, Sicily, Salerno, and Venafro. In less than two years an outfit that had begun as an experiment in the countryside of Northern Ireland had lived up to its illustrious name by leading four invasions and fighting in battles in African deserts, on mountains of Sicily and Italy, and finally on the marshy killing grounds of Cisterna di Littoria.

While able-bodied survivors of the First and Third who were not original Rangers would be attached to the Canadian-American First Special Service Force on February 19, and then assigned to conducting a scouting and patrolling school for the Fifth Army at Civitavecchia, near Naples, the Fourth Battalion was assigned to guard lines of communication from February 1 to 3, then moved into a forward bivouac area, where they came under intermittent enemy fire for a week. During this period, Captain Roy Murray was hospitalized with jaundice. Command of the battalion was temporarily assumed by Walter Nye.

Noting that the First Division had fared little better in the effort to break out from Anzio than the Sixth Corps and the Rangers had done in taking Cisterna, General Truscott had orders from General Lucas to "stop all attacks, dig in for defense, and hold the Corps Beachhead Line at all costs" against an expected assault aimed at smashing the Anzio beachhead and thwarting the Allied drive toward Rome. The 100,000 Americans faced the German Fourteenth Army, which had swollen to 125,000 men. The German counterattack began on the morning of February 4.

With the battle still raging on February 10, the Fourth Battalion, with Roy Murray back in command, was attached to the 504th Parachute Infantry Regiment and placed in reserve near the Mussolini Canal. The area that quickly became known to the Rangers as "Hell's Corner" was described by Altieri as a "patch of bitterly contested beachhead real estate." He wrote, "We didn't like this kind of defensive fighting, we weren't trained or equipped for it, but we knew the situation was so desperate that every soldier, be he paratrooper, Ranger, or infantryman, was needed to save the beachhead."

Seven days after the Fourth moved into position, Darby, although slightly wounded by a bomb fragment on the night of February 15, was relieved as commander of the Ranger Force and assigned to the Third Infantry Division. The shock of losing command of the outfit he had built and led was followed the next day by orders placing him—at long last—in command of a regular regiment. Apparently having rebounded from the Cisterna disaster, he was described as smiling and showing "contagious confidence, energy and enthusiasm" that "invigorated" headquarters of the 179th Infantry Regiment, Forty-fifth Infantry Division. Dug in north of the Padiglione Woods, it was taking heavy losses and being forced back to a defensive perimeter close to the original beachhead. When Darby took command at 1400, he learned that its shattered Third Battalion had been withdrawn for reorganization and the Second was at less than half strength and nearly exhausted. Only the First Battalion was capable of organized resistance.

Communication lines between the regiment and the battalions were out, complicating the task of creating a coordinated defense. Calling together his battalion commanders, Darby told the First Battalion to hold the left sector. The Second Battalion commander was ordered to take over the right sector with whatever troops he could find. Major Merlin O. Tyron, commander of the Third Battalion, was to "endeavor to get all stragglers and pick all men physically fit in the rear echelon" to join in the battle.

Confronted with the possibility of seeing the destruction of his second command in three weeks by an overwhelming enemy force, Darby saw no recourse but for the battered regiment to fall back to the woods to reorganize. Contacting Forty-fifth Division Commander Major General William W. Eagles by radio, he reported, "We are getting attacked all along the front. We will have to get out of here. We can't keep this CP here any longer and still function. These people are pretty shaken. There are men streaming back from all directions and it's going to be a job to get them organized."

Eagles replied to the request with an order to hold the final beachhead line "at all costs" and promised the support of the First Battalion, 157th Infantry. By good fortune or a failure of the Germans' intelligence gathering, the tide of the fight abruptly shifted from the 179th's position to that of another regiment, and after two days the five-day counterattack ended. For the rest of February and into March the Anzio beachhead became a reminder of the stalemate of the Western Front in World War I, with Rangers, in Altieri's words, "fighting from dugouts and trenches." For Darby the situation was an opportunity to show why he had gained a reputation for effective use of artillery support.

In a telling example of his regard for employing technology and making the maximum use of his assets, Roy Murray on a visit from the Fourth Battalion found Darby testing a grenade-throwing machine that consisted of an inner tube tied to the crotch of a tree to form a slingshot. He fashioned it, he explained to Murray, because he had "more grenades than men."

A few days after Murray's visit, the Fourth Battalion was detached from the parachute unit and moved to a bivouac area and divided into two groups. Those who were not considered "veteran personnel" were transferred to the First Special Service Force. Murray and the others (19 officers and 134 enlisted men), whom Altieri called "the old, war-weary surviving Ranger veterans," were informed that they were being sent home to train other troops and tour the United States for "inspirational purposes." They sailed from Naples on March 27, 1944.

Still the diligent chronicler of the Rangers, James Altieri recorded:

> Of our original Fox Company, about one-third
> survived. Sergeant Dunn, Corporal Fuller, Tech Ser-
> geant Junior Fronk and First Lieutenant Harris, along

with Major Nye, Colonel Murray and I, came back together.

Carlo Contrera—my old buddy—who had been with Colonel Darby throughout the bitter Anzio battle, came back to marry his Brooklyn sweetheart. Sergeant Smith, my old First Armored battery mate, came through unscratched. And Phil Stern—Hollywood's best photographer—was on hand as a full-fledged photographer for *Life* magazine, which did a spread on us.

Wounded in a salvo of German shells at El Guettar, Stern had tried to rejoin the Rangers, but was finally discharged because of his wounds. The *Life* article, published on July 31, 1944, featured a photo of Darby on his motorcycle (taken by Stern in Sicily). Chuck Shunstrom, who had returned to the Rangers after his escape from Stalag II-B, was depicted at home with his wife and "playing gently with his child," but described in the caption as the Rangers' "outstanding solo killer." Roy Murray appeared lying on an army cot in a barracks identified by Murray as "the most comfortable home I've had in years." A full page was devoted to before-and-after portraits of Second Lieutenant Gino Mercuriali. In the first, he was a brand-new Ranger with a "boyish face," wearing a cloth garrison cap, which contrasted with the second as a "wiser but much older" veteran in a helmet with a rifle slung over his shoulder. Two pages contained Phil Stern's fresh portraits of twelve of the returned Rangers.

A large photo that was taken by Stern at Camp Butner, North Carolina, showed "the Rangers' terrible loss." Ninety-seven of the original Rangers stood in a formation in front of troops representing the original First Battalion's strength (about fifteen hundred).

The article's headline read:

THE RANGERS

SURVIVORS OF TOUGHEST, MOST BITTERLY LACERATED U.S. INFANTRY
FORCE ARE HOME FOR WELL-EARNED REST

The story began, "The survivors of the First, Third and Fourth Ranger Battalions are home. These men have exposed themselves to danger in more actions, with higher casualties, perhaps also with a greater fierceness of spirit, than any other American Army units."

Because General Clark felt that their founder and leader needed and deserved a rest, and because it was feared that the famous commander of the heroic Darby's Rangers might be killed in action, Darby would follow them home in early April with orders to report to Washington for duty with the Operations Division of the War Department. Tasked with issuing orders down the chain of command for execution of the directives from Chief of Staff George C. Marshall, the office was divided into the Strategy and Policy Group, Executive Group, Logistics Group, and Theater Group, which was organized by sections according to theaters of operation. Darby was assigned to the North African and Mediterranean sections. But before assuming his duties, he was granted a leave.

For his first furlough in four years, he headed to Arkansas by plane on Monday, April 24, with a promise by the officials of his hometown, as announced in the newspaper *Southwest American*, that he would receive "the greatest ovation for a military hero in Fort Smith since General Zachary Taylor rode away to the Mexican war." Plans for a parade on April 25 that was organized by members of the Fort Smith American Legion called for it to commence at four in the afternoon in front of the redbrick, neo-Gothic Immaculate Conception Catholic Church and go down Garrison Avenue, wheel left near the bridge, pass a statue honoring Confederate heroes, and halt at the courthouse. All streetlamp posts and building fronts were clad in red-white-and-blue bunting and American flags.

When the parade began with a police detail in the lead, followed by ranks of Fort Smith's State Guard Unit, commanded by Captain Randolph Sengel, the marching tempo was set by the Fort Smith High School Band. A line of open cars carrying city, state, and federal dignitaries and members of the American Legion was followed by Darby seated between his beaming parents in the rear of a convertible, with Doris Nell in the front. As the parade reached Sixth Street to turn toward the courthouse, confetti and streamers cast from the windows of the First National Bank resembled a multicolored snowstorm. When Darby stepped from the car to cheers from more than twenty-five hundred Fort Smithians, the west steps of the courthouse were flanked by banks of red roses and white snapdragons. The 203rd Army Band from nearby Camp Chaffee played the Army's anthem, "The Caisson Song."

Introduced by master of ceremonies J. E. Garner, Mayor Chester Holland presented Darby with a parchment scroll bearing greetings and expressing "the esteem of the citizens of Fort Smith" for the city's "foremost citizen and soldier."

Darby began his remarks by recalling how Mayor Holland used to "shoo" Billy Darby from his front porch and thanked him for not "scatting" him off the courthouse steps. He told the crowd, "The thing I was fighting for was to come back to such a wonderful family, and to come back to the most beautiful community in the world. And I feel qualified to say it. You can never sell me any travel tickets to Sicily, Italy, or North Africa."

The ceremony ended with the army band playing "The Star-Spangled Banner."

Reporting the festivities the next day, the *Southwest Times Record* noted, "Following the ceremony, the colonel received hundreds of friends, admirers, and autograph seekers in the foyer of the courthouse building."

Among the crowd that thronged the courthouse that day was Virginia Gardner. Recalling the event more than two decades later in the tribute to Darby published by the ninth-graders of the William O. Darby Junior High School, she said:

> The town was going to give him a big reception; a parade down the avenue and over to the courthouse, but [his mother] said, "I don't think Bill will do it. He doesn't like attention." So they asked my brother to go with them to the airport to convince him. So Carnell [her brother] went out and met Bill. On the way to town he said, "Bill, the avenue is lined on both sides of the street with people waiting for you."
>
> Bill said, "I'm no hero. I'm not going to do that."
>
> After about two blocks [of looking at the cheering crowds along the street while seated in the back of the car], Bill turned to Mrs. Darby and said, "You know these people want to see that I'm here."
>
> She said, "I told you so, son."
>
> So he stood up in the convertible and they went down the avenue.

Two days after the homecoming an Associated Press story from Washington, D.C., read:

> **To get to the enemy first and leave last is the job of the Army's Rangers, their young commander, Colonel William O. Darby, disclosed today in the first official account of how the little band of night fighters and marauders operates.**
>
> **Darby is a veteran of battles in North Africa and Italy (he wears the Distinguished Service Cross, Purple Heart, Silver Star and the British**

Distinguished Service Order) and the organizer of the Ranger force. The Rangers went into action for the first time when they slipped ashore on North Africa in the pre-dawn darkness of November 8, 1942, before the enemy knew the Rangers were there. When the Nazis pushed the Allies back at Kasserine Pass, the Rangers held off the Germans until the main body of Allied troops could take up defensible positions. At Anzio, Italy, they went ashore to move into the seacoast towns and then advance as the beachhead moved inland. Orders came to infiltrate German lines in a night operation. "We accomplished the mission; the initial part was successful; the Germans had more stuff than we did, so we sort of got sawed off and lost quite a few Rangers," Darby said of that operation.

Back in Washington only briefly, Darby inspected training facilities at Fort Meade, Maryland; Camp Croft, South Carolina; Fort McClellan, Alabama; and Camp Wheeler and Fort Benning, Georgia, where he had a reunion with five former Ranger officers who were instructors at the Infantry School. While there he also appeared on the NBC radio program *The Army Hour* and told the national audience that the Rangers were not supermen. They were "just infantry foot soldiers, well-trained, eager" and "willing to go through the toughest kind of training to insure the success of their mission." In early June he visited Camp Robinson, Arkansas, and Camps Wolters, Hood, and Fannin in Texas.

Shortly after he returned to Washington from the tour, a West Point classmate, William A. Baumer, Jr., reported to the Operations Division from duty as a liaison officer in Moscow and in London in Eisenhower's Supreme Headquarters, Allied Expeditionary Force. Also the author of popular books for relatives of servicemen and for brand-new soldiers (*He's in the Army Now, 21 to 35: What the Draft and Army Training Mean to You*, and *How to Be an Army Officer*), and a recent history of the U.S. Military Academy, *West Point: Moulder of Men* (1942), Baumer had learned that his New York publishing house was interested in a book on Darby's Rangers. When he informed Darby of this, Darby and Herman Dammer met Baumer at his home in the evenings. With his account of Rangers' history recorded by a stenographer in an adjoining room, the manuscript was completed after six weeks of "night work," in Baumer's words, during which the long-anticipated invasion of France had occurred. When Baumer told his publisher the story of the Rangers was written, he was informed that since D-day (June 6, 1944) "the market for war books had taken a nosedive." With no interest in a book about the Rangers, and Baumer himself transferred to France, the manuscript was consigned to Baumer's file cabinet.

Darby passed the time reading stacks of classified documents that crossed his War Department desk on the status and progress of the action in the theater of war assigned to him. He followed the campaign in Italy through newspapers and the radio. He felt as though he were an actor who had strode the stage for the first two acts of a great drama and then been written out of the last.

After leading the Rangers through nearly two years of almost constant fighting, he was now an ocean away from the action and relegated to touring training camps and writing reports brimming with suggestions for improvements. He found himself contending with a capital city awash with certainty that victory was within reach and populated by hostesses who believed they had a right to expect a certified war hero to accept invitations.

Less than two months after Cisterna, he had been thrust into a place that David Brinkley, who had served in World War II and in the final months of the war as the NBC White House correspondent, would describe in his 1988 book *Washington Goes to War* as "socially the most aggressive and most tireless city in the western world." Because Darby was not only the highly decorated leader of the celebrated "Darby's Rangers," but a handsome, young, and unmarried officer, he received invitations to dinners, luncheons, Sunday brunches, receptions, and cocktail parties. "Often there were fifty to one hundred a night," wrote Brinkley of the latter, "and from the mezzanine floor of the Statler Hotel downtown on across town through Northwest into the suburbs there was the rattle of ice and glass, the drone of conversation and the loud shriek of alcoholic laughter."

Darby's frustration over not being at the front became even more acute when he learned on June 4 that the Allies had at long last entered Rome. It had taken five months of fighting to get there, but the triumphal taking of the city was for Darby's Rangers a sweet payback for the humiliation the Germans had inflicted on the Rangers who had been captured at Cisterna and paraded around the Colosseum. But the liberation was eclipsed two days later by landings at Normandy, with the Second and Fifth Ranger battalions leading the way. Two days after these triumphs, Darby traveled south to Camp Butner, North Carolina, for a melancholy reunion with remnants of his original Rangers on the second anniversary of the activation of the First Ranger Battalion. While they relived their fights from Arzew to Cisterna, they were mindful that at Normandy the Second Ranger Battalion that had been formed and trained in the United States had climbed the sheer cliffs of Pointe du Hoc of Omaha Beach. Noting that they were "proudly carrying on the Ranger traditions," James Altieri recalled that the Second Battalion was led by original Darby Ranger Max Schneider.

Throughout a hot and humid Washington summer, Darby enjoyed the companionship of several West Point classmates who had been assigned to staff positions in Washington. Edward T. Ashworth,

Morris O. Edwards, Guy C. Lothrop, Edwin D. Marshall, Jack W. Rudolph, and Lawrence J. Lincoln discerned his "unhappiness at not being in combat."

In a conversation with Lincoln, Darby speculated on the success Ranger techniques might have against the Japanese and gave the impression that he yearned for the job. This idea was also presented to James Altieri. During a lunch with Altieri at the Pentagon, Darby said, "I hate this job. I'd like to get up another Ranger outfit and go out to the Pacific. Would you come along?"

Altieri answered that he would, and that "every Ranger would do the same."

With a smile, Darby replied, "That's the old spirit."

Although Darby was unhappy with his position as a staff officer, his annual efficiency report by Brigadier General J. DeF. Baker described him as "an energetic and forceful officer." In language reminiscent of that of Darby's classmates and teachers at Fort Smith and officers and enlisted men of the Rangers, he depicted "a very agreeable personality which complements his energy and force." These were qualities that marked Darby's astonishing rise in a period of two years from captain and aide-de-camp to General Hartle to colonel. But they were not the sole factors. Nor was he simply lucky. He was certainly brave, but courage and valor were ample commodities in all the ranks of every branch of the armed services in World War II. What he had that was not common is found in the 1929 essay. He wrote, "I intend to become great."

Reminiscing about his childhood friend, Ross Rhodes observed, "He wasn't the most brilliant guy in the world, but he was a hard worker, dedicated and ambitious." Noting that the "ambitious officer who has a practical understanding of the army's bureaucracy can use it to his advantage," the military historian and Darby biographer Michael J. King wrote, "Darby's career is proof of this. His promotions were swiftest and most predictable when he made certain peculiarities of the army's bureaucracy, but were frustrated when he misperceived or disregarded those peculiarities."

Unwilling to accept being removed from combat command and the frustration of his ambition by being confined to a desk job in Washington, Darby elected to attempt to use the army's bureaucracy by appealing to Fifth Army commander Mark Clark to use his "influence" to arrange a transfer to Italy. While Clark was sympathetic, he informed Darby that he was unable to help. On a visit with Herman Dammer and his wife, Elizabeth, Darby expressed "distaste for staff work" and admitted to "despairing of ever again seeing combat." When the Darby-Dammer team addressed the faculty of the Army and Navy Staff College in Washington on lessons to be learned in the history of the Rangers, he became so energetic that he cut a finger on a sliding map board. Gazing at the wound, he joked that he had not lost "that much blood" in the war.

In the autumn of 1944, certification of his heroism on the battlefield came with the official awarding of decorations for which he had been recommended, including the Legion of Merit, the French Croix de Guerre, the Soviet Union's Order of Kutuzov Third Class, and the Oak Leaf Cluster to the Purple Heart. His work in the Operations Division was rewarded with his promotion to the head of the North African and Mediterranean theater sections. With it came a ten-day leave that he spent visiting Fort Smith. Back at his desk, he read reports of the German attack in Belgium at Christmas, known as the Battle of the Bulge; noted that in the Pacific War the "Ranger spirit" motivated the Sixth Ranger Battalion in assaulting a notorious Japanese prison camp at Cabanatuan, the Philippines, in January, liberating American POWs, including survivors of the 1941 Bataan death march; and followed the steady progress of the Second and Fifth Ranger battalions as they moved into Germany. And he read with great interest of the Tenth Mountain Division fighting in the mountains of northern Italy.

Convinced that the European war was in its final throes, and that his only hope of seeing action lay in the Pacific, where he anticipated that the final act would be the invasion of Japan, he arrived at his office on March 29, 1945, and found orders assigning him to a ninety-day tour of the European theater, along with the Army Air Forces chief General Henry (Hap) Arnold, with the main purpose of evaluating aerial support of ground combat. The next day, the orders were amended to allow him to visit other theaters if he thought it was "necessary." Knowing it was accepted army practice that an officer visiting a major command might be transferred to it if the commanding general agreed, he seized the opportunity to appeal to the commander of the Tenth Mountain Division. He happened to be Darby's old friend, Major General George P. Hays. He was a lieutenant colonel and commander of the Ninety-ninth Field Artillery (Pack) in 1940 and 1941 when Darby was commander of its Battery A. So confident was Darby that Hays would welcome him to his staff that he informed Dammer that he was "going to Italy to join the Tenth Mountain Division."

Once again, Darby's ambition was the beneficiary of a coincidence. As he had been in the right place at the right time when General Hartle was empowered to pick the man to set up the Rangers in Northern Ireland, he arrived at Hays's headquarters when Hays needed someone to take over as assistant division commander, replacing Brigadier General Robinson E. Duff, who had been wounded and evacuated. With General Clark's approval and the assent of the high command in the War Department that Darby be transferred (entitling him to promotion to brigadier general), Darby assumed the post on April 25, 1945.

★CHAPTER 20★

ITALIAN SPRING

"Don't let me do anything stupid."

W~HEN~ B~RIGADIER~ G~ENERAL~ D~UFF~'S ~AIDE-DE-CAMP~, S~ECOND~ L~IEU~-tenant Kenneth S. Templeton, Jr., returned to Tenth Mountain Division headquarters on the northern outskirts of San Benedetto after two days in the rear attending to the hospitalized Duff in Castelfranco, Lieutenant Muldrow Garrison told Templeton they had a new boss and that they should be prepared "to take off at any moment" on a mission that had been assigned to what was now "Task Force Darby" to capture Verona. The unit was composed of the Eighty-sixth Mountain Infantry Regiment, Thirteenth Tank Battalion, the

1125th Armored Field Artillery Battalion, Company B of the 701st Tank Destroyer Battalion, Company B of the 751st Tank Battalion, and elements of the 126th Engineer Battalion and the Tenth Medical Battalion.

Templeton recalled, "Darby greeted me in what I should call his typically friendly, efficient manner and came straight to the point: 'Templeton, there are just two things I want you to be sure to do. First, be able to keep me informed at all times of our position, and secondly, don't let me do anything stupid!' "

Templeton assured him he would try to do his best, but he admitted later that he had "misgivings" about the second assignment because he had learned that keeping assistant division commanders out of trouble presented "even more difficulties and frustrations than the camel's passing through the eye of the needle. If Colonel Darby were to operate in the same manner as had Duff, I knew that every day we would find ourselves in 'hot spots,' any one of which might prove disastrous."

Later that afternoon (April 25), Task Force Darby began to move across the Po River. The crossing had been delayed for several hours because of last-minute bridging difficulties. During the preceding three days, the Eighty-fifth and the Eighty-seventh Mountain Infantry regiments had established and expanded a bridgehead on the north bank of the Po.

Darby in his jeep proceeded to the head of the task force column shortly after its leading elements crossed the river. He then drove ahead in order to make certain that the route had been cleared and units had successfully reached Villafranca, about ten miles southwest of Verona.

Reaching the town shortly after 1900 hours, he ascertained that the entire town and its neighboring airfield had been secured so that everything was in readiness for Task Force Darby to use it for its assault on Verona. He then left Villafranca and returned along Highway

62 to the head of the task force, which by this time had moved up to a point within about five miles of Villafranca.

Darkness had fallen, but a nearly full moon provided good visibility.

About ten o'clock the commanders of the various task force elements conferred with Darby at a command post in a small stone house on the northern outskirts of Villafranca. As he spelled out with the aid of various maps his plan of attack on Verona and issued his final orders, Templeton was impressed by his "carefully and minutely worked-out tactics," as well as by his "lucid and vigorous explanation of the plan of attack" to his subordinate commanders. At the same time he called for suggestions and integrated them into his final plans.

Throughout the night a number of German vehicles stumbled into outposts that the First Battalion of the Eighty-fifth had established around Villafranca. The sky was repeatedly lit by flashes of German ammunition dumps being blown up, either by partisans or the Germans.

According to Templeton, at 0400 hours Task Force Darby began the advance on Verona. The main force of one battalion of the Eighty-sixth Regiment and attached tanks moved down Highway 62 and dispersed small pockets of resistance before reaching the outskirts of the city. A second force composed of another battalion of the Eighty-sixth and attached tanks closed in on the city along a secondary road that roughly paralleled Highway 62 about one mile to the west. Both of these columns began their penetrations into the city proper about 0530, shortly after dawn. Meeting only scattered and disconnected groups of enemy personnel, the infantry and tanks cleared the entire city south of the Adige. The main body of German troops had apparently already fled north from the city into the Italian Alps. Elements of the Eighty-fifth Infantry's 351st Infantry, motoring up Highway 12 from Ostiglia, had entered Verona the previous evening and by dawn had largely silenced German opposition there.

Darby had moved forward to direct these final operations and rode through the streets on a tank, with Italians "jamming the streets and leaning out windows" and cheering. Satisfied that the Germans had effectively demolished every bridge across the Adige, he ordered the task force to swing northwest along the southern bank of the Adige, with the objectives of capturing Bussolengo about seven miles from Verona and trying to take any Adige bridges that might remain intact between Verona and Bussolengo. One battalion of the Eighty-sixth was ordered to mop up the Verona area and temporarily police the city.

When Darby returned to Villafranca at 1000 hours on April 26, he reported to Hays at the advance division command post. Hays called a conference of staff and commanders. By noon it was decided that the division would swing westward and continue its advance northward along the eastern shores of Lake Garda, rather than try to cross the Adige and pursue the Germans up Highway 12, the main route to the Brenner Pass.

During the early afternoon Darby returned to Verona and then followed the route of his task force northwest from the city, arriving at Bussolengo about 1600 hours. A wooden bridge crossing the Adige had been found intact in the vicinity of Bussolengo, so that infantry patrols of the task force had crossed the river and were patrolling the northern bank. German vehicles were intercepted trying to flee northward on Highway 12. Darby recalled these patrols to the southern bank of the Adige and, in line with the division's new objective, ordered one battalion of the Eighty-sixth with supporting tanks to continue the drive west and by nightfall seize Lazise on the southeastern shores of Lake Garda, sealing off a possible German escape route along the highway running northward on the eastern shores of Lake Garda.

In one day of operations, Templeton noted, Task Force Darby "had not only spearheaded the second longest, twenty-four-hour divisional advance of the campaign (22.5 miles), but successfully cleared all enemy personnel from the area of its advance and had physically occupied a thirteen-mile front along the southern bank of the Adige from Verona to Bussolengo and overland to Lazise." On April 27 the division's advance up the eastern shores of Lake Garda was continued by regimental and battalion operations performed by the Eighty-fifth and Eighty-seventh with tank support.

"Darby's mission," recalled Templeton, "was to keep in close contact with our leading elements and provide General Hays with on-the-spot information. He succeeded in doing this so well that, on entering a house in the town of Garda, he could have eaten the German officers' luncheon, which was still warm on their plates. Another twenty-mile advance was made on this day to Malcesine, just ten miles short of the northern end of the lake."

On April 28 the advance was limited to five miles because the Germans had successfully blown up the first of six tunnels on a road that passed at that point. Attempts by partisans who had been instructed to try to prevent their demolition had failed.

The cliffs rose so sharply and so high from the edge of the lake, Templeton recorded, that the advance was continued by means of an amphibious operation using DUKWs, supported by tank destroyers and artillery. This caught the Germans off balance, so that remaining tunnels were captured intact.

On the morning of April 29 Darby went forward by means of a speedboat and then by jeep to investigate the progress of the Third Battalion of the Eighty-sixth, held up because of enemy direct fire into the fifth tunnel by self-propelled guns at the head of the lake. Five men had been killed and approximately fifty wounded by a German shell that exploded ten yards into the tunnel. General Hays joined Darby a short time later to assess the situation. Around noon, they climbed into a speedboat and went out into the lake to return to the division command post. A few seconds later, a shell burst in the water about fifty yards to the right rear of the boat. The driver "turned on the gas," going back down the lake as fast as possible. Seven more shells burst about the same distance wide and short as the boat scooted the next half mile before swinging in for cover behind a small promontory. "No sooner had this maneuver been executed," noted Templeton, "than the engine died—out of gas! Fortunately, the Krauts had not been as accurate in their naval gunnery as they had been in zeroing in on the mouth of tunnel number five. All during the 28th and 29th we could observe German vehicles fleeing northward on Highway 45, which ran along the shore on the opposite side of the lake. Our attached British 5.5-inch guns opened up periodically on this traffic."

At 2400 hours on April 29, Darby took charge of an amphibious operation. This involved sending Company K of the Eighty-fifth across the lake in DUKWs to seize Gargnano and cut the escape route up Highway 45. The operation was successfully completed by 0200 hours.

Later in the morning Darby and division officers crossed the lake to inspect Mussolini's mansion and estate on the outskirts of Gargnano. Other elements of the Eighty-fifth were ferried across the lake and by noon of April 30 the division had two columns closing in on the town of Riva at the head of the lake. The Eighty-sixth had taken Torbole and was pushing on toward Riva, three miles away. At about 1400 hours, Darby arrived by DUKW at Torbole. Germans on high ground to the north had almost perfect observation of troop movements. After landing, he walked immediately to the Eighty-sixth regimental command post, located in a small hotel close to the waterfront. For about half an hour he conferred with the regimental commander and his staff concerning pushing the attack northward from Torbole and Riva to Trento and Bolzano.

Templeton recalled, "About three minutes before Darby concluded this conference, a single 88mm round was heard bursting somewhere nearby in the town. Of course, the Germans, seeing our DUKWs put in and out of Torbole, had periodically shelled the town's waterfront that day but had not inflicted any serious damage on us. Nevertheless, why just one round should come in was a question that should certainly have given pause to any artilleryman and also, perhaps, to any battlewise infantryman."

Darby stepped outside, intending to take a jeep back along the eastern shore to examine the road and tunnels. Since the engineers were supposed to have unblocked tunnel number one, he wanted to be sure that everything was clear for a rapid movement forward by tanks and heavy artillery to provide proper support to the projected infantry attack into the mountains to the north. As he paused in the warmth of the Italian springtime with the sunlight glinting off the placid lake to talk with the regimental commander, Lieutenant Colonel Robert L. Cook, and Brigadier General David L. Ruffner, the division artillery commander, he and every officer and soldier around him knew that the end of the war was close at hand.

The day before, Italian partisans in Milan had captured Benito Mussolini and hanged his battered corpse upside down from a lamppost by the heels. The German commander in Italy had also announced that all his forces would surrender unconditionally at noon on May 2. The U.S. Army was deep inside Germany. The Russians were in Berlin. Hitler had committed suicide. All that was left was for Ike to accept an official German surrender.

Two weeks earlier, Darby had feared that when it occurred all that anyone was likely to remember about William Orlando Darby was that after he had allowed the Rangers to get wiped out at Cisterna, he had been sidelined behind a desk. Now he was back in combat in a job that meant a brigadier general's star—the first of his West Point class—and he was only thirty-four years old. In the war from the start and present at the finish, he could claim that he had met the challenge of turning a concept of a new kind of American soldiering into a reality called the Rangers, and then led them from Arzew, Sened Station, and El Guettar to Gela, Salerno, Chiunzi Pass, Venafro, Anzio, and Cisterna. Together, they'd enshrined those names in the battle history of the U.S. Army with as much deserved glory as those of Bunker Hill, Gettysburg, San Juan Hill, Château-Thierry, Guadalcanal, and Bastogne in the Battle of the Bulge.

When the jeep driven by Regimental Sergeant Major John T. Evans swung around the corner and stopped, Templeton heard the whine of an incoming artillery shell. Half of the dozen men surrounding him were wounded by exploding shards of the shrapnel. General Ruffner was unhurt, but a large chunk of hot metal nearly decapitated Evans. He died instantly. McLellan was hit in a thigh and ankle. Cook took shrapnel in the left hip.

Darby was slammed to the ground. A piece of shrapnel about the size of a dime had sliced into his heart. As he was taken from the porch by Cook, who was so dazed that he was unaware of his own wound, Darby was breathing, but unconscious. He was put on a cot. Two medics were summoned from a nearby building.

Two minutes later, Colonel William Orlando Darby was declared dead.

★ EPILOGUE ★

LEGEND AND LEGACY

"Your record speaks for itself."

WHEN PERCY DARBY WALKED INTO FORT SMITH HIGH SCHOOL'S auditorium on the afternoon of May 1, 1945, and interrupted a rehearsal of the annual senior class play, his daughter, Doris Nell, knew from the grim expression on his face that he must be bearing bad news about her brother. Had something happened to Doris's mother, she reasoned, he would have stayed with Nellie and there would have been a phone call to the school and someone in the principal's office would have come to the auditorium. As she left the school in tears with Percy's arm around a shoulder, her classmates, lifelong friends, and teachers knew that she and her brother had always been exceptionally close.

She enjoyed recalling that when she was a little girl, Billy would "swoop through the house," grab her and sling her over his shoulder, put her on the handlebars of her bicycle and then pedal her around the block. When he was home on leave from the army and she felt sad that the end of his visit was near, he would say, "Keep your chin up, sis. Everything is all right."

She'd giggled with delight when he showed her his West Point yearbook with a part in a passage below his picture that read, "As for vices, he has a baby sister for whom he blows soap bubbles full of smoke." (Despite this evidence that Darby indulged in cigarettes, and photos showing him with a drink in hand, Doris insisted years later that he neither smoked nor imbibed alcohol.)

No one in the welcome-home parade had looked prouder than Doris Nell as she rode in the front seat of the car carrying him and his parents to the courthouse ceremony. A few weeks before she was informed of his death, she had reported excitedly to everyone in the senior class that he'd phoned her from Washington to promise that after the trip to Europe to tour army bases, he would be home to see her graduate.

The War Department telegram to the Darby home said that he was killed in action but gave no details. So well known was he in Fort Smith that the writer of the headline above the story in the *Southwest American* reporting that he had been killed in action felt no need to give his first name. It read:

COLONEL DARBY IS DEAD IN ITALY

The Darby family listened to an eyewitness account of how he was killed, several months later during a visit to their home by Major General Ruffner, then serving at Camp Chaffee just outside of Fort Smith. After recalling having first met Darby at Fort Bliss, Texas, in

1935, and encountering him four years later at Fort Lewis, Washington, he related not seeing him again until Darby arrived in the Po Valley in Italy as second in command of the Tenth Mountain Division, replacing General Duff. According to a report on Ruffner's visit with the Darbys in the *Arkansas Gazette*, Ruffner said:

> **I had already crossed the Po River, and I came back that night, when General Hays told me Bill was taking over. There followed seven days of continuous action. By the way, did you know Bill was in an amphibious operation? Well, we were inland, all right, but Bill led a task force from the Po River north, and he used "ducks"—those vehicles that can go over land or over water. I'll bet you never knew that Bill did some fighting on water.**
>
> **But I didn't see too much of Bill during those last seven days. He fought around the clock, day and night. There was no off-duty for Bill, then. He was a hell of a good soldier.**

Mrs. Darby asked, "You were with him when he was killed?"

"I was shoulder to shoulder with him when he got hit," said Ruffner. "We were standing there—a group of nine of us. That area was supposed to be safe. But a shell exploded over us. It was a freak shell, you might say. A one-in-a-million shell that came close to that area by pure accident. We had just taken the village the night before. The shell burst ten feet overhead. I was standing right next to Bill. All of us were knocked down. I got up and Bill was lying at my feet. I bent down and felt of him. I thought he was unconscious. A man came over and looked at him. He felt inside Bill's jacket. The aide looked up at me and said, 'He's dead.' "

Mrs. Darby asked, "Was Bill butchered by the shell?"

"No. He got a chunk of shrapnel right here," said Ruffner, placing a hand over his heart. "He never knew what hit him. He died instantly."

"I always feared that Bill might have been torn up by the shell. I'm glad he went quickly." Thus the conversation went. Small talk. Informal conversation. Reminiscing tales. And so a commanding general, visiting a print shop owner and his wife, again brought to life the memory of an already legendary army figure, General William O. Darby, who in the words of General Ruffner, was "a fine man, a wonderful officer, a hell of a good soldier!' "

Darby's promotion to brigadier general was an event without army precedent. He had gone from captain to one-star general in three years and eleven months. The promotion had been recommended before his death, and when Secretary of War Henry L. Stimson presented the papers to President Harry Truman on May 15, 1945, the rise in rank was approved as if Darby were alive. It was the only such promotion to star rank in the war.

Having created the First Ranger Battalion in June 1942 and then organized the Third and Fourth a year later, Darby had outlived them all. The First and Third were officially deactivated on August 15 and 16, 1944, and the Fourth was disbanded on October 24. In a formal farewell in a message in April 1945 to "the officers and men who served," he had said:

> Whether it was in training or battle, your unwavering, indomitable spirit forged by painstaking and diligent zeal has always persevered. Your resourcefulness and initiative have earned for you the respect and esteem of all true fighting men the world over. You have done much to aid the Allied cause in this war.
>
> As your commanding officer, I am justly proud to have led such an outstanding group of American

fighting men. Never was I more sad than on the day of our parting. Never was I more content than being with you on our many exciting operations. You trained hard, you fought hard, and always you gave your best regardless of discomfort or danger. From the great Allied raid at Dieppe through the exacting, bitter campaigns culminating with the Anzio beachhead battles, the First, Third, and Fourth battalions have performed in a capacity unsurpassed by the highest traditions of the American army. Your record speaks for itself.

We—the living Rangers—will never forget our fallen comrades. They and the ideals for which they fought will remain forever present among us. For we fully understand the extent of their heroic sacrifices. We will carry their spirit with us into all walks of life, into all corners of America. Our hearts join together in sorrow for their loss, but also our hearts swell with pride to have fought alongside such valiant men. They will never be considered dead, for they live with us in spirit.

Darby's last words to his men concluded, "Commanding the Rangers was like driving a team of very high-spirited horses. No effort was needed to get them to go forward. The problem was to hold them in check."

When his body was brought from an American military cemetery in Italy to be interred in Fort Smith National Cemetery on March 3, 1949, Rangers formed the honor guard in what was the first of numerous commemorations by the people of Fort Smith of its famous war hero. The tributes included bestowing his name on the junior high school in 1955 (the building had been the high school that Darby attended) and, three years later, changing the name of the school's sports teams from "Cubs" to "Rangers." The Darby boyhood house on East Eighth Street, which was renamed General Darby Street, became headquarters of the William O. Darby Ranger Memorial Foundation (begun in 1977), as well as a museum with the first floor as it was on the day the death-notice telegram was delivered. Darby artifacts were also preserved in the city's Old Fort Museum. Acknowledging the tragedy that befell the Rangers after the Anzio invasion, Fort Smith declared Cisterna a "sister city" and hosted a delegation from Cisterna on a tour of Fort Smith and a ceremony at Darby Junior High School.

In March 1950, the Army Transport Service acquired the World War I U.S. Navy ship *Admiral William M. Sims*, renamed it *General William O. Darby* and used it to transport troops home from Europe. Manned by a civilian crew, she operated out of New York between 1950 and 1953, completing more than twenty round-trip voyages to Bremerhaven and back to rotate troops and transport military dependents and civilian refugees. In June 1953, she traversed the Panama Canal to Yokosuka, Japan, to embark homebound veterans of the Korean War. After returning to Seattle, Washington, in July, she made five more troop lifts from Japan. Resuming transatlantic transport duty, she completed thirty-two voyages between Bremerhaven and New York and was deployed to the Mediterranean in 1956 to support peacekeeping operations of the Sixth Fleet. In the 1960s, the ship was used to shuttle troops to and from South Vietnam, then put in reserve.

The army also memorialized Darby in 1951 by establishing Camp Darby in northern Italy as a facility for sending troops home from World War II and then as a permanent supply base. The camp was created near Livorno by agreement between the United States and Italy and has remained a strategic asset of American power in the Mediterranean and the Mideast. It was headquarters of the Eighth

Support Group (logistical) of the South East Command of the North Atlantic Treaty Organization (NATO) and a rest and recreation area for U.S. forces in Europe.

Of Darby's death James Altieri wrote in *The Spearheaders*, "We old Rangers were hit hard by the news. It was hard to believe that his luck had run out." Determined to leave a written record of the Rangers, and his own experiences, he used the diary he kept from Carrickfergus to Cisterna to write *Darby's Rangers* (published in 1945). That year, three of his comrades in arms (Roy Murray, Walter Nye, and Chuck Shunstrom) served as technical advisers on a movie based on the experiences of Scripps-Howard correspondent Ernie Pyle, played by Burgess Meredith. Titled *The Story of GI Joe*, it dealt with the men of Company C, Eighteenth Infantry Regiment, whom Pyle accompanied in campaigns in North Africa and Italy.

Possibly with the assistance and encouragement of Murray, Nye, and Shunstrom, Altieri also served as a technical adviser for a 1951 movie. Directed by Michael Curtiz, *Force of Arms* starred William Holden as a U.S. Army sergeant in Italy in love with a WAC (Women's Army Corps) in what one critic described as a World War II version of Ernest Hemingway's World War I romance *A Farewell to Arms*. It was advertised as "the most beautiful love story ever told." Five years later, when the director of *The Story of GI Joe*, William Wellman, acquired the film rights to *Darby's Rangers*, Altieri was hired as technical adviser. Wellman chose Charlton Heston to play Darby, but when Heston quit the film, the part went to James Garner. The star of the hit television series *Maverick*, he had been signed for a supporting role. Released by Warner Bros. in 1958, with all the characters fictionalized, except for Darby and General Truscott, the film devoted as much time to Darby dealing with Rangers' romances and antics as with battle scenes.

Two years after the release of *Darby's Rangers* to broad acceptance by film critics and audiences, Altieri published *The Spearheaders*. In a ceremony at the Brooklyn Army Terminal in New York, he presented a copy of it and *Darby's Rangers* to the master of the *General Darby*, Captain Harold C. Campbell. Settled in Santa Barbara, California, Altieri organized a reunion of the Rangers in 1965, where the guest of honor was their training nemesis in Scotland, Colonel Charles Vaughan.

Dedicating himself to keeping the memory of Darby and "the Ranger spirit" alive, and to help Rangers and their families remain in touch with each other, Altieri was instrumental in fostering the Ranger Battalion Association of World War II, which established the William O. Darby Award to outstanding graduates of the Ranger School at Fort Benning, Georgia.

On orders from the army chief of staff, General J. Lawton Collins, in October 1951, the United States Army Infantry School extended Ranger training to all combat units in the army. The first class for individual candidates graduated on March 1, 1952. On November 1, 1987, the Ranger Department was reorganized into the Ranger Training Brigade, with four battalions. The mission was to conduct the Ranger, Long Range Surveillance Leader and Infantry Leader courses and to develop "leadership skills, confidence and competence of students by requiring them to perform effectively as small unit leaders in tactically realistic environments."

Training during the course is 19.4 hours per day, with students averaging only a couple hours of sleep every night and two or fewer meals per day. Field instruction composes the major part of the course, in which students plan and execute attacks on widely dispersed objectives, as the original Rangers did at Achnacarry, followed by a rapid movement to a new patrol base. Graduates earn the black-and-gold Ranger arm patch. Lieutenant General J. D. Lock in his book *The Coveted Black and Gold* described the Ranger School course as "a handshake with reality, a rite of passage," and initiation into a highly select band of warriors. Of those Ranger candidates who begin the grueling nine-week course each year, less than half graduate. Of the half who graduate, half of them will have repeated one of the course's three phases.

The "Camp Darby" portion begins with students assembled in a clearing near the camp's headquarters to begin three days of intense classroom instruction on patrolling fundamentals, advanced land navigation techniques, troop leading procedures, battle drills, and leadership responsibilities. Day four of Camp Darby starts with the students assaulting the "Darby Queen" obstacle course. Consisting of twenty obstacles set along a densely wooded hillside, it tests each student's endurance, tenacity, and dedication. Crawling, jumping, sliding, and climbing through, over, and around obstacles, each Ranger negotiates the course with his Ranger Buddy (the "me and my pal" system devised by Colonel Vaughan at Achnacarry). Assisting each other along the way, the buddies complete the course as a team, or they do not complete it at all. Later in the afternoon, the students engage in survival training. This teaches them how to catch, prepare, and cook rabbits, chickens, and fish.

With the basic training, the Darby Queen, and survival training out of the way, states a description of the program, the remainder of the student's time at Camp Darby is devoted to field training exercises focusing on reconnaissance operations. Utilizing the crawl, walk, and run method of training, instructors first demonstrate and guide the students through the task prior to conducting a field training exercise. The exercises are for squad level missions. During the final four days of this phase, students attempt to accomplish the mission against an opposing force that is determined to "kill" or capture them. As an additional incentive against capture, there is a "prisoner of war" compound.

This training regimen was intended to realize the original Ranger concept proposed to Truscott by General Marshall in 1942, in which Americans were to learn Commando tactics and return to their units to instruct others, but which was not carried out. With establishment of the Ranger School in 1951, the goal was to place one Ranger-qualified officer in each company and one Ranger-qualified noncommissioned officer in each rifle platoon. In 1954 it became mandatory that all newly commissioned Regular Army officers attend either Ranger or Airborne school. But during the Vietnam War, it became army policy to assign Ranger companies to divisions and brigades, as Darby's Rangers had been employed, without a central Ranger headquarters. Following Vietnam (for the first time since Darby's Rangers were disbanded in 1944), two Ranger battalions were formed, with the First Battalion, Seventy-fifth Infantry (Ranger) at Fort Stewart, Georgia, and the Second Battalion, Seventy-fifth Infantry (Ranger) based at Fort Lewis, Washington.

Today there are three. Headquartered at Fort Benning, with the mission to "plan and conduct special missions in support of U.S. policy and objectives," they are the First Battalion, Hunter Army Airfield, Georgia; Second Battalion, Fort Lewis, Washington; and Third Battalion, Fort Benning. Each battalion can deploy anywhere in the world with eighteen-hour notice.

A statement of purpose that might have been written by Colonel Darby states, "Training at night, during adverse weather, or on difficult terrain multiplies the benefits of training events. Throughout training, Rangers are taught to expect the unexpected."

All officers and enlisted soldiers in the regiment are four-time volunteers for either the Army, Airborne School, the Ranger Regiment, or Ranger School. They must meet "tough physical, mental and moral criteria." All commissioned officers and combat-arms NCOs must be airborne- and Ranger-qualified and have demonstrated proficiency in the duty position they are seeking. Upon assignment to the regiment, officers and senior NCOs attend an orientation that is intended to integrate them into the regiment by familiarizing them with regimental policies, standing operating procedures, the commander's intent, and Ranger standards. Enlisted soldiers assigned to the regiment go through the Ranger Indoctrination Program that assesses physical qualifications and indoctrinates basic regimental standards. Junior enlisted soldiers who are not Ranger-qualified must attend a Pre-Ranger course, which ensures that they are administratively, physically, and mentally prepared before they attend the U.S. Army Ranger Course.

Each Ranger battalion is authorized 660 personnel assigned to three rifle companies and a headquarters company. The battalions are light infantry and have only a few vehicles and crew-served weapons systems.

Because Darby remained at heart an artilleryman, it may be assumed that he would approve of the standard weapon systems of today's Rangers (84mm Ranger Antitank Weapons System, 60mm and 81mm mortars, Mark 19 RP MM Grenade Launcher, and 120mm Stinger mortars). He would also appreciate that their purposes are those of his Rangers in the form of "infiltrating and exfiltrating" by land, sea, and air; carrying out nighttime raids, recovery of personnel and special equipment, and conducting conventional or special light-infantry operations, and that their training encompasses desert and mountain operations, as well as amphibious instruction.

Colonel William Orlando Darby might have slipped into the mists of history if James Altieri had not written *Darby's Rangers* and *The Spearheaders*. Although these books were an intensely personal view of Altieri as a member of Fox Company of the First Ranger Battalion, they were the only record outside of official U.S. Army archives on the exploits of the Rangers in North Africa, Sicily, and Italy until 1980, when, at the urging of Darby's sister, William H. Baumer retrieved from his file cabinet the 1944 transcripts of six weeks of Darby's reminiscences that were published with the title *We Led the Way* (later changed to *Darby's Rangers: We Led the Way*). Coincidentally, Michael J. King published his scholarly volume *William O. Darby: A Military Biography*, based on his doctoral dissertation.

Because Darby did not survive the war to write an autobiography, and without Altieri's books, Baumer's preservation of the Darby transcripts, King's insights as a soldier and military scholar into Darby's career, and the various perspectives and viewpoints of each of them, writing the life story of this unique and worthy individual who strode the stage with the great generals of World War II and kept pace with them would have been difficult, if not impossible.

A U.S. Military Academy publication that summarized the lives of West Point graduates killed in World War II said about the man who created and led the Rangers from the front, "Had he lived through the war, he would still be justly famous, and there is no ceiling to the heights that he might have attained. In death, he remains an inspiration to higher achievement for those more fortunate of us who live—for the spirit and the tradition of Bill Darby will never die or even dim; they will be enhanced through the years to come."

CHRONOLOGY

WILLIAM ORLANDO DARBY

February 8, 1911	Born at Fort Smith, Arkansas
1929–1933	U.S. Military Academy, West Point
1933–1937	Assistant Commander, Battery A, First Battalion, Second Field Artillery, Fort Bliss, Texas; and Assistant Communications Officer
	Married Natalie Shaw in El Paso, Texas (they divorced in 1939)
	Commanding Officer, 205th Motor Transport Company, Quartermaster Train, First Cavalry Division
	Promoted to first lieutenant (June 13, 1936)
	CO, Headquarters Battery, First Battalion, Second Field Artillery
September 1937–June 1938	Field Artillery School, Fort Sill, Oklahoma
1938–1941	Eighty-fourth Field Artillery, Fort Riley, Kansas

	Army maneuvers, Camp Beauregard, Louisiana (May– June 1940)
	Ninety-ninth Field Artillery, Fort Hoyle, Maryland (September 1940–January 1941)
	Fleet Landing Exercise Number 7, Puerto Rico (January–February 1941)
	Landing operation training exercises with Carib Force, Fort Bragg, North Carolina (July–August 1941)
	Orders for transfer to Hawaii (November 1941)
January 5, 1942	Ordered to New York City as aide-de-camp to Major General Russell P. Hartle, Commanding Officer, Thirty-fourth Infantry Division
January 26, 1942	Leading elements of the Thirty-fourth Division arrive in North Ireland; Hartle assumes command of United States Army Northern Ireland Forces (USANIF) and Fifth Army Corps (Reinforced)

RANGERS

April 1942	Colonel Lucian K. Truscott appointed to head a group of American officers to organize an American Special Operations force like the British Commandos; Truscott confers with British in London
May	Truscott drafts letter of instructions to Hartle to organize the "1st Ranger Battalion"
June 1	Darby promoted to major
June 7	Hartle appoints Darby as commander
June 8	Darby begins interviewing officers; chooses Captain Herman Dammer as second in command
June 11	First group of three hundred volunteers from Thirty-fourth Division arrive at Camp Sunnylands, Carrickfergus, Northern Ireland
June 19	General Order Number 7 officially activates First Ranger Battalion; Darby promoted to lieutenant colonel
July 1	Rangers move to Commando Depot, Achnacarry, Scotland, to be trained by British Commandos

July 12	First Ranger casualty: Private Lamont D. Hoctel drowns while swimming a creek during training exercise
August 1	Battalion moves to training at Royal Navy base at Argyll, Scotland
August 19	Six Ranger officers and forty-four enlisted men participate in Commando Raid at Dieppe, France
September 1	Battalion moves to Dundee, Scotland, for amphibious training
September 11	British Commando chaplain Father Albert E. Basil becomes unofficially attached to the Rangers
September 24	Battalion moves to Glasgow, Scotland, and is attached to First Infantry Division
October 13–25	Training in exercise Mosstrooper for invasion of North Africa
October 26	Battalion sails with convoy from Clyde, Scotland
November 8	Landings at Arzew, Algeria, spearheading Operation Torch; capture of port and two French artillery batteries
November 10	Company C "badly shot up" in battle at St. Cloud
December–January 1943	Battalion detached from First Division and placed in Second Corps reserve; Darby appointed mayor of Arzew; retraining exercises
February 8	Battalion airlifted to Tebessa, Tunisia, assigned to Second Corps
February 9	Battalion moved by truck to Gafsa to conduct harassing raids and carry out reconnaissance
February 12–14	Raid and battle at Sened Station
February 19–22	U.S. forces defeated in Battle of Kasserine Pass
February 15–March 1	Patrolling in support of First Division at Feriana and Gafsa
March 6	General George S. Patton takes command of Second Corps
March 21	Rangers attack Italian position at Djebel el Ank Pass
March 23–April 5	Patrol and reconnaissance at Djebel Berda, Gafsa, and Sidi Bou Zid
April 10–18	Bivouac at Gafsa, move to Nemours
April 18–June 8	Formation, training, and activation of Third and Fourth battalions

July 9–10	First and Fourth battalions spearhead invasion of Sicily at Gela; Third Battalion lands at Licata; Darby declines offer from Patton, with promotion to full colonel, to leave Rangers and command an infantry regiment
July 15–16	Third Battalion participates in taking Montaperto and Porto Empedocle
July 17–23	Darby heads Task Force X, including First and Fourth Ranger battalions, as Third Battalion supports Patton's drive to capture Palermo.
July 22	Task Force X captures Marsala
July 25–August 17	First and Fourth battalions encamp near Corleone; Third Battalion takes part in Patton's drive to capture Messina; Darby writes letter to Eisenhower, seeking to form a Ranger regiment, but the request is denied; Germans withdraw from Messina to Italy
September 1	Darby forms a Ranger cannon company under the command of Captain Charles Shunstrom
September 9	Rangers land north of Salerno, Italy, at port of Maiori
September 9–18	While Allied breakout from Salerno beachhead stalls in the face of strong German defenses, the Rangers hold out at Chiunzi Pass to block enemy tank movements
September–December	Mountain fighting in Venafro region
January 15–16, 1944	Field Order Nineteen and Ranger Force Administrative Order for the invasion at Anzio, Italy (Operation Shingle), and creation of the 6615th Ranger Force (Provisional); Darby is promoted to colonel
January 21	Rangers sail from Pozzouli Bay for Anzio
January 22	Altieri describes landing at Anzio as the Rangers' "most successful"
January 22–28	While Sixth Corps commander Major General John P. Lucas is slow in launching a breakout from the beachhead, the Germans rush in reinforcements that Allied intelligence fails to recognize as the preparations for a counterattack
January 28	Darby receives orders for Ranger infiltration and reconnaissance of the strategically important town of Cisterna di Littoria

January 29–30	First and Third battalions encounter a massive force of German tanks and infantry and are decimated, with more than seven hundred Rangers taken prisoner
February 1	Germans parade captured Rangers around the Colosseum in Rome and through streets before confining them to prisoner-of-war camps; an estimated 10 percent of them will escape
February 15	Darby is slightly wounded by a bomb fragment; relieved as commander of the all-but-destroyed Ranger Force
February 16	Darby is given command of badly battered 179th Infantry Regiment
March 25	Fourth Battalion assigned to First Special Service Force
March 27	First Battalion survivors ordered stateside
April 15	Remnants of Third Battalion sent home
April–June	Darby is assigned to War Department General Staff Operations Division, Washington, D.C.; receives hero's welcome during homecoming visit to Fort Smith; tours training camps in the United States
June 19	Darby has a reunion with Fourth Battalion Rangers at Camp Butner, North Carolina, to mark the second anniversary of the formation of the first ranger battalion
August 15–16	First and Third Battalions deactivated
October 24	Fourth Battalion disbanded at Camp Butner
March 29, 1945	Darby is sent on a ninety-day tour of the European theater; in Italy, he is named assistant commander of the Tenth Mountain Division
April 1–29	Tenth Mountain Division in action in the Villafranca-Verona area near Lake Garda in northeastern Italy
April 30	Following a conference in a hotel in the town of Torbole, Darby is killed by a small chunk of shrapnel from a German cannon that struck him in the heart; he was thirty-four years old
May 15	President Harry Truman approves Darby's promotion to brigadier general

THE ORIGINAL DARBY'S RANGERS

Darby, William O., Major and Lt. Col.

Basil, Albert E., Capt. (British Catholic chaplain)

Dammer, Herman W., Capt.

Manning, Jacob, Capt.

Martin, William E., Capt.

Meade, Stephen J., Capt.

Miller, Alvah N., Capt.

Murray, Roy A., Capt.

Ahlgren, Frederic F., 1st Lt.

Anderson, Axel W., 1st Lt.

Carran, Earl L., 1st Lt.

Dirks, Leonard F., 1st Lt.

Flanagan, Robert, 1st Lt.

Jarrett, William A., 1st Lt.

Klefman, Gordon L., 1st Lt.

Knudson, Dean H., 1st Lt.

Lanning, William B., 1st Lt.

Lyle, James B., 1st Lt.

Nelson, Alfred H., 1st Lt.

Nye, Walter F., 1st Lt.

Schneider, Max F., 1st Lt.

Young, Leilyn M., 1st Lt.

Johnson, Robert L., 2nd Lt.

Karbel, Howard W., 2nd Lt.

Loustalot, Edwin V., 2nd Lt.

Randall, Joseph H., 2nd Lt.

Saam, Frederic J., 2nd Lt.

Shunstrom, Charles M., 2nd Lt.

Sunshine, George P., 2nd Lt.

Butler, Walter, 1st Sgt.

Munro, Kenneth J., 1st Sgt.

Hanson, James B., T/Sgt.

Porter, Richard W., T/Sgt.

Baccus, Edwin V., S/Sgt.

Bertholf, Merritt M., S/Sgt.

Dalquist, Clyde, S/Sgt.

Honig, Richard P., S/Sgt.

Hooker, Dean, S/Sgt.

Hooker, John F., S/Sgt.

Kness, Lester E., S/Sgt.

McCauley, Robert, S/Sgt.

Mercuriali, Gino, S/Sgt.

Musegades, William M., S/Sgt.

Musselman, Chester V., S/Sgt.

Rembecki, John S., S/Sgt.

Sorrell, Charles A., S/Sgt.

Stempson, Kenneth D., S/Sgt.

Yambor, Steve P., S/Sgt.

Adams, Harold, Sgt.

Ball, John J., Sgt.

Beaver, Corwin W., Sgt.

Butler, Grant R., Sgt.

Butts, Theodore Q., Sgt.

Castle, Gene, Sgt.

Clarey, John C., Sgt.

Church, Lloyd, Sgt.

Dew, James R., Sgt.

Dye, Joe, Sgt.

Earhart, Thomas A., Sgt.

Evans, Warren E., Sgt.

Fox, Arlo G., Sgt.

Gabriel, Martin J., Sgt.

Gollinger, Bernard H., Sgt.

Greene, Richard, Sgt.

Greenland, Dale E., Sgt.

Gustafsen, Maurice E., Sgt.

Harris, Randall, Sgt.

Hartin, Maurice D., Sgt.

Heacock, Mervin, Sgt.

Hendrickson, Robert S., Sgt.

Huckle, William J., Sgt.

Hudson, Jack, Sgt.

Jacobsen, Albert T., Sgt.

Jensen, Ernest, Sgt.

Johnson, Warren L., Sgt.

Jones, Donald L., Sgt.

Kavanaugh, Marvin L., Sgt.

Kenyon, Kenneth, Sgt.

Klebanski, Walter, Sgt.

Knapp, John J., Sgt.

Kunkle, Ronald, Sgt.

Laseter, Douglas E., Sgt.

Maginn, Francis T., Sgt.

Mahoney, Edwin, Sgt.

Mattivi, Frank, Sgt.

McCollam, Donald, Sgt.

Minarsich, Clifford E., Sgt.

Northrup, Arthur J., Sgt.

Parish, Earl, Sgt.

Perry, Paul E., Sgt.

Pfrunder, David L., Sgt.

Prudhomme, Thomas H., Sgt.

Reagan, Harry M., Sgt.

Rensink, Gerrit J., Sgt.

Rowe, Ronald L., Sgt.

Sandage, Garnett, Sgt.

Sellers, Richard, Sgt.

Sieg, Walter R., Sgt.

Sorby, Tom, Sgt.

Spangler, Theodore, Sgt.

Sporman, Leonard E., Sgt.

Stern, Phil, Sgt.

Swank, Marcell, Sgt.

Szima, Alex J., Sgt.

Taylor, Robert, Sgt.

Thompson, Clyde C., Sgt.

Thompson, Ed, Sgt.

Torbett, Donald K., Sgt.

Vanskoy, John R., Sgt.

Wojcik, Walter J., Sgt.

Woods, Wayne, Sgt.

Yandell, Ray C., Sgt.

Yurko, Michael S., Sgt.

Arimond, William, Cpl.

Arnbol, Andrew K., Cpl.

Barnes, William B., Cpl.

Bacon, Robert, Cpl.

Beckham, Robert, Cpl.

Bolton, Floyd H., Cpl.

Brady, William R., Cpl.

Buona, Wayne A., Cpl.

Edstrom, Robert, Cpl.

Ehalt, Robert E., Cpl.

Eklund, Robert D., Cpl.

Elwood, William O., Cpl.

Finn, John N., Cpl.

Fisher, Chester, Cpl.

Foley, John J., Cpl.

Ford, Richard, Cpl.

Frederick, Donald S., Cpl.

Gallup, Wilbur L., Cpl.

Gangath, Phillip, Cpl.

Gilbert, Nolan M., Cpl.

Gramke, Melvyn P., Cpl.

Haines, James, Cpl.

Hancock, Victor, Cpl.

Henry, Howard M., Cpl.

Hermsen, Paul S., Cpl.

Hunt, Russell W., Cpl.

Keegan, John E., Cpl.

Key, James N., Cpl.

Kness, Marvin E., Cpl.

Koons, Franklin M., Cpl.

Kuhl, Howard V., Cpl.

Lacosse, Frank, Cpl.

Ladd, Garland S., Cpl.

Masalonis, Edward W., Cpl.

McAllister, Harold, Cpl.

Rada, Anthony, Cpl.

Rote, Edgar W., Cpl.

Runyon, Oscar L., Cpl.

Ryan, Thomas L., Cpl.

Schmirler, Robert C., Cpl.

Schon, Clarence M., Cpl.

Sexton, Donald R., Cpl.

Shippy, Zane G., Cpl.

Shuff, Joseph, Cpl.

Silkwood, Monzell, Cpl.

Skarie, Robert, Cpl.

Spackman, Arthur, Cpl.

Torneby, Samuel C., Cpl.

Trabu, Edward W., Cpl.

Trynoski, Joseph R., Cpl.

Vetcher, Peter, Cpl.

Vickmark, Clayton O., Cpl.

Wilson, Gilbert E., Cpl.

Wojcik, Louis J., Cpl.

Altieri, James J., T/5

Bierbaum, Kenneth, T/5

Chesnut, J. T., T/5

Coomer, Jennings, T/5

Cundriff, Woodrow, T/5

Dunn, Donald E., T/5

Earl, Llewellyn, T/5

Elliott, Richard C., T/5

Greene, Leonard L., T/5

Halliday, Robert H., T/5

Heid, Ivan R., T/5

Kerecman, Michael, T/5

McGee, William A., T/5

Merrill, Von D., T/5

Polus, Matthew, T/5

Phillips, Joseph C., T/5

Reid, Lawrence, T/5

Rouse, Claude, T/5

Salkin, Aaron A., T/5

Smith, John H., T/5

Stojewski, Raymond A., T/5

Urban, Henry A., T/5

Yoder, William H., T/5

Aasve, Kermit E., Pfc.

Bailey, Raymond L., Pfc.

Bannister, Floyd R., Pfc.

Beitel, Clare P., Pfc.

Bevan, Robert M., Pfc.

Blake, Fred E., Pfc.

Boudreau, Burton, Pfc.

Brake, Douglas E., Pfc.

Bresnahan, Walter A., Pfc.

Bristol, Jess B., Pfc.

Brown, Roy A., Pfc.

Brown, William E., Pfc.

Bruder, Robert, Pfc.

Bruun, Mervyn P., Pfc.

Bunde, Clar R., Pfc.

Bush, Stanley, Pfc.

Campbell, Joseph S., Pfc.

Contrera, Carlo, Pfc.

Cook, Lester B., Pfc.

Crandall, Claude D., Pfc.

Eskola, Elmer I., Pfc.

Deeb, Peter, Pfc.

Demick, Eugene L., Pfc.

Drost, Carl, Pfc.

Dudrow, Douglas S., Pfc.

Eastwood, Philip H., Pfc.

Fronk, Junior, Pfc.

Garrison, Elmer W., Pfc.

Gaskill, Robert K., Pfc.

Girdley, William S., Pfc.

Grafton, Thomas A., Pfc.

Gust, Joe V., Pfc.

Harr, Gerald J., Pfc.

Hedges, Richard, Pfc.

Heiser, Robert, Pfc.

Higgins, John J., Pfc.

Hoffiens, John R., Pfc.

Holy, Norman F., Pfc.

Jacobs, Shirley G., Pfc.

Johnson, Robert O., Pfc.

Joiner, William, Pfc.

Jondal, Ozonville, Pfc.

Ketzer, Steve, Pfc.

Knox, John K., Pfc.

Kopanda, George, Pfc.

Kopp, William G., Pfc.

Legg, Sherman L. Pfc.

Leighton, Charles F., Pfc.

Lienhas, William E., Pfc.

Marty, Raymond E., Pfc.

Mayberry, Howard M., Pfc.

McLenson, Stanley P., Pfc.

Miller, John A., Pfc.

Moffatt, Rollin, Pfc.

Mosely, James, Pfc.

Nagengast, Jerome J., Pfc.

Nanny, James, Pfc.

Nickirk, Charles, Pfc.

Powell, Waiter R., Pfc.

Pfann, William, Pfc.

Preston, Pete M., Pfc.

Pruitt, Charles R., Pfc.

Puccio, Charles, Pfc.

Quinn, Leslie, Pfc.

Rodriguez, Raymond, Pfc.

Rutledge, Raymond, Pfc.

Sivil, Charles, Pfc.

Stewart, Estel, Pfc.

Stovall, William, Pfc.

Sugrue, John E., Pfc.

Sumpter, Gerald C., Pfc.

Swanson, Robert, Pfc.

Szcesniak, Steven S., Pfc.

Taylor, Alpha O., Jr., Pfc.

Tiggelaar, Samuel, Pfc.

Traufler, Donald A., Pfc.

Trent, Nelson, Pfc.

Wells, Royal H., Pfc.

Westerholm, Harold S., Pfc.

Wood, William, Pfc.

Yenzer, Ronald K., Pfc.

Anctil, Roland, Pvt.

Andre, Howard W., Pvt.

Archer, James, Pvt.

Avers, Robert H., Pvt.

Back, Harley, Pvt.

Baker, Clarence H., Pvt.

Barefoot, James H., Pvt.

Barker, Jack, Pvt.

Baum, John L., Pvt.

Bergstrom, Dennis A., Pvt.

Bills, Perry E., Pvt.

Biro, Imre, Pvt.

Bock, Woodrow C., Pvt.

Bond, Fred, Pvt.

Brassfield, John S., Pvt.

Brinkley, William S., Pvt.

Brown, George D., Pvt.

Bullington, Lee M., Pvt.

Burdine, Carl C., Pvt.

Buringrud, Wendell, Pvt.

Cain, Paul W., Pvt.

Calahan, Rollie F., Pvt.

Calfayon, Varton, Pvt.

Calhoun, Edward T., Pvt.

Card, Earl E., Pvt.

Carlson, Douglas, Pvt.

Chesher, Robert T., Pvt.

Christensen, Alfred E., Pvt.

Colbert, Paul E., Pvt.

Coon, Lyle, Pvt.

Cooney, James D., Pvt.

Corrin, Thomas, Pvt.

Cote, Jules E., Pvt.

Coy, Charles R., Pvt.

Creed, George H., Pvt.

Dean, Edward L., Pvt.

DeGennareo, Steven N., Pvt.

Delski, John, Pvt.

Diehl, Charles W., Pvt.

Dlugas, Adam, Pvt.

Donnelly, William, Pvt.

Doss, John F., Pvt.

Dunn, Robert C., Pvt.

Earnest, Charles A., Pvt.

Earnwood, Don A., Pvt.

Eaton, Richard E., Pvt.

Edwards, James O., Pvt.

Eineicher, Clarence W., Pvt.

Elliott, Clyde W., Pvt.

Evans, Charles, Pvt.

Fergen, Thomas B., Pvt.

Fernandez, Adelfeo, Pvt.

Ferrier, Leslie M., Pvt.

Fitzhugh, Norman R., Pvt.

Folsom, Harold, Pvt.

Fontenot, Lee J., Pvt.

Fortenberry, Ike S., Pvt.

Freeman, Roy, Pvt.

Fulks, Warren, Pvt.

Fullerton, Edward, Pvt.

Furru, Edwin R., Pvt.

Galbraith, John, Pvt.

Gavins, Raymond, Pvt.

Gilardi, Americo, Pvt.

Goins, Archie, Pvt.

Gomez, Simon R., Pvt.

Gonzolas, Lalo, Pvt.

Gorman, John E., Pvt.

Grant, Charles F., Pvt.

Gray, James E., Pvt.

Gray, Lyman, Pvt.

Greene, Othel, Pvt.

Grisamer, George W., Pvt.

Gummel, Kenneth E., Pvt.

Hall, Cornelius, Pvt.

Hambrich, Clifford H., Pvt.

Harrington, Lester C., Pvt.

Harris, Lemuel G., Pvt.

Harris, Thurman E., Pvt.

Harrison, Elby W., Pvt.

Hathaway, Charles, Pvt.

Hauck, Cecil, Pvt.

Hawkins, George, Pvt.

Hayes, Charles E., Pvt.

Hayes, Donald L., Pvt.

Haywood, Edward, Pvt.

Hedenstad, Howard, Pvt.

Hedrick, Vernon, Pvt.

Hoctel, Lamont, Pvt.

Hoffman, George C., Pvt.

Hyatt, Lloyd O., Pvt.

Ingram, John R., Pvt.

Jackson, William A., Pvt.

Jantz, Irvin W., Pvt.

Jernberg, Innes A., Pvt.

Johnson, Charles, Pvt.

Johnson, Donald G., Pvt.

Johnson, Everett L., Pvt.

Johnson, Francis K., Pvt.

Johnson, John J., Pvt.

Kallis, Milton, Pvt.

Karboski, Stanley, Pvt.

Katzen, Murray A., Pvt.

Kazura, Charles, Pvt.

Keberdle, Robert C., Pvt.

Keener, Vance, Pvt.

Kopveiler, Eugene N., Pvt.

Lambert, Daniel, Pvt.

Larson, Kenneth E., Pvt.

Launer, Harvey L., Pvt.

Lehmann, Carl H., Pvt.

Lodge, Vernon W., Pvt.

Logsden, Chester, Pvt.

Loman, Robert B., Pvt.

Longona, Paul, Pvt.

Low, Austin G., Pvt.

Lowell, Bob L., Pvt.

Lucas, Joseph P., Pvt.

Madson, Marvin K., Pvt.

Mahoney, James, Pvt.

Martin, Edwin W., Pvt.

Martin, Grant E., Pvt.

May, Joseph C., Pvt.

McClain, LeRoy J., Pvt.

McGraw, Elvis G., Pvt.

McMahon, Regis M., Pvt.

Merritt, James M., Pvt.

Miller, Seymour, Pvt.

Mitchell, Dencil E., Pvt.

Moffett, Walter, Pvt.

Moger, Edwin, Pvt.

Montgomery, George C., Pvt.

Morasti, Victor A., Pvt.

Moses, Robert L., Pvt.

Mozzetti, Eric C., Pvt.

Mulling, Jullien, Pvt.

Najomowicz, Walter J., Pvt.

Neal, Charles, Pvt.

Nelson, Trent, Pvt.

Nelson, George P., Pvt.

Nixon, Jacque M., Pvt.

Nochta, John E., Pvt.

Norman, John R., Pvt.

Nystrom, Alder, Pvt.

Oneskunk, Samson P., Pvt.

Ostlund, George L., Pvt.

Pagunano, Charles E., Pvt.

Palade, Weslie W., Pvt.

Palmer, Frank W., Pvt.

Parker, Walter A., Pvt.

Parsons, William T., Pvt.

Patterson, Francis B., Pvt.

Petersen, Henry, Pvt.

Peterson, Ronald I., Pvt.

Petty, Clarence A., Pvt.

Pierce, Raymond, Pvt.

Puchinski, Walter, Pvt.

Ratliff, Vinson, Pvt.

Reed, Robert, Pvt.

Reilly, Charles, Pvt.

Reiter, Leonard, Pvt.

Retig, Roland, Pvt.

Rinard, Harold L., Pvt.

Roane, George H., Pvt.

Rorex, John R., Pvt.

Ruschkewicz, James R., Pvt.

Ryan, Patrick, Pvt.

Sander, Richard, Pvt.

Sandlin, William G., Pvt.

Sausen, William L., Pvt.

Schooley, Clayton, Pvt.

Schrader, Arthur C., Pvt.

Schultz, Edward A., Pvt.

Schumacher, Dennis L., Pvt.

Schwartz, Joey H., Pvt.

Shain, Edward, Pvt.

Shuput, Michael M., Pvt.

Shurmak, Sylvester, Pvt.

Sosh, James, Pvt.

Stanton, John J., Pvt.

Stark, Ernest, Pvt.

Stoopes, Leslie, Pvt.

Stroud, Presley P., Pvt.

Sullivan, Thomas, Pvt.

Surratt, Robert C., Pvt.

Swanson, Allan E., Pvt.

Sweazey, Owen, Pvt.

Swicker, Howard B., Pvt.

Thompson, Evan, Pvt.

Thompson, Richard N., Pvt.

Thurman, George W., Pvt.

Tongate, Kenneth C., Pvt.

Treumer, Clarence, Pvt.

Troxell, Lawrence F., Pvt.

Turner, Robert E., Pvt.

Wallsmith, Clotis, Pvt.

Walters, Charles, Pvt.

Wensle, Charles L., Pvt.

Whited, Murel, Pvt.

Wilkerson, Edward N., Pvt.

Wilkerson, Kimbrell M., Pvt.

Williams, Joe O., Pvt.

Williams, Thomas, Pvt.

Wilson, Harold, Pvt.

Winsor, Thomas G., Pvt.

Wisniewski, John, Pvt.

Wood, Virgil H., Pvt.

Woodhall, John B., Pvt.

Yarboro, Jessie, Pvt.

Zaccardi, Dominico, Pvt.

Zielinski, Herman A., Pvt.

RANGERS AT DIEPPE

WITH NUMBER THREE COMMANDO, HEADQUARTERS TROOP (FROM F COMPANY):

Captain Roy A. Murray
Sergeant Edwin C. Thompson
Sergeant Tom Sorby
PFCs
Howard W. Andre
Stanley Bush
Don A. Earnwood
Pete Preston

WITH NUMBER THREE TROOP (FROM A COMPANY):

First Lieutenant Leonard F.
  Dirks

Sergeant Harold A. Adams
Sergeant Mervin T. Heacock
T/5 Joseph C. Phillips
PFCs
Howard T. Hedenstad
Edwin J. Moger
James A. Mosely

WITH NUMBER THREE TROOP (FROM D COMPANY):

Sergeant Marvin L. Kavanaugh
Sergeant Gino Mercuriali
T/5 William S. Brinkley
T/5 Michael Kerecman
PFC William S. Girdley
Private Jacque M. Nixon

**WITH NUMBER FOUR TROOP
(FROM C COMPANY):**

Second Lieutenant Charles M.
  Shunstrom
Sergeant John J. Knapp
T/5 John H. Smith
PFCs
James O. Edwards
Charles F. Grant
Donald G. Johnson

**WITH NUMBER FOUR TROOP
(FROM E COMPANY):**

Staff Sergeant Lester Kness
Sergeant Theodore Q. Butts
PFCs
Clare P. Beitel
Charles R. Coy
Charles Reilly
Owen W. Sweazey

**WITH NUMBER SIX TROOP
(FROM B COMPANY):**

Second Lieutenant Edwin V.
  Loustalot
Staff Sergeant Merritt M. Bertholf
Sergeant Albert T. Jacobsen
PFCs
Edwin R. Furru

Donald L. Hayes
William E. Lienhas

**WITH NUMBER FOUR COMMANDO
(ALL WITH A TROOP)
(FROM RANGERS HQ COMPANY):**

Staff Sergeant Kenneth D.
  Stempson
Sergeant Alex J. Szima

(FROM C COMPANY):

Corporal William R. Brady

(FROM D COMPANY):

Corporal Franklin M. Koons

WITH CANADIAN UNITS:

Sergeant Marcell G. Swank,
  Headquarters Company
Sergeant Lloyd N. Church, A
  Company
Second Lieutenant Joseph H.
  Randall, C Company
Sergeant Kenneth G. Kenyon, D
  Company
T/4 Howard M. Henry, E Company
First Lieutenant Robert Flanagan,
  E Company

BIBLIOGRAPHY

BOOKS

Allen, William. *Anzio: Edge of Disaster*. New York: Dutton, 1978.

Altieri, James. *Darby's Rangers*. Arnold, Missouri: Ranger Book Committee, 1977.

————. *The Spearheaders*. Indianapolis, Indiana: Bobbs-Merrill, 1960.

Astor, Gerald. *The Greatest War: Americans in Combat, 1941–1945*. Novato, California: Presidio Press, 1990.

Atkinson, Rick. *An Army at Dawn: The War in North Africa*. New York: Henry Holt and Company, 2002.

Bahmanyar, Mir. *Darby's Rangers: 1942–1945*. Wellingborough, United Kingdom: Osprey Publishing, 2003.

————. *Shadow Warriors: A History of the U.S. Army Rangers*. Wellingborough, United Kingdom: Osprey Publishing, 2006.

Black, Robert W. *Rangers in World War II*. Novato, California: Presidio Press, 1992.

Blumenson, Martin. *Anzio*. Norwalk, Connecticut: Easton Press, 1963.

Bowditch, John. *Anzio Beachhead*. Washington, D.C.: United States Army Center of Military History, 1990.

Darby, William O., and William H. Baumer. *We Led the Way*. New York: Jove Books, 1985.

297

BIBLIOGRAPHY

Department of the Army Historical Division. *Anzio Beachhead*. Nashville: The Battery Press, 1986.

Farrar, Jackie Marie, editor. *William Orlando Darby: A Man to Remember*. Claremore, Oklahoma: Country Lane Press, 1987.

Gilchrist, Donald. *Castle Commando*. London, England: Oliver and Boyd Limited, 1960.

Hogan, David W., Jr., *Raiders or Elite Infantry*. Westport, Connecticut: Greenwood Press, 1992.

————. *U.S. Army Special Operations in World War II*. Washington, D.C.: Center of Military History, 1992.

Jeffers, H. Paul. *Theodore Roosevelt, Jr.: The Life of a War Hero*. Novato, California: Presidio Press, 2002.

King, Michael J. *Rangers: Selected Combat Operations in World War II*. Honolulu, Hawaii: University Press of the Pacific, 2004.

————. *William Orlando Darby: A Military Biography*. Hamden, Connecticut: Archon Books, 1981.

Ladd, James. *Commandos and Rangers*. New York: St. Martin's Press, 1978.

Lock, John D. *To Fight with Intrepidity*. New York: Pocket Books, 1998.

Meltesen, Clarence R. *After the Battle . . . Ranger Evasion and Escape*. San Francisco: Oflag 64 Press, 1997.

O'Donnell, Patrick K. *Beyond Valor: World War II's Ranger and Airborne Veterans Reveal the Heart of Combat*. New York: Touchstone, 2001.

Shapiro, Milton. *Ranger Battalion: American Rangers in World War II*. New York: Julian Messner, 1979.

Suominen, Edwin, and Mary Suominen. *Twice to Freedom*. Kearney, Nebraska: Morris Publishing, 1999.

Taylor, Thomas H. *Rangers Lead the Way*. Paducah, Kentucky: Turner Publishing Company, 1996.

Truscott, L.K., Jr., *Command Missions*. New York: E. P. Dutton and Company, 1954.

Vaughan-Thomas, Wynford. *Anzio: The Massacre at the Beachhead*. New York: Holt Rinehart Winston, 1961.

BIBLIOGRAPHY

PERIODICALS

Abati, Anthony J. "Cisterna di Littoria, a Brave but Futile Effort," *Army History* (Fall 1991).

Hull, Michael D. "Rangers' Rendezvous with Destiny," *World War II History* (July 2004).

McManus, John. "Bloody Cisterna," *World War II* (January 2004).

Morris, Mack. "Rangers Come Home and Bring Stories of Their Tough Campaigns in Africa and Europe," *Yank* (August 4, 1944).

Ossad, Steven L. "The Last Battle of Gen. William Orlando Darby," *The Army* (January 2003).

Rule, Richard. "Tragic Dress Rehearsal," *World War II History* (July 2005).

Templeton, Kenneth S., Jr. "The Last Days of Col. William O. Darby: An Eyewitness Account," *Army History* (Spring 1998).

Young, Leilyn M. "Rangers in a Night Operation," *Military Review* (July 1944).

GOVERNMENT DOCUMENTS

1st Ranger Battalion, Report of Action. Combined Arms Research Library, Archives, Fort Leavenworth, Kansas, January 31, 1944.

3rd Ranger Battalion, Report of Action. Combined Arms Research Library, Archives, Fort Leavenworth, Kansas, April 3, 1944.

4th Ranger Battalion, Report of Action, Period 22 to 31 January 1944. Combined Arms Research Library, Archives, Fort Leavenworth, Kansas, February 15, 1944.

4th Ranger Battalion, Journal of Operations. Combined Arms Research Library, Archives, Fort Leavenworth, Kansas, January 1944.

4th Ranger Battalion, Journal of Operations. Combined Arms Research Library, Archives, Fort Leavenworth, Kansas, February 1944.

Ranger Force Headquarters. Field Order 1. Combined Arms Research Library, Archives, Fort Leavenworth, Kansas, January 1944.

Ranger Force Headquarters. Field Order 2. Combined Arms Research Library, Archives, Fort Leavenworth, Kansas, January 1944.

Reports of Action. Captain Charles M. Shunstrom. "Capture of the First and Third Ranger Battalions." United States Military Academy Library, Archives, West Point, New York, July 10, 1944.

OTHER SOURCES

Allen, Major. Combat Studies Institute Battlebook, "Operation Shingle." Fort Leavenworth, Kansas: Combat Studies Institute, 1984.

Haggerty, Jerome J. "A History of the Ranger Battalions of World War II." Dissertation, New York: Fordham University, 1982.

Smith, D. B. "The 1st, 3rd, and 4th Ranger Battalions in World War II." Student paper, Fort Leavenworth, Kansas: U.S. Army Command and General Staff College, 1972.

Stewart, Jeff R. *The Ranger Force at the Battle of Cisterna.* Thesis, Fort Leavenworth, Kansas: U.S. Army Command and General Staff College, 2004.

★ INDEX ★

INDEX